Events That Changed Germany

Events That Changed Germany

Edited by
Frank W. Thackeray

GREENWOOD PRESS
Westport, Connecticut • London

Library of Congress Cataloging-in-Publication Data

Events that changed Germany / edited by Frank W. Thackeray.
    p. cm.
  Includes index.
  ISBN 0–313–32814–5
  1. Germany—History—1789–1900. 2. Germany—History—20th century.
3. Germany—History—Unification, 1990. I. Thackeray, Frank W.
DD89.E84 2004
943.08—dc22   2004017663

British Library Cataloguing in Publication Data is available.

Library of Congress Catalog Card Number: 2004017663
ISBN: 0–313–32814–5

First published in 2004

Greenwood Press, 88 Post Road West, Westport, CT 06881
An imprint of Greenwood Publishing Group, Inc.
www.greenwood.com

Printed in the United States of America

The paper used in this book complies with the
Permanent Paper Standard issued by the National
Information Standards Organization (Z39.48–1984).

10 9 8 7 6 5 4 3 2 1

Contents

Illustrations

Preface

Few would argue that the "issue" of Germany lies at the heart of much recent history. The world has struggled painfully and earnestly to answer such questions as what is Germany, who comprises it, what are its borders, what does it have to offer, what fears does it raise, what role should it play in Europe and in the world, what are its positive attributes, and what are its negative characteristics. Now, at the start of the twenty-first century, answers to these questions are at hand; one can only hope that these answers are permanent and acceptable ones and that the "issue" of Germany will fade from the scene.

Key to any understanding of modern German history is the matter of unification. Although the drive for German unification had grown steadily throughout the early nineteenth century, it received an apparent setback with the seemingly unsuccessful Revolutions of 1848. Nevertheless, a united Germany appeared in 1871, and this new German state was populous, prosperous, self-confident, and—above all—militarily powerful. Germany's rise continued unabated during the next few decades, leading to a case of extreme hubris that helped to provoke the disastrous World War I. The Germany that emerged from that debacle reluctantly accepted liberal democracy, but the Weimar Republic often seemed to teeter on the brink of chaos. When the Great Depression brought economic calamity, Germany sank to the depths. First Hitler and his Nazi demons enslaved a not-unwilling Germany, and then *der Führer* led his Third Reich over the precipice into the abyss of World War II. Broken, beaten, and lifeless in 1945, Germany was divided by the victors whose existence the Nazis had so recently threatened. Amazingly enough, Germany—or at least West Germany—arose like a phoenix from the ashes of the war. West Germany emerged as Europe's economic powerhouse; it also achieved a heretofore unattainable political and social stability, and successfully integrated itself into a larger European superstructure. By the end of the twentieth century, Germany was once again unified, strong, prosperous, and respected.

The impetus for this book derives from my interaction with thousands of students over many years. While almost all the students proved to be very nice people, their knowledge of the world in which they live in general and that world's history in particular was less than impressive. When teaching courses on recent German history, it became apparent that the standard textbooks available presumed that the students entered the class knowing more than they actually did. Moreover, in their race through the decades, the textbooks sometimes failed to distinguish clearly between truly important developments and events of a secondary nature. Nor, at times, did the textbooks do a superb job of analyzing and evaluating events. Thus, the objective of this book is to provide both students and laypeople with a short but organized, lively, and coherent synopsis of the ten most important events or developments that shaped German history over the past century and one-half or so. The hope is that this book will enable students and lay readers to place modern Germany in its proper world historical context and also to appreciate the fascinating history of Germany itself.

The volume is presented in a straightforward manner. First, the editor has provided an introduction that presents factual material about each event in a clear, concise, chronological order. Each introduction is followed by a longer interpretive essay by a specialist exploring the ramifications of the event under consideration. Each essay concludes with a selected bibliography of the most important works about the event. The 10 chapters are followed by 3 appendices that provide additional information useful to the reader. Appendix A is a glossary of names, events, organizations, and terms mentioned but not fully explained in the introductions and essays. Appendix B is a timeline, and Appendix C is a statistical compendium of elections from 1871 through 2004.

The events covered in this volume were selected on the basis of the editor's combined teaching and research activities. Of course, other editors might have arrived at a somewhat different list, but it is the editor's belief that he has assembled a group of events that truly changed Germany in the nineteenth and twentieth centuries.

As with all published works, numerous people behind the scenes deserve much of the credit for the final product. Kevin Ohe and Michael Hermann, Greenwood Publishing Group editors, unfailingly lent their support, insight, and patience. The staff of the Photographic Division of the Library of Congress provided helpful assistance in the selection of the photographs that appear in this book. Megan Renwick served as student research assistant. Her excellent editorial skills and her perceptive comments proved invaluable. Brigette Colligan, who was always ready to type or retype whatever was asked of her, also deserves special mention. Various staff members of the Indiana University Southeast (IUS) computer center cheerfully unscrambled disks and turned mysterious word-processing programs into something with which one could work. The IUS library staff also provided helpful assistance. Thanks also go to IUS for funds that allowed for the student research assistant and covered other costs associated with the project. Special thanks go to Roger Baylor, Amy O'Connell, and Kate Lewison for making their establishment available, thereby enabling the editor to confer about this project and discuss its many facets with his colleagues and former students in a congenial atmosphere. Among those who helped in one way or another to make this a better book are John Findling, John Newman, Sam Sloss, Sheila Anderson, Stephanie Bower, Cliff Staten, Yu Shen, A. Jack, Glenn Crothers, and Roz Tate. Most importantly, the authors—whose essays were well-conceived and thoughtful and whose patience when the project seemed to lag was much appreciated—deserve sincere thanks.

Heartfelt thanks go to Kathy, Sasha, and Max, whose interest in the work—to say nothing of their tolerance of the editor's idiosyncrasies—made it all worthwhile. Finally, a hearty "danke schön" to all the editor's students—past, present, and future. After all these years, they continue to inspire.

Frank W. Thackeray

1 ——————————————————————

The Revolutions of 1848, 1848–1849

INTRODUCTION

In 1848, a mighty wave of revolution rolled across the European continent and the German-speaking world did not escape its fury. To a large extent, this revolutionary outburst sought to overthrow the system that Europe's Great Powers (Great Britain, France, Prussia, Austria, Russia) established at the close of the Napoleonic Wars. At the Congress of Vienna (1814–15), the major states and their smaller brethren molded a Europe that was mostly monarchical and aristocratic. Kings reigned; the nobility enjoyed their ancient privileges; established state religions demanded allegiance; and the upper levels of both the bureaucracy and the officer corps remained the exclusive preserve of the landed aristocracy. Those who did not fall within this magic circle of favor found tough sledding. The rising middle class saw its ambitions set aside; the peasantry was relegated to its traditional, subservient role; the artisans were ignored; the embryonic working class failed to make an impression; and those who harbored nationalist aspirations were viewed with suspicion, if not outright hostility.

The acknowledged leader of the forces that had put Europe back together again was the Austrian chancellor, Prince Clemens von Metternich. Metternich's authority was so great and so enduring that the 1815–48 period is often called "The Age of Metternich." However, the Revolutions of 1848 not only challenged Metternich's status quo, but also proved strong enough to drive him from power and send him into exile.

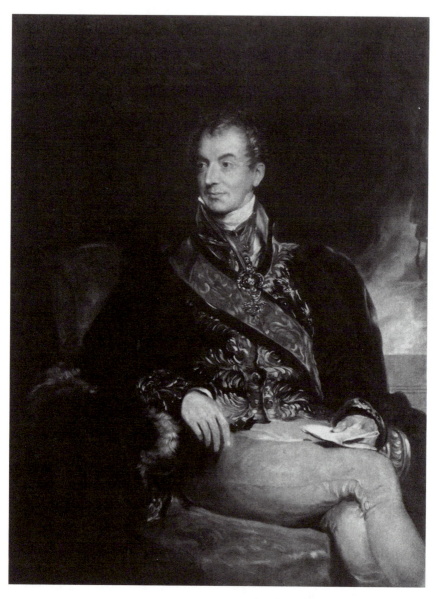

Austrian chancellor Clemens von Metternich dominated Europe from the conclusion of the Napoleonic Wars until the Revolutions of 1848. The intelligent, urbane, and magisterial Metternich opposed both liberalism and nationalism. (Reproduced from the Collections of the Library of Congress.)

A variety of causes—sometimes mutually incompatible—sparked the revolutions. European liberals, who traced their heritage back to the previous century's Enlightenment and French Revolution, rejected the status quo in favor of far-reaching change. Inspired by revolutionary slogans such as "Liberty, Equality, Fraternity" and committed to the Enlightenment's belief that human reason could create institutions that would bring a more perfect world, the liberals demanded constitutions, representative assemblies, religious toleration, an economic system based on laissez-faire or the free market, and a judicial system resting on the principle of equality under the law. In addition to educated idealists, liberalism drew much of its support from those engaged in trade and manufacturing who saw liberalism as a way to maximize their profits and to gain political power and social prestige equal to their growing wealth.

Europe's nationalists also opposed the status quo. They objected to political units and boundaries that rested upon tradition or dynastic considerations. Rather, they viewed the world through a national or ethnic perspective. They presumed that each national group had intrinsic value and brought something to the table. That being the case, they sought ways to enable each national group to reach its full potential in the belief that this would enrich the whole. To achieve this laudable goal, nationalists felt that each national group should be able to make its own decisions and that the best way to accomplish this would be for each national group to be unified and independent. Of course, in order to succeed it would be necessary to destroy the status quo and to remake the map of Europe.

The peasantry also supported revolution, but its commitment was less ideological and more personal in nature. Unlike the liberals and nationalists, the peasants did not want major systemic change. Instead, they called for an end to the vestiges of feudalism and greater control over their lives and land.

Europe's workers also demanded change. Those who worked in factories objected to the gross exploitation that they experienced. They hated their long hours, low wages, poor working conditions, and lack of job security. Although continental Europe had few factories at this time, the handwriting was on the wall. The industrial plant was the wave of the future, a prospect that terrified artisans, or traditional handworkers. In an increasingly frantic manner they sought protection against the machine age that would render them superfluous and unable to compete economically. When the ruling authorities failed to heed their cries, they turned to revolution.

Two specific events hastened the coming of the revolutions. The industrial expansion of the early 1840s suddenly ended, and economic hard times began. The unemployment level rose dramatically, and those who lost their jobs had no safety net to protect them. Governments everywhere left the problem of the unemployed to private institutions such as the church; however, the needs of those thrown out of work were too great and much misery ensued. Even worse, in mid-decade the potato crop failed. Potatoes provided sustenance for millions of Europeans, and when the crop failed, hunger stalked the land. In some areas, such as Ireland, peasants died of starvation. As was the case with unemployment, governments made no real effort to alleviate the misery. Thus, it should have come as no surprise that desperate people would seek desperate solutions.

The first of the major Revolutions of 1848 broke out in February in France. The conflagration spread rapidly, and by early March, the German states lying closest to France buzzed with excitement. In Baden, Württemberg, and Bavaria, the old structures came under attack as the revolution moved toward the north and east from the German southwest. Nevertheless, for German history events in Vienna and Berlin proved to be of much greater importance. On March 3, the Hungarian nationalist Louis Kossuth demanded that the Austrian Empire grant a constitution to its Hungarians. A few days later, rioting broke out in Vienna. While it appeared that most of Vienna sided with the forces of change, the movement's leadership fell to radical students who increasingly relied on undisciplined Viennese artisans and workers to get their points across. On March 13, Metternich resigned and fled into exile in Great Britain. The great architect of the past 30 years was gone! At the same time, the feeble-minded emperor Ferdinand promised a constitution, and preliminary steps were taken to call a constituent assembly. Shortly thereafter, serfdom was abolished in both the Austrian and Hungarian lands. Nevertheless, the revolutionaries remained unsatisfied, and in May, the emperor and his court left the city for the safer climes of Innsbruck. Furthermore, the Habsburg Empire's Slavic populations, especially the Czechs, demanded autonomy, and Piedmont attempted to seize Austria's Italian provinces. As Austria's difficulties mounted, its weakened condition prevented it from exercising its customary authority over German affairs.

For the defenders of the status quo, the situation in Berlin was not much better. Rioters took to the streets on March 15, reacting to massive industrial layoffs earlier in the month and news of events from Vienna. Three days later, Frederick William IV, the enigmatic Prussian king, announced a number of concessions. However, confusion prevailed, shots were fired, and before nightfall, more than 200 people lay dead in the streets. More confusion led the army to withdraw from Berlin, unintentionally leaving the king unguarded. On March 19, the king was forced to pay homage to the dead whose bullet-ridden and bayoneted bodies were paraded before him. Caught up in the emotion of events, the rather unstable Frederick William endorsed the formation of a unified German state with the announcement that henceforth "Prussia is merged in Germany." Indications are that Frederick William almost immediately regretted this commitment.

At this juncture, the focus of the revolution in Germany turned back to the western lands and Frankfurt, where a national assembly gathered. This was the Frankfurt Parliament, a revolutionary successor to the old German Confederation, a loose body of 39 German states that had been formed at the Congress of Vienna and dominated by Austria ever since. The revolutions in Germany swept away the Confederation's authority, and in late March, a preparliament, or *Vorparlament*, met at Frankfurt to lay the foundations for the parliament that would decide Germany's fate. Although a significant minority of the 500 or so delegates wanted the immediate creation of a unified, liberal Germany based in part on the example provided by the United States, most of the delegates hoped to plan Germany's future in conjunction with Germany's hereditary rulers. Ultimately, the decision was made to hold elections for representatives to the parliament. The right to vote was extended to all adult, "independent" (an imprecise stipulation that disenfranchised many) males. Elections were held on May 1, and on May 18, the delegates assembled at Frankfurt's St. Paul's Church for the opening of the National Assembly or Frankfurt Parliament.

The Parliament's composition was decidedly moderate. Of the more than 500 delegates, judges and lawyers made up a plurality. Additionally, there were 150 bureaucrats, more than 100 educators, about 40 businessmen, and an equal number of clergy. Only one peasant and four artisans attended. As one might expect from that lineup, the Parliament was long on debate and rather short on action. As their president, the delegates elected Heinrich von Gagern, a liberal nobleman and administrator from Hesse-Darmstadt; for the unpopular German Confederation they substituted a quasi-government of their own headed by Archduke Johann of Austria, the youngest brother of the late emperor Francis and something of a liberal by reputation.

While the Frankfurt Parliament claimed to speak for the German people, it never established any real authority over the country. Rather, it endlessly debated the nature of the future Germany and its boundaries as the various German states and their shaken but gradually recovering rulers continued to exercise real power. Proof of this came in mid-July when the German princes ignored Frankfurt's demand that their armies accept Parliament's authority. A few weeks later, in the wake of an almost unfath-omable dispute over the north German duchies of Schleswig and Holstein that had grown into a thorny international crisis, the Parliament reversed its earlier position and accepted Prussia's highly unpopular and antina-tionalistic solution to the issue. Obviously, the Parliament could not act independently in matters concerning the German states and international relations. In this particular instance, Berlin—not Frankfurt—prevailed.

Moreover, the Schleswig-Holstein matter exacerbated a problem that had plagued the Frankfurt Parliament since its inception. It clearly revealed the split between moderates and radicals. In the wake of the Schleswig-Holstein fiasco, many of the Parliament's radicals raised the red flag of revolution. While the forces of the princes easily suppressed the revolutionaries, their actions alienated many German burghers who now began to shift their support from the Parliament to the princes since the lat-ter now seemed best able to maintain law and order and to guarantee the burghers' property.

Meanwhile, in both Austria and Prussia, the revolution was flagging and the traditional authorities were regaining their nerve. In the Habs-burg Empire, loyal troops bombarded revolutionary Prague into submis-sion, defeated the Piedmontese invaders at the Battle of Custozza, and mounted an effective campaign against the rebellious Hungarians. In Vienna itself, wild mob action in October underlined the radical turn that the revolution there had taken. Moderates of all shades reconsidered their support for the revolution and concluded that the former status quo offered a more secure future. In late October, the Austrian army under Prince Alfred von Windischgrätz occupied the city after bloody fighting. The victors annihilated the radicals and restored traditional order. The immediate future of the empire was entrusted to the brilliant conservative Prince Felix von Schwarzenberg, and in December, the incompetent emperor Ferdinand abdicated in favor of his 18-year-old nephew Franz Joseph, who would rule the Habsburg lands until his death in 1916.

In Prussia, Frederick William IV, who early on regretted the concessions that he had made to his subjects, saw his feeling of remorse deepen when the newly elected Prussian National Assembly convened in Berlin in May and much against his will began to write a democratic constitution. How-ever, the assembly dawdled. Meanwhile, economic conditions in Berlin worsened, and the restless working class expressed disappointment with the work of the relatively moderate assembly. Perhaps most importantly, the officer corps, the Junkers, and the bureaucracy—traditional centers of monarchical power—remained steadfast in their opposition to the revo-lution and resolute in their determination to destroy it. The end of the

Prussian revolution came in November when Prussian general Friedrich von Wrangel's troops occupied Berlin. The National Assembly was dissolved, and Frederick William issued a new constitution that included a fairly liberal veneer but had the practical effect of restoring most of the prerevolutionary status quo.

The Frankfurt Parliament also passed into history. The liberal-radical divide had sapped its energies; the Schleswig-Holstein failure had demonstrated its weakness; and now this body took on the difficult and complicated task of establishing the new Germany's borders. Although a deep and sincere sense of German nationalism motivated many delegates, it soon became apparent that Parliament's sympathy for national ideals did not extend to non-Germans such as the Poles. It was decided that the new German state would include these non-Germans regardless of their wishes.

The question of how to fit the multinational Austrian Empire into this configuration loomed large. Although a very complex issue, one proposed solution—the *Grossdeutsch*, or great Germany, option—called for the inclusion of Austria and a fair number of its non-Germanic peoples. However, by the end of 1848 Schwarzenberg's Austria had made clear that it had no interest in the *Grossdeutsch* solution. The Frankfurt Parliament then turned to the *Kleindeutsch*, or little Germany, solution, one that excluded Austria and its non-Germanic possessions from the new Germany.

Naturally, the *Kleindeutsch* option placed Prussia at the head of the new German state. Consequently, in March 1849, the Frankfurt Parliament voted to make Frederick William IV emperor of Germany. However, Frederick William refused the honor, privately denigrating the offer as "a pig crown" and "a crown from the gutter." With this refusal, the Frankfurt Parliament broke up. A rump Parliament reassembled at Stuttgart, but Württemberg troops dispersed it in June 1849. The revolutions that had begun so promisingly now proved barren.

INTERPRETIVE ESSAY
Robert D. Billinger, Jr.

"The past is never dead. It's not even past," the U.S. author William Faulkner said about the American South. The same could be said about the Revolutions of 1848–49 in Germany: each generation rewrites the history of this significant period and each ideological grouping reflects its own political perspective. The Revolutions of 1848–49 are events that changed Germany. Their symbols remain; most obviously, the flag of the Federal Republic in both its 1949 and 1990 incarnations is the black, red, and gold tricolor of the revolutionaries of 1848–49.

Complicating historical memories and interpretations is the fact that there were *many* revolutions in German-speaking central Europe in 1848–49, not just one revolution. Though the popular uprisings in Vienna and Berlin and the later meetings of the National Assembly in Frankfurt figure prominently in the literature, it is important to remember that there were revolutions not only in the capitals of the 39 states of the German Confederation, but also uprisings in many rural areas as well. Though revolutionary Europe is not the subject of this essay, the many revolutions of the German-speaking world took place in a European context in which revolutions in Italy and France in 1848 provoked emulation in cities as disparate as Brussels, Budapest, Milan, Prague, Rome, and Venice. The so-called Springtime of the Peoples is an appropriate name for these popular uprisings, which, despite their differing causes, goals, and results, had in common the attempt to replace aristocratic governments with more popular ones. Europe in 1848–49 saw the mobilization and politicization of groups as never before. That politicization, in Germany as in other revolutionized areas, would be a major factor in the politics of all of Europe thereafter. Even restored monarchies would have to pay deference to democratic and nationalistic feelings. Aristocrats would mobilize their own popular support through the creation of conservative newspapers and clubs to rival and counter the liberal and democratic ideologies of the revolutionary years.

Before attempting to interpret the German Revolutions of 1848–49 within their unique historical contexts, as recent historians have tried so hard to do, it is important to reject some of the more ahistorical though commonly propagated interpretations of the German Revolutions of 1848–49. One must first categorically discard views that suggest that the German revolutions were total failures and that those failures were inevitable because of the uniqueness of German national character. To be disdained even more is the view that German revolutionary failures led inevitably to the rise of a unique German Caesarism under Otto von Bismarck and ultimately to the horrors of Adolf Hitler's regime. To do otherwise is to read history backward, requiring one to overlook the strong liberal, democratic, and socialist political strands in German history that, inspired by the heroes of the 1848–49 Revolutions, continually arose to trouble conservatives, reactionaries, and fascists ever since. It attributes a negative uniqueness to German history that is absurd.

What is most important for an understanding of the revolutions in Germany in 1848–49 is to put them in their proper historical context. Midcentury Germanic central Europe was a world in which peasants predominated, craftsmen displaced by machines advocated governmental paternalism and spoke against free enterprise, Karl Marx's "proletariat" was probably less than four percent of the population, and Marx himself was a revolutionary democrat. Likewise, in the 1840s the color red stood for democratic revolution rather than for socialism, religious conflicts were more important than economic ones, and the king of Prussia was still an opponent of national unification.

While we must guard against the tendency to read history backward, we must not forget that people have always acted based on what they learned or thought they learned from their past. The German fascination with the French Revolution of 1789 that would bring the planting of freedom trees, the turning of scythes into weapons, the wearing of Phyrigian hats, and the proclaiming of human rights in the German states in 1848–49 were not symbols that were suddenly rediscovered in 1848. The coals in the ashes—the liberal, democratic, and even socialist ideals of the French Revolution of 1789—did not die despite the Carlsbad Decrees of 1819, their renewal in 1824, and the Six Articles and Ten Acts of 1832. The repression of liberals and nationalists by the particularistic German princes and their states' rights- and monarchy-protecting German Confederation only radicalized German intellectuals. Recent studies have revealed that despite the ban on political parties in the pre-1848 period, crypto-political associations not only politicized large numbers of the educated middle classes, but also trained them in the procedures of a civil society. Members learned to use rules and procedures to organize debates and decision making through use of the ballot. Training in party organization and discipline, policy making, and balloting would be evident in the first German national assembly.

It was through numerous preexisting political associations that educated Germans expressed their interest and hopes for political reform and possible German unification on the eve of 1848. Naturally, means and ends varied depending on the political ideologies and aspirations of varying groups. In September 1847, radical democrats including Friedrich Hecker and Gustav von Struve met in Offenburg to call for the democratization of the German Confederation, including Austria. Within a month, in October 1847, moderate liberals like Karl Mathy and Adam von Itzstein of Baden, Friedrich Römer of Württemberg, Heinrich von Gagern of Hesse, and David Hansemann of the Rhineland met in Heppenheim to urge the unification of Germany through the Prussian Tariff Union.

These men could dream and agitate for change, but revolutions are made by frustrated people in city streets and peasant villages. These so-

called little people were the ones who produced the revolts that led to
monarchic concessions that the intellectuals would turn to their purposes.
But the men and women who made the revolutions were moved by specific local social grievances that often had little in common with the
dreams of the ideologues. Common folk revolted against what was called
progress and for the return to the supposed good old days. In rural villages, there were revolts against the abandonment of traditions like common land and peasant forest gleaning rights. In the cities, revolts were
against a free enterprise industrialism that was pauperizing traditional
artisans and craftsmen. Economic frustrations frequently led to anti-
Semitic disturbances, which were denounced by liberal leaders.

It was mobs of common people that first reacted to the news of the outbreak of revolution in France during the last week of February 1848. Their
antifeudal uprisings frightened the monarchic establishments of the German states. Frustrated by the poverty of the lean years between 1845 and
1847, on March 2, 1848, irate peasants appeared in Wiesbaden and forced
Duke Adolf of Nassau to end serfdom. Trouble hit the huge estates of the
imperial nobility of Baden and Württemberg, too. Nobles were terrorized,
feudal' privileges renounced, and estate records were destroyed. Mobs
took to the streets of Karlsruhe and Stuttgart, leading the grand duke of
Baden to appoint liberal ministers to work on a new constitution and the
king of Württemberg to do the same. Similar developments occurred in
Munich, where King Ludwig I of Bavaria decreed freedom of the press
and ministerial responsibility to the Diet before abdicating in favor of his
son, Maximilian.

As early as March 3, 1848, the Diet of the German Confederation, a collection of the diplomatic representatives of the 39 German states,
announced that each state might repeal the hated Carlsbad Decrees if it
chose. Within a week the otherwise monarchic Diet declared black, red,
and gold the official colors of Germany and called for representatives of
the German states to draft a new constitution for Germany. All of this
occurred before the momentous revolutionary events of March 13 in
Vienna and those of a week later in Berlin.

While leaders of the opposition met in Heidelberg on March 5 to prepare a call for an all-German constitutional convention, violence rocked
the German states. It intimidated aristocrats, rulers, and reformers alike.
But this violence was the motive force of the revolutions. It was a violence
that felled trees in royal forests, destroyed ditches that divided formerly
common lands, burned feudal castles, and destroyed machines that took
away the living of artisans. It was the violence of artisans and students
that led to the downfall of Clemens von Metternich in Vienna on March

13. It was violence in Berlin on March 18 that led King Frederick William IV of Prussia on March 21 to don a German tricolor and proclaim his intention to lead a united Germany, an intention that he had long resisted and would soon reject again. But for the moment, Frederick William, like the other intimidated aristocrats of the German states, tried to hold on as best he could by bending rather than breaking. He introduced freedom of the press and appointed a reform ministry. Throughout the German states, the new "March ministries," like the French National Assembly back on the night of August 4, 1789, took the first steps to restore order by antifeudal reforms to quell peasant revolts.

The ministries of the newly reformed German states felt it necessary not only to appease peasants, but also to repress republican movements. When a preparliament of nearly 600 reformers met in Frankfurt to draft procedures for an all-German election in May, Friedrich Hecker and Gustav von Struve of Baden called for the abolition of monarchies and the creation of a United States of Germany. Moderates led by Heinrich von Gagern, later president of the Frankfurt National Assembly, argued that Germany was not ripe for a republic and that reformers should work with existing kings. The Baden radicals returned home to raise an army of 4,000 peasants, workers, and soldiers that was crushed on April 20 by regular troops of Baden's new liberal government.

When one thinks of the German Revolutions of 1848–49, a key image will always be the Frankfurt National Assembly meeting in the Pauluskirche (St. Paul's Church), a structure still venerated in Germany today. But one also thinks of the unkind images of the Frankfurt Assembly created by Bismarck and other conservatives of a useless, impractical gathering of 800 so-called professors. Indeed there may have been as many as 812 different members of the parliament between May 18, 1848 and June 18, 1849, but that is counting replacement deputies. The membership laid down by law was 649, but the assembly probably never had more than between 400 and 450 members at any one time. More importantly, the National Assembly was a parliament of civil servants rather than professors. Most of its members had university degrees, and perhaps 60 percent had studied law. Through their training and experience, these Germans, not unlike U.S. senators today, were not representative of the average citizen. They were moderately conservative in their historical and constitutionalist leanings rather than pro-parliamentary or democratic. Yet because of their training they were practical men and modern in their formation and use of political factions.

The eight factions of the Pauluskirche, named from the eight different cafés in which they met after hours and ranging from the rightist Café

Milani group through the leftist Deutsche Hof and Donnersberg groups, functioned very much like twentieth-century political parties in Western Europe. The presence of these factions, rather than being decried as evidence of revolutionary divisiveness, should be understood as an important step on the way to political modernity in Germany. It was through them that the business of the National Assembly was ordered, subjects for debate determined, plenary debates shared, and constituents outside the Assembly kept aware of political developments. Out of confusion, coherence was achieved with four broad political blocs emerging: right, center right, center left, and left. Their interests ranged from support for constitutional monarchy and states' rights on the right and shaded over to greater emphasis on the power of a central German parliament. Further to the center and left were found attitudes in favor of universal suffrage, parliamentary democracy, and even support for national plebiscites. In the Frankfurt Parliament, much to the chagrin of contemporary radicals and latter-day critics, the right and center right were the majority factions.

The National Assembly's first and initially most important decision, one achieved by a vote of 450 to 100, was the creation of a new provisional Central Power, composed of an imperial regent, a minister president, and a ministerial cabinet made up of ministers of foreign affairs, home affairs, war, finance, justice, and trade. The selection of Archduke Johann of Austria as the imperial regent indicated the inclination of the majority of the Assembly for Germany to create a unified, constitutionally monarchic Germany, a *Grossdeutschland* that would include Austria.

The new Central Power generated apprehension both abroad and within the German states. Foreign powers and states' rights-protective German March ministries were reluctant to countenance the creation of what the French feared would be an "Empire Germanique." Great Britain hoped for a strong liberal Germany able to resist both French revolutionary republicanism and a reactionary Russia. Russia hoped for a strong conservative Germany to resist a potentially expansive French Republic. Both Great Britain and Russia adopted a cautious wait-and-see attitude. In fact, the only foreign power to recognize the diplomatic status of the new Central Power was the United States of America. Individual German states refused to pay homage to the imperial regent, though they did provide him with command of "imperial troops"—the army corps of the former federal troops of the German Confederation—to put down republican uprisings. When the Central Power acted on behalf of "law and order," it had the full support of the German states. Yet by doing so, it became associated with the repression of democratic political associations and alienated some of its popular base.

The most important and lasting impact of the National Assembly was undoubtedly its creation of a statement of Basic Rights for German citizens. Those rights, which were to be extended to all peoples living within territories of the former German Confederation, including German Jews and "non-German Germans," such as Poles and Italians, were remarkable for their time and would be the basis for the Basic Rights of Germans again after 1949. In this connection, it is worth mentioning that German Jews played a major role in the Revolutions of 1848–49 despite the occasional anti-Semitism of some revolutionaries. A vice president of the National Assembly, Gabriel Riesser, a Jew from Hamburg, was applauded when he resisted an attempt by several deputies to exclude Jews from the Basic Rights.

A powerful blow to states' rights and protested as such by Austria, Prussia, and several other states, the Basic Rights were to be guaranteed to all citizens in all of the German states. They were aimed at guaranteeing personal and political freedoms as well as personal property. Rights mentioned included freedom of the press, assembly, and association. The Basic Rights also abolished all feudal bonds, though with individual financial compensation. The fact of compensation was an irritant to democrats at the time. Individual German states were guaranteed constitutions with representative bodies and responsible ministries. Finally, religious freedom along with the separation of state and canon law were recognized, laying the basis for a modern secular German state.

Parenthetically, despite the importance, symbolic and real, of the National Assembly in Frankfurt, it is important to remember that there was more than one popularly elected assembly functioning in Germany during the Revolutions of 1848–49. The assemblies of the individual states were the scene of German parliamentary experience as well. Though these assemblies, like the one in Frankfurt, would eventually be pushed aside or relegated to mediocrity by resurgent princes, it is important to note that these attempts at democratic government did not fail; they were defeated militarily. The revolutionary parliamentary initiatives of 1848, unlike those of the equally startling Revolutions of 1989, were defeated by reactionary armies.

While German state assemblies existed in 1848–49, they gave proof of the diversity of possibilities that existed in terms of representation and policies. In Berlin, for instance, the so-called Prussian National Assembly had a higher percentage of peasants, craftsmen, and clergymen than did the Frankfurt Parliament. More representative of the lower middle classes and the poor, it refused to accept a constitution suggested to it by Frederick William IV and produced its own draft. This draft proposed a general right to arms, a people's army under parliamentary control, parliamentary advice and consent for foreign treaties, and only a suspensive veto for the king on parliamentary bills. It is important to note that since the monarchy had abolished serfdom in 1807, this was not an issue in Prussia as it was in Austria. Prussians were beyond feudalism and ready to move further along the line to political freedoms, political participation, and political equality. But the Prussian assembly embittered the king by passing resolutions aimed at eliminating "by the Grace of God" from the royal title and ending aristocratic titles all together. Its innovative work was doomed when royalist troops restored control in Berlin in November. On December 5, 1848, the Prussian National Assembly was dissolved, and a new monarchic constitution was promulgated by Frederick William IV. He was to remain monarch "by the Grace of God," the army was not to take an oath to the constitution, and noble titles were secured. Yet there was a Prussian constitution. Though it instituted a three-tiered suffrage system that favored the wealthy and protected royal authority, one result of the Revolutions of 1848 in Prussia was that the king triumphed over revolution by accepting a constitution that would ultimately remain in force until the end of the monarchy after World War I.

Rather than bringing a new constitution to Austria, the most lasting result of the Revolutions of 1848–49 was a new monarch. Franz Joseph replaced Ferdinand in December 1848 after the success of the counterrevolution. Unlike in Prussia, personal rule rather than constitutionalism was the ultimate impact of the revolutions in the Habsburg Monarchy. Experimentation with constitutionalism was brief. In Vienna a Reichstag (parliament) composed of 383 deputies from all of the Habsburg states, except for separatist Hungary and Lombardy-Venetia, opened in July 1848 in multiethnic splendor. Almost one-fourth of the deputies were farmers or small landowners, and most agreed to end agrarian feudalism. However, in a victory for the moderates and private property interests, feudal obligations were abolished with compensation by those involved. With the end of feudal obligations, peasant demands were satisfied, and this large group became supporters of the monarchy. For the agrarian population, the reason for revolts was ended. Liberals lost their support. As for the Reichstag itself, the conquest of Vienna by Imperial troops in October led to its transfer to Kremsier in Moravia and ultimately to its dissolution by the Kaiser's army in March 1849. Any possibility of a revolutionary *Grossdeutschland* was at an end.

Meanwhile, the National Assembly in Frankfurt continued to meet, and its German nationalism aroused controversy among contemporaries and has provoked criticism ever since. The crux of the matter is the degree to which the liberal and cosmopolitan nationalism of the *Vormärz* period was replaced at the Pauluskirche by a more aggressive, expansionist, and antagonistic nationalism. Certainly there were a variety of perspectives represented at Frankfurt, and a seemingly antagonistic nationalism appeared when the Assembly was confronted by the questions of Posen, South Tyrol, Bohemia-Moravia, and Schleswig-Holstein. But casting stereotypes of a later nineteenth- and twentieth-century aggressive German nationalism aside, a more benign, though competitive, bourgeois nationalism seems evident. The Assembly was willing to give non-German nationalities room for cultural expression and cultural autonomy but felt that its own honor and that of the German cultural nation demanded a defense against the aggressiveness of other nationalities. Convinced of the superiority of German culture, most deputies felt that in the free play of cultural competition, even non-Germans would recognize and seek an attachment to German culture. Only where German openness to cultural competition was met by militant aggression should Germany defend its honor and possessions. Thus, when Prussian troops put down a Polish uprising in Posen in May 1848 and the Prussian government claimed two-thirds of the province as German-Posen, the Frankfurt Assembly sanctioned the decree and resisted proposals for German claims to the entire province.

In the question of South Tyrol, the Assembly has been accused of aggressive nationalism for not allowing Italian-speaking portions of the German Confederation to leave the new German state. Yet this attitude can be seen less as an example of German aggressiveness than as an attempt to maintain traditional territories in the face of the aggressiveness of others. The same can be said of the Assembly's rejection of Czech demands for exclusion from Germany. The Czechs refused to send deputies to Frankfurt from 48 of 68 of their constituencies. But as with the South Tyrol, Bohemia and Moravia were seen as traditional areas of the German Confederation and not to be turned over to another nationality. At the same time, however, the Pauluskirche deputies did recognize the concerns of non-German minorities and voted unanimously for measures to protect the cultural and political rights of these minorities.

The cases of Limburg and of Schleswig-Holstein are also interesting because they were cited at the time and by some historians since as examples of German aggressive nationalism. The fact that Limburg and Holstein were parts of the German Confederation and therefore not subject to abdication from the perspective of most members of the Frankfurt National Assembly was countered then and now with the international reality that both Limburg and Schleswig-Holstein were German territories attached personally, but not constitutionally, to the Dutch and Danish crowns, respectively. From the point of view of the governments of England, France, and Russia, such considerations placed Limburg and Schleswig-Holstein in a special category of territories whose princely sovereignty was to be protected. From the point of view of the delegates at Frankfurt, these territories, like all of the German-speaking territories of the German Confederation were traditionally "German." Claiming them for the new "Reich" was not an act of aggression but an assertion of traditional and rightful national honor. When the king of Denmark annexed Schleswig to Denmark in March 1848 and Danish troops moved into this area, which had its own German revolutionary provisional state government, the Diet of the German Confederation declared a federal war against Denmark. The Frankfurt Assembly continued the conflict. It was the Prussian government, under pressure from Russia and England, that agreed in August to the Truce of Malmö that divided Schleswig according to nationality, thus circumventing and undercutting the new Central Power at Frankfurt. The National Assembly rejected the Central Power's reluctant acceptance of the Truce of Malmö and actually forced the Charles von Leiningen cabinet to step down. This is an interesting example, though a frustrating one, of the adhesion to the principles of parliamentary government observed by the new German National Assembly.

Concern for the exigencies of international relations ultimately led the Assembly to accept the provisions of the Truce of Malmö, though that provoked further uprisings throughout Germany, including one in Frankfurt in September 1848. The very moderation of the National Assembly alienated its more nationalistic and democratic constituents. The resulting revolutionary outbreaks forced the Assembly to seek protection from radicals by relying on conservative and antirevolutionary German monarchs and their troops. Thus the Schleswig-Holstein issue correlates to, if it did not cause, a turning point in the flow of events in the Germany of 1848–49. Instead of risking an international war with Russia and England over Schleswig-Holstein, the National Assembly associated itself with upholding the European international status quo and provoked what amounted to a German civil war instead. In that German civil war, the Pauluskirche would be blamed by democrats and nationalists for siding with the forces of reaction. In response, Germany's moderate parliamentary liberals ever since have blamed radical democratic excesses for undermining the Frankfurt Assembly.

The moderate Frankfurt Assembly and radical democratic provincials stood opposed after the fall of 1848. Likewise, advocates of a greater Germany, *Grossdeutschland*, which would have included Austria, found themselves opposed not only by pro-Prussian constitutional monarchists, but also by the restored reactionary governments in Berlin and Vienna. In

Vienna, the Felix von Schwarzenberg ministry declared that the Habsburg Empire was indivisible and would not be part of a new German empire. Almost simultaneously, Frederick William IV of Prussia rejected an overture made by the new Heinrich von Gagern cabinet in Frankfurt that would have had the Prussian king solve the nationality question by accepting a role as the hereditary emperor of a smaller German state, a *Kleindeutschland*. The proposal rejected by Frederick William in November 1848 would be renewed in April 1849, only to be rejected again. But by then the fate of the revolutions in Germany was determined. It is easy to see why moderate liberals in Germany have blamed Frederick William ever since for not accepting a challenge that might have created a unified and constitutional Germany. But that thinking seems ahistorical: first, because of Frederick William's traditionalist personality; second, because Russia and Austria would probably have resisted; and finally, because except for revolutionary centers in Saxony, the Palatinate, and Baden, counterrevolutionary feelings were ascendant in the Germanies.

With the rejection by Frederick William IV of the proffered imperial crown, the Revolutions of 1848–49 were all over but for the shooting. The shooting of democratic nationalists by Prussian troops after the fall of the last revolutionary holdouts in Dresden and at the southwest German fortress at Rastatt formed the denouement after a spectacular climax to the German Revolutions of 1848–49. That climax was a demonstration of the popularity, organizational skill, and zeal on the part of radical democrats. A recent study by Jonathan Sperber of democratic groups in the Rhineland has revealed the specific historical concerns, particularly religious concerns, that motivated these grassroots democrats and put them at odds with the moderates of the Frankfurt Assembly as well as with the reigning princes.

What motivated them gives us insight into the uniqueness of the world of mid-nineteenth-century Germany. It was a world in which religious differences still mattered, leading Catholics of the Prussian Rhineland and Protestants of the Bavarian Palatinate to reject the rule of a Protestant monarch in Berlin and a Catholic monarch in Munich. The republicans of the Prussian Rhineland and the Bavarian Palatinate, areas recently grafted onto new states in the wake of the Napoleonic Wars, expressed their opposition to far-away princes of differing religious sympathies through an enthusiasm for a future republican national German state. When in April 1849 Frederick William IV rejected the Frankfurt Assembly's constitution and its offer of a hereditary monarchy despite the approval of both by 29 of the 39 German states, the Rhineland republicans staged their last revolt. This uprising, like that in Dresden, was suppressed by Prussian regular army troops who as early as 1849 were equipped with rapid-fire needle guns.

The Revolutions of 1848–49 in Germany, like the revolutions through-out Europe in those years, ended with victorious princes, disappointed moderates, and fugitive or dead democrats. Those executed by the author-ities of the restored German states, like every 10th prisoner in the Rastatt fortress in Baden, were "pardoned," as the German expression went at the time, "to powder and lead." Had *a* German Revolution of 1848 failed? How does one assess failure when there were many revolutions in many German states and with many diverse goals? As the German historian Wolfram Siemann has pointed out, there were many revolutionary events in the Germanies in 1848–49, and even those that took place at the same time occurred in isolation from each other and often with conflicting motives. What was consistent despite the diversity of aims of Germans in 1848–49 was the new political mobilization in all areas and by advocates of all political positions across the spectrum: democrats, liberals, monar-chists, and even members of the Protestant and Catholic religious right. By the fall of 1849, reaction had triumphed, but politically mobilized Ger-mans would never return to their pre-1848 inertness. Henceforth, even reactionaries would mobilize the masses through newspapers, associa-tions, popular demonstrations, and nationalistic flag-waving. But the course of German history did not lead directly from "white revolutionar-ies" like Bismarck, manipulators of popular participation, nationalism, and paternalistic social policies to beguile Germans, to the fascism of Adolf Hitler. After the Revolutions of 1848–49, all of the German states made concessions to parliamentary movements within several decades.

Historians may still argue about a "failure" of a German Revolution in 1848, as though there were only one, and about that failure being caused by dissension among the revolutionaries. In fact, dissension and its artic-ulation is a characteristic of the modern world, and a modern world was being born in Germany in 1848–49. Despite the dissension, cooperation led to the expression of constitutional ideals and assertions of national character that were exemplary in their idealism and moderation com-pared to the ideals and actions of mid-twentieth-century Germans. The idealism and moderation of the German revolutionaries of 1848–49 was astounding compared to that of citizens of most other European countries during a later and darker period of European history in the twentieth cen-tury.

SELECTED BIBLIOGRAPHY

Anderson, Margaret Lavinia. "History in the Comic Mode: Jonathan Sperber's
    1848." *Central European History* 25 (1992): 333–42. An analysis of Sperber's

award-winning study of the Rhineland radicals of the Revolutions of 1848–49, it contrasts Sperber's positive tone with the more "conscience-stricken" analyses of revolutionary "failure" common among German historians.

Barclay, David E. *Frederick William IV and the Prussia Monarchy, 1840–1861.* Oxford: Clarendon Press, 1995. Chapters 6–8 present the best current analysis of the despair, confusion, and delusions of this most interesting and complex of monarchs and of the advisors who surrounded him during the Revolutions of 1848–49.

Brose, Eric Dorn. *German History, 1789–1871: From Holy Roman Empire to the Bismarckian Reich.* Providence and Oxford: Berghahn Books, 1997. Excellent, up-to-date and readable. Chapter 14, "The Revolutions of 1848 and 1849," captures the latest scholarship.

Elon, Amos. *The Pity of It All: A History of Jews in Germany, 1743–1933.* New York: Henry Holt and Company, 2002. Most interesting book with an excellent chapter on the leadership roles and aspirations of German Jews during the Revolutions of 1848–49.

Eyck, Frank. *The Frankfurt Parliament of 1848–9.* London and New York: Macmillan and St. Martin's, 1968. This is the classic, detailed, and judicious analysis of the Frankfurt Parliament, stressing the difficulties facing the German governments and the various revolutionary factions represented at Frankfurt.

Felix, David. "Heute Deutschland! Marx as Provincial Politician." *Central European History* 15 (1982): 332–50. Interesting analysis of Karl Marx's role as a Rhineland advocate of a single democratic German republic during the Revolutions of 1848–49.

Hamerow, Theodore S. *Restoration, Revolution, Reaction.* Princeton, NJ: Princeton University Press, 1958. Excellent, if now somewhat dated, study of the social movements that formed the background to the German revolutions.

Hammen, Oscar J. *The Red '48ers: Karl Marx and Friedrich Engels.* New York: Charles Scribner Publishing, 1969. A densely detailed biographical account of the activities of these two men during the Revolutions of 1848–49.

Harris, James F. "Rethinking the Categories of the German Revolution of 1848: The Emergence of Popular Conservatism in Bavaria." *Central European History* 25 (1992): 123–48. Based on an analysis of petitions sent to the Bavarian Lower House supporting and opposing the Frankfurt National Constitution and its Basic Rights, the author reveals the existence of a strong, outspoken, and strongly populist and "conservative" constituency in Bavaria during the revolutionary period.

Judson, Pieter M. *Exclusive Revolutionaries: Liberal Politics, Social Experience, and National Identity in the Austrian Empire, 1848–1914.* Ann Arbor: University of Michigan Press, 1996. Chapter 2, "1848: The Transformation of Public Life," of this award-winning study skillfully evaluates the conundrums facing German liberals in multiethnic Austria.

Lensink, Paul D. "The Revolutions of 1848." In *Events That Changed the World in the Nineteenth Century,* edited by Frank W. Thackeray and John E. Findling, pp. 75–92. Westport, CT and London: Greenwood Press, 1996. Good, brief introduction to the history, analysis, and bibliography concerning all of the European Revolutions of the 1848–49 period.

Mattheisen, Donald J. "History as Current Events: Recent Work on the German Revolution of 1848." *American Historical Review* 88 (1983): 1219–37. Excellent review of the evolving historiography of the German revolutions up through the early 1980s, with special emphasis on the ideological and political nature of the historical disagreements.

———. "Liberal Constitutionalism in the Frankfurt Parliament of 1848: An Inquiry Based on Roll-Call Analysis." *Central European History* 12 (1979): 124–42. Uses quantification to analyze Pauluskirche roll-call votes to conclude that its midcentury liberals were at least as strongly opposed to democracy as they were to the old regime.

———. "Voters and Parliaments in the German Revolution of 1848: An Analysis of the Prussian Constituent Assembly." *Central European History* 5 (1972): 3–22. Provocative statistical study of Prussian parliamentary voting patterns that suggests the unexpected: that rural districts elected men of the Left and urban districts men of the Right.

Mosse, W. E. *The European Powers and the German Question, 1848–71: With Special Reference to England and Russia.* Cambridge: Cambridge University Press, 1958. Chapter 1, "The Powers and the German Revolution, 1848–51," rejects the late-nineteenth-century German view of Great Power opposition to German unification and suggests initial sympathies for that unification, especially under Prussia, until the emergence of the Schleswig-Holstein Question.

Namier, Lewis. *1848: Revolution of the Intellectuals.* Garden City, NY: Doubleday, 1946. Very readable older study, but influenced by the bloody nationalisms of the twentieth century. Namier unjustifiably portrayed the Frankfurt Parliament as made up of aggressive nationalists who in their attitudes toward Poles and Czechs were the true forerunners of Hitler.

Nipperdey, Thomas. *Germany from Napoleon to Bismarck, 1800–1866.* Translated by Daniel Nolan. Princeton, NJ: Princeton University Press, 1996. Chapter 5, "The Revolution of 1848–49," of this 1983 classic German grand narrative is a good analytical survey that concludes that the split between the center and left did not cause the "failure" of the revolution, but that it resulted because the resistance to change within the various German states was too diverse and problems such as the *Grossdeutsch/Kleindeutsch* question were too great.

Rath, R. J. *The Viennese Revolution of 1848.* Austin: University of Texas Press, 1957. A marvelously detailed narrative based on and with extensive quotation from contemporary literature; now somewhat dated in style and interpretation.

Robertson, Priscilla. *Revolutions of 1848: A Social History.* Princeton, NJ: Princeton University Press, 1952. This is the most colorful read of the older romantic revolution school, with vivid chapters on the revolutions in the German states.

Sheehan, James J. *German History 1770–1866.* Oxford: Clarendon Press, 1989. Chapter 9, "Revolution and Reaction," of this masterful survey is a very readable and well-footnoted analysis of the continuities and changes of the revolutionary period.

Siemann, Wolfram. *The German Revolution of 1848–49.* Translated by Christiane Banerji. New York: St. Martin's Press, 1998. This 1985 analytical survey of the diverse revolutionary movements of 1848–49 is also an excellent introduction to the evolving German scholarship on these topics.

Sperber, Jonathan. *The European Revolutions, 1848–1851.* Cambridge: Cambridge University Press, 1994. Best and most up-to-date analytical survey of the European revolutions with particularly good chapters on Germany and a very useful bibliography.

———. *Rhineland Radicals: The Democratic Movement and the Revolution of 1848–1849.* Princeton, NJ: Princeton University Press, 1991. This is an award-winning and brilliantly written, innovative regional study.

Stadelmann, Rudolph. *Social and Political History of the German 1848 Revolution.* Translated by James G. Chastain. Athens: Ohio University Press, 1975. A classic 1948 German study, now greatly supplemented by Siemann and Sperber, but good on social origins, pre-Marxian worker consciousness, the concerns of the European powers, and the ultimately positive impacts of a "failed revolution" that the author blames in part for the lack of positive initiatives by Frederick William IV of Prussia.

Vick, Brian E. *Defining Germany: The 1848 Frankfurt Parliamentarians and National Identity.* Cambridge, MA: Harvard University, 2002. Provocatively revisionist analysis of the moderation of the nationalism of the Frankfurt Parliament, marred by theoretical and literary verbiage.

Zucker, Stanley. "German Women and the Revolution of 1848–49: Kathinka Zitz-Halein and the Humania Association." *Central European History* 13 (September 1980): 237–54. This is a fascinating and groundbreaking study of the leader of a women's organization of about 1,600 members in Mainz that was organized first to support democratic revolutionaries and then to give humanitarian aid to the defeated revolutionaries and their dependents.

The Unification of Germany, 1871

INTRODUCTION

Prior to the creation of the German state in 1871, the word "Germany" more accurately described a geographical location rather than a political unit. For centuries, the German-speaking lands were divided into hundreds, if not thousands, of principalities, free cities, ecclesiastical states, counties, duchies, earldoms, and the like. Each of these states varied in size, natural resources, population, wealth, and military might. An institution called the Holy Roman Empire exercised nominal command over the German states, but as the eighteenth-century French writer Voltaire noted, "the Holy Roman Empire was neither holy, nor Roman, nor an empire."

The Habsburg dynasty ruled Austria, and it also controlled the Holy Roman Empire. Periodically, the Habsburgs made attempts to convert the Holy Roman Empire into something resembling their Austrian holdings, over which they exercised great authority. Always their efforts came to naught.

Between 1618 and 1648, the Thirty Years' War ravaged the German-speaking lands. The devastation was so great that most observers do not detect many signs of a Germanic revival until the nineteenth century. Certainly the war further entrenched German particularism, or the tendency of each German state to go its own way without regard for—and even with hostility toward—the putative central government or Holy Roman Empire.

When change did come, it came from the outside in the form of the French conqueror Napoleon Bonaparte. On the heels of a series of military

General Karl von Steinmetz led the victorious Prussian forces during the 1870 Battle of Saarbrücken. The Franco-Prussian War (1870–71) successfully ended the intense campaign to unify Germany under Prussian auspices. (Reproduced from the Collections of the Library of Congress.)

successes, in 1806 Napoleon dissolved the Holy Roman Empire and created in its place the Confederation of the Rhine. With Napoleon's final defeat in 1815, no serious consideration was given either to resurrecting the numerous small states that he had extinguished or to reviving the Holy Roman Empire itself. Rather, the Congress of Vienna that settled Europe's affairs after the Napoleonic Wars created a loose political unit called the German Confederation that consisted of 39 states, the largest of which were Austria and Prussia. Like the Holy Roman Empire, the German Confederation lacked power and authority; German particularism continued to dominate.

During the German Confederation's life, Austria and Prussia competed for preeminence in the German-speaking world. The former usually held the upper hand, and the Habsburg rulers of Austria were not slow to convey this superiority to their Hohenzollern cousins who ruled Prussia.

The Revolutions of 1848 that swept across the Continent did not bypass Germany. Revolutionary outbreaks in Prague, Budapest, Milan, and Vienna itself seemed to threaten Austria's very existence. Similar disturbances occurred in other German locales, but especially in Prussia, where in March 1848 revolutionaries effectively swept aside the government. While a number of factors account for the revolutionary storm, nationalism played a central role as a growing body of Germans demanded unification.

Ultimately, the Revolutions of 1848 failed, and Germany would not be unified at that time. However, as the uprising had run its course, the Prussian king, the erratic Frederick William IV, had rather ambiguously and thoughtlessly placed himself and his kingdom at the head of the movement to unify Germany. This greatly angered Austria, which was rapidly recovering from its close call with the revolution. Realizing that a Germany unified under Prussian auspices would do irreparable harm to Austria's interests, Vienna called Berlin to task with the so-called Humiliation of Olmütz in 1850, which reconfirmed Austria's paramount role in German affairs. After Olmütz, Austria worked to maintain the status quo while Prussia retired to lick its wounds. Nevertheless, among a sizable portion of the German-speaking population the desire for unification was not destroyed; rather, it grew stronger.

It is against this backdrop that the man responsible for German unification, Otto von Bismarck, assumed the chancellorship of Prussia in 1862. Although a domestic crisis propelled Bismarck to the top of the political heap, he soon turned his prodigious energies to the question of unification.

Otto von Bismarck was born in 1815, the son of a Junker, or Prussian landed aristocrat. Although Bismarck liked to boast that his paternal ancestors had put down roots in Prussia well before the arrival of the royal Hohenzollerns, his maternal forebears were merchants and governmental officials rather than nobility. Physically, Bismarck was a huge man distinguished by a massive head sitting atop broad shoulders. Gargantuan appetites matched Bismarck's size. His ability to consume massive amounts of both food and, especially, drink was legendary. An indifferent student, Bismarck spent his university years drinking, dueling, and generally carousing. However, this picture of an out-of-control "student prince" is not a complete one. Bismarck was also highly intelligent and very well read.

After the university, Bismarck entered the Prussian civil service; however, he soon resigned out of boredom and retired to his estates where he righted the family's listing financial ship. By the late 1840s, Bismarck clearly identified himself as an archconservative or reactionary. At the height of the 1848 crisis, Bismarck offered to arm his peasants and send them to Berlin to put down the revolution and to restore the monarchy to its fullest powers. Needless to say, Frederick William IV politely declined Bismarck's offer, but the reputation of "Wild Bismarck" as a fire-eating conservative was enhanced. While Bismarck became a bit less pugnacious in his later years, throughout his life he remained consistently loyal to three things: the institution of the monarchy, his Junker class, and Prussia. Bismarck was no liberal, nor—it can be argued—was he a German nationalist.

In 1851, Bismarck returned to government service as Prussia's representative to the German Confederation then meeting at Frankfurt. Initially sympathetic to conservative Austria, Bismarck soon concluded that Austria stood as the chief obstacle to any and all ambitions that Prussia might have. Accordingly, he spent the rest of his tenure opposing Austrian initiatives and personally annoying the Austrian delegates. In 1859, he moved to St. Petersburg where, as Prussian ambassador, he familiarized himself with the court of Tsar Alexander II. In 1862, he was named Prussian ambassador to France. Although he spent only about six months in Paris, he got to know (and take the measure of) the French emperor Louis Napoleon, or Napoleon III.

Bismarck's ambassadorial career ended when he was recalled to Berlin in 1862 to become Prussian prime minister, or chancellor. As before, the Bismarck who now guided Prussia's destiny remained a bundle of nervous energy. When the spirit moved him, he could be charming, urbane, and witty. However, most of the time Bismarck was blustery, intolerant, egotistical, and volcanic. Although a cultured man, the new chancellor loved to play the role of the straight-shooting, plain-talking, rustic squire.

In fact, he was quite wily, canny, and nimble of thought. Like most out-standing statesmen, Bismarck possessed an ability to read complex situations clearly and, perhaps most importantly, to keep in play a multitude of options. However, at the heart of Bismarck's *Weltanschauung,* or worldview, was a reliance upon *macht,* or power/force. Shortly after his recall to Berlin, Bismarck made his most famous speech in which he told members of the Prussian legislature, "The position of Prussia in Germany will be determined not by its liberalism but by its power.... Not through speeches and majority decisions are the great questions of the day decided—that was the great mistake of 1848 and 1849—but through blood and iron."

Germany's march to unification began unexpectedly in late 1863 with a crisis over the disposition of Schleswig and Holstein, two duchies located on the Jutland Peninsula. The latter was populated by Germans; the for-mer was populated by a mixed Danish-German population. The details surrounding the crisis are complicated enough to have launched a thou-sand doctoral dissertations. Suffice it to say that by fall 1864 Austria and Prussia, acting in concert, had defeated a badly overmatched Denmark. The final disposition of the provinces occurred only in August 1865, when Austria and Prussia signed the Gastein Convention. This agreement called for Austria to administer Holstein, which shared a border with Prussia, and for Prussia to administer Schleswig, which was now separated from its Prussian masters by Austrian-governed Holstein. As confusing as this arrangement was, it gave to Bismarck a ready-made excuse to provoke a quarrel with Austria whenever he wished, and in 1866, the Prussian chan-cellor did just that.

Bismarck intentionally either initiated or intensified several disputes—each of which could have been settled peaceably—that eventually resulted in war in June 1866. Observers expected the Austro-Prussian War to be a lengthy one; however, it lasted just seven weeks. On July 3 the Prussians crushed the Austrians at the Battle of Sadowa (Königgrätz), and the road to Vienna lay open. Austria quickly sued for peace, and the Treaty of Prague followed. Bismarck purposely made a lenient treaty since he now wished to mollify Austria and make an ally of his vanquished enemy. Nevertheless, the treaty had the practical effect of expelling Austrian influence from the bulk of the German-speaking world and directing that nation's future toward the east and south, rather than the Germanic north and west. The terms of the treaty dissolved the old German Confederation and allowed Prussia to annex Schleswig, Holstein, Hanover, Hesse, Nas-sau, and Frankfurt. In the wake of its victory, Prussia also created the North German Confederation, thereby bringing the remaining independent German states lying north of the Main River firmly under Prussian control.

During the course of his duel with Austria, Bismarck had managed either to engage or to neutralize the other major European states. Italy allied itself with Prussia; Russia looked on benignly; and Great Britain expressed disinterest. France, however, was a special case, since a Prussian triumph—however unexpected—might very well change the balance of power on that country's eastern doorstep. To keep France from intervening, in 1865 Bismarck met with Napoleon III at Biarritz where he satisfied the French emperor with vague promises of future "compensation" for French neutrality in the upcoming war. As it turned out, Prussia's stunning triumph set off alarm bells in Paris, as French officials belatedly recognized the rise of a powerful Germanic state. After the Austro-Prussian War, an aroused France and an expansionistic Prussia seemed to be on a collision course.

The collision—due in no small measure to the arrogance, duplicity, treachery, and bellicosity of both parties—occurred in 1870. The ouster of the queen of Spain in 1868 opened a can of worms not dissimilar to the Schleswig-Holstein mess in its complexity. Thanks to Bismarck's anti-French intrigue, it appeared as though a prince from an auxiliary branch of the Hohenzollern family would win the vacant Spanish crown. Once France caught on to the game, it placed enormous pressure on William I, head of the house of Hohenzollern, to force the Hohenzollern candidate to withdraw. Without consulting Bismarck, the Prussian king acquiesced, and the crisis seemed about to end peacefully. However, France now overplayed its hand. Its ambassador to Prussia, Count Vincent Benedetti, confronted King William at Bad Ems where the Prussian monarch was "taking the waters." An informal encounter between the two was civil, if not cordial. Benedetti, on behalf of France, demanded that William make future commitments regarding Spain; William declined. Immediately after this encounter, William sent a telegram to Bismarck—the Bad Ems Dispatch—describing the events. His telegram reached Bismarck in Berlin where, according to the chancellor, he and the leaders of the Prussian army were consoling each other over their failure to provoke war with France. Seeing in the Bad Ems Dispatch the opportunity to achieve his goal, Bismarck skillfully edited the telegram to make it appear as though each side had grievously insulted the other. He then released the edited version to the newspapers. Within hours, patriotic mobs were in the streets clamoring for action, and on July 19, 1870, France obliged them by declaring war.

The Franco-Prussian War proved to be yet another sweeping victory for Prussia. The main French garrison at Sedan surrendered on September 2, and more than 100,000 French were taken prisoner, including Emperor Napoleon III. Eight weeks later, the garrison at Metz fell. This time Prussia took an additional 150,000 prisoners. The surrender of Paris on January 28, 1871, completed France's humiliation. The Treaty of Frankfurt, signed on May 10, 1871, formally ended the Franco-Prussian War. By the terms of this treaty, Germany received the province of Alsace and about two-fifths of the province of Lorraine. France also had to pay an indemnity of 5 billion francs, with the stipulation that German troops would occupy France until that sum's final payment.

In the meantime, the political map of the German-speaking world changed dramatically. With the opening of hostilities, the independent south German states of Baden, Württemberg, and Bavaria—Catholic, moderately liberal, and fearful of Protestant Prussia—joined the war against France. Bismarck's ability to convince the southerners that Napoleon III intended to dominate them merged with a strong surge of German nationalist sentiment to produce this unexpected result. Then, in the wake of Prussia's victory, Bismarck engineered the final unification of Germany when he persuaded the German princes to offer the crown of a unified Germany to William I. On January 18, 1871, in the Palace of Versailles' ornate Hall of Mirrors, William I was crowned German emperor. Germany was now unified.

INTERPRETIVE ESSAY
Gesine Gerhard

In 1871, the first German nation-state—called an empire, or *Reich*—was founded. Germany had finally caught up with other European countries and had replaced a fragmentary confederation of small territories with a centralized state. The first attempt to create a unified Germany with a liberal constitution had failed with the 1848 revolutions, but the unification under Otto von Bismarck was achieved relatively quickly. It took 3 wars in less than 10 years to overcome all obstacles and to bring together a mixture of independent states as one country. The history of unification does not, however, begin with Bismarck, the conservative prime minister and first chancellor of the German Reich, who is usually credited with accomplishing the difficult task. It does not end with the declaration of the Empire in the Hall of Mirrors in Versailles, either. In many ways, 1871 marks only the beginning of the building of a nation, the making of "Germans" living in a unified state. Bismarck's unification from "above" took years to build up from "below." The road was marked by many hurdles.

The first challenge in the unification process was to define what and where "Germany" actually was. Germany meant quite different things to German-speaking Austrians and Saxons, to workers and landowners, and to Catholics and Protestants. In 1871, the country that bore this name existed more on maps than it did in the minds of the people. Germany included territory and areas populated with millions of Poles, Danes, and Alsatians who did not particularly desire to be members of the new German Empire. At the same time, the boundaries excluded many others who had always considered themselves German. People living within the German borders, if asked, proudly called themselves Bavarians, Prussians, Saxons, or Frankfurters. For a Bavarian, traveling to the duchies of Schleswig or Holstein in the north felt like a journey to a foreign land, just as it would have to a French or Dutch person. The new German state had boundaries that were clearly marked on a map, but the people living in the designated area did not identify strongly with it.

In addition to this undeveloped sense of German national identity, the political, social, and economic unification of the new nation-state had a long way to go. The foremost task was to create common institutions and symbols of a unified state. The new government's departments and policies had to overcome memories of the past when local authorities could issue their own money and pass their own laws. Social integration required connecting people with different histories, dialects, religions, and livelihoods. Cake recipes, beer-brewing customs, dress codes, and laws varied from region to region. Living in the countryside around Hanover implied cultivating and inheriting land according to customs that were different than those practiced around Munich. In the new Germany, Catholics found themselves a large minority in a Protestant-led empire and longed for the days when the Habsburg monarchy had provided protection. During the first decades of the young empire these feelings increased. In the *Kulturkampf,* a domestic war of the state against the Catholic Church, Catholics were treated as enemies of the empire. Priests were sent into exile, and the state extended its control to include education and the appointment of the clergy, domains that had formerly belonged to the Catholic Church.

In the economic realm, industrialization took off after unification. It followed very different paths in the Ruhr, the center of heavy industry in the west, and in the south, where industrialization made great advances in textile production. The growing working class had just started to organize itself and emphasized class solidarity across borders. German statesmen felt threatened by the internationalism and radicalism of the new socialist movement. Anti-Socialist laws were introduced that sent the Socialist party and its press into the underground and many party leaders into prison. The repression of Catholics and Socialists only made the unification more difficult.

German unification was further complicated by the many competing ideas of what the German nation-state would look like. In hindsight, it seems almost natural that Germany took the shape that it did in 1871. For contemporaries, however, this was just one model of a German state, and for many it was not the most desirable one. Other proposals for a new Germany had circulated, and they made just as much sense. There was, first of all, the *Grossdeutsch,* or "greater German," position. Advocates of a greater German nation-state imagined the German-speaking areas of the Austrian empire to be part of a federal state. This plan attracted many, since it built on the recollections of a common past. It was directly opposed to the "little German," or *Kleindeutsch,* solution that depicted a German nation-state excluding Austria-Hungary. Prussia favored the *Kleindeutsch* model, for this would turn Prussia into the largest part of the new Germany. The smaller German states advocated yet another possibility. Their concept of a "third Germany" combined all smaller and midsized territories into a union. These states resented both Prussian and Austrian dominance and favored a federal state without one central authority.

Despite the flaws and problems of the young nation-state, many contemporaries regarded Bismarck's work as a great achievement. To them, unification seemed an overdue step toward a European order of constitutional and national states. Germany was finally catching up with the nation-building frenzy of the nineteenth century that replaced the old and dysfunctional multinational dynasties. Historians after 1945 have taken a more critical stand. They see Bismarck's German Empire as a fateful solution to the question of national unity that was to cause major problems in the years to come. According to this interpretation, these problems exploded in 1914 with the outbreak of World War I and ultimately led to Adolf Hitler's plan for a new—"third"—German Reich. The division of Germany after World War II is understood in this interpretation as a means to avoid the mistakes of the past.

The 1870s and 1880s were crucial years for building a sense of German national identity. But before looking at the developments that eventually would bring Germans closer together, we need to examine how the creation of the German Empire came about. It was called the "second" German Empire in reference to the "Holy Roman Empire of German Nations," a thousand-year-old entity that encompassed lands in central

Europe. At the beginning of the nineteenth century, the Holy Roman Empire was a loose conglomeration of more than 300 small independent principalities, dynastic kingdoms, and free cities. They were held together by little more than a name and the German emperor, or *Kaiser*. Territorial rulers could issue their own money and laws, decide on the religion of their subjects, and charge tolls at their state borders.

The fragmented political character and decentralized structure weakened the Holy Roman Empire. When Napoleon's revolutionary armies invaded and occupied the German lands west of the Rhine River, the Holy Roman Empire caved in. Napoleon reorganized the territories and created the Confederation of the Rhine (*Rheinbund*). Napoleon's victories, however, were short-lived. A coalition of Austria, Prussia, and Russia defeated the French army and undid Napoleon's territorial changes. The conservative statesmen of the European monarchies met in Vienna in 1814–15 under the leadership of the Austrian chancellor, Prince Clemens von Metternich, to come up with a settlement for Europe after the Napoleonic Wars. They replaced the Holy Roman Empire with a loose confederation of states called the German Confederation (*Deutscher Bund*). The *Bund* covered about the same geographic area as its predecessor, but the territory was now reorganized into 35 states and 4 free cities. The size of these political units varied from the large territories of Prussia, Austria, and Bavaria to the small city-republics of Bremen, Frankfurt, Hamburg, and Lübeck. In theory, all the member states were sovereign. In reality, however, Prussia and Austria dominated and controlled the Confederation. The *Bund* had a parliament—the first national German parliament—that met in Frankfurt with representatives from all German states, but it lacked real legislative power. The German Confederation was part of the "Concert of Europe" created at the Congress of Vienna. The Concert of Europe was a defensive alliance of monarchical states to maintain peace and the status quo in the face of revolutions and social upheavals.

One of the revolutionary ideologies of the nineteenth century that threatened to upset the old order was nationalism. It was a powerful ideology that undermined the large multinational empires such as the Ottoman Empire and the Austrian Empire. Polish, Hungarian, Greek, and Italian national causes found wide support, and nation-building proceeded successfully in Japan, the United States, and Italy. At first, the German concept of nationalism was rather diffuse and vague. It was based on the romantic recollection of a common past, on fairy tales and songs. Napoleon's foray into Germany ignited the patriotic fire. Everywhere in the German lands nationalist organizations mushroomed, especially during and after the German War of Liberation against French domination in parts of Germany. The nationalist idea spread to student fraternities, gymnastic and choral societies that organized festivals to celebrate and cultivate a sense of nationality and ideas of Germandom. Reading clubs and art societies promoted German literature and folk songs. German nationalism was promoted with religious fervor, even though no concrete concept of a nation-state had been outlined yet. The idea of a German Fatherland was more a poetic and utopian idea than a solid plan.

As uncertain and ill-defined as the agendas of these nationalistic groups were, by the time of the 1848 revolutions, their political potential was indisputable. Radical ideas circulated, and many of the groups' leaders became the spokesmen of political parties. The goals and ideologies differed from group to group, but their common denominator was the idea of a nation. It seemed as if all the different ideas about boundaries, constitutions, and political systems were unimportant in the face of the one enthusiastic call for German unity. People longed for something new and bigger; they wanted to get rid of the old dynastic empires and small states. The German nation-state they envisioned would have popular support and constitutional legitimacy. National unification, according to these liberal and nationalist groups, would come from below. It would be the result of popular action and lead to a democratic state. Equal political representation and equal rights to all citizens were part of this vision.

This is not, however, how German unification happened. By the time Bismarck embarked on his mission, much of the national enthusiasm had disappeared. The most radical leaders of the movement had left, and the idea to unify Germany from below was nothing but an unrealistic dream. What had happened? After the collapse of the 1848 revolutions, the conservative political climate in the following decades choked much of the national enthusiasm and revolutionary fervor. Liberal political changes were reversed, the new ministers replaced, and constitutions withdrawn. Conservative statesmen set out to restore the old order. Princes reclaimed their authority and noble privileges which they had lost so abruptly in the revolution. The Frankfurt parliament that had met since May 1848 lacked experience, practicality, and national authority. The chances to write a new constitution for a united Germany dwindled. With the crushing of the revolutions and the onset of the counterrevolution, the hopes and dreams of a united, more liberal German nation-state crumbled as well. Prussia became the leader of the conservative powers that took over the political stage during the reactionary decade. To quench any future political revival, the most active leaders of the liberal camp were put under surveillance or purged. Many found security and freedom only in exile. Liberal newspapers were censored, and police forces were enhanced to stop any grassroots activism.

It was, however, impossible to return to the status quo of the past. Economic growth had started in the first part of the century, and even conservative politicians understood that more liberal economic and fiscal policies were necessary to further stimulate industrial progress. Germany was on its way to a modern, capitalist society, and the old system had to give way. Serfdom had been abolished, and peasants were no longer the subjects of noble landowners. They were on their way to becoming free farmers and independent entrepreneurs. The idea of legal equality replaced the old notion of privilege linked to birth and status.

The return to political conservatism was not uniform in all German states, either. Although the liberal constitutions were withdrawn, most princes ruled on the basis of constitutions. Concessions were made to the moderate liberals, and Prussia, for example, introduced a three-class electorate in 1849 to elect its lower house. The new voting system divided Prussian men 25 years and older into 3 classes according to income. Each voting group contributed one-third of the tax revenue and had an equal number of representatives. The three-class electorate was clearly unjust because it ensured the power of the small group of wealthy landowners, while the third class, consisting of the large majority of the lower class, possessed only one-third of the electoral power. Nevertheless, it was an electoral system based on taxes rather than on birth and privileges. It was a step in the direction of a constitutional political system.

With the fiasco of the first national parliament in Frankfurt, the nature of the German question changed. It now focused increasingly on the rivalry between Prussia and Austria. The Olmütz agreement of November 1850 had restored both of them as the largest and most powerful members of the German Confederation, but the two old allies were fighting for the economic and political dominance of Germany. An event on the international front changed the situation in the 1850s and, in the long run, helped Prussia establish itself as the new powerhouse in central Europe. The Crimean War of 1853–56 represented the first major European conflict since the settlement after the Napoleonic Wars at the Congress of Vienna. It disrupted the monarchical alliance system and seriously eroded Austria's position as the leader of the "European concert." The system had worked for the conservative European powers by maintaining a balance of power and quelling any revolutionary threat that might have disrupted the status quo. In the Crimean War, however, former allies found themselves on different sides. Austria had entered the war to block Russia's advance into territory of the disintegrating Ottoman Empire. By doing so,

Austria abandoned its old ally Russia and fought on the side of Britain and France. The period of conservative alliances to defend each other against radical and national upheaval had come to an end. Once again, war replaced diplomacy as the means to achieve political goals. The outcome of the Crimean War was not, however, what Austria had anticipated. Once at the pinnacle of conservative European powers, its position grew more and more isolated.

Austria felt the consequences of its international isolation even more severely when Italy embarked on its road to national unification. In trying to oust Austria from northern Italy, the prime minister of the Kingdom of Piedmont, Count Camillo di Cavour, was supported by France. Prussia did nothing to help its old ally Austria. In the fight against Piedmontese and French troops, Austria lost one battle after another until it finally had to ask for a cease-fire on July 8, 1859. These events clearly weakened Austria. The once-powerful Habsburg dynasty was unable to stop the decay of its empire. For Prussia, this was yet another proof that it was destined to become the sole master of a German state without Austria. The possibility to form a "little" German Reich under Prussian hegemony seemed more realistic than ever.

The 1860s marked a new era, inaugurated by the accession of William I to the Prussian throne. Prussian politics embarked on a more conciliatory course after years of reaction. Soon, however, a new conflict between the crown and the parliament poisoned the political atmosphere. The conflict started with the king's proposal for a radical military reform aimed at strengthening the Prussian army. The bill introduced to parliament suggested doubling the size of the army by increasing the number of conscripts. It extended military service from two to three years and foresaw full training for the recruits. Even though the Liberal Party supported the idea of strengthening the army, the bill was blocked because the Liberals were concerned about the high costs of the reform—financed with tax increases—and its political implications. The proposed reform would enlarge the number of reserves, but it would also limit their role to rear-line duties. The reserve was a bastion of middle-class and lower middle-class men in a Prussian military dominated by the nobility. The Liberals feared reducing the role of the reserve would enhance the army as a powerful tool for the crown. While the liberal opposition in parliament blocked the bill, William was determined to push the reform through, even without the consent of the parliament. The minor issue turned into a major political crisis that brought Bismarck into the game. In September 1862, two years after the controversial bill had been proposed, Bismarck was called to Berlin in order to resolve the standoff between the liberal opposition and the crown. It would take, however, several more years to end the constitutional crisis.

Otto von Bismarck's name is closely intertwined with the history of German unification. The "iron" chancellor of Germany from 1871 to 1890 is often credited with uniting Germany. His political style and actions have impressed and horrified people at the same time, and the judgments of his achievements vary greatly. Who was Bismarck? Was he a political genius, or a ruthless manipulator? Did he make history, or was he just in the right place at the right time?

At the height of his career, Otto von Bismarck described himself as "God's chosen instrument," destined to complete a great task. His career, however, had not shown any promising signs of the major role he would play in Germany's future. He was the son of a Pomeranian noble landowner who liked to brag about his family's longstanding Prussian roots. Otto earned a law degree and in 1836 took his first job in the Prussian civil service. He did not stay for very long. The clerical work bored him, and he left his job to move back to manage his family's estate in Brandenburg. In 1847, Bismarck returned to politics when he was elected as a substitute to the Confederation's parliament. In this position, he soon became well known as a conservative spokesman for the crown. He resented the revolution and its liberal and nationalistic leaders and was unshaken in his belief that the great majority of people did not support the revolutionaries. Peasants, the darlings of the conservatives, would be the first to stand behind their kings and would protect their way of life from dramatic changes.

The revolutionary spirit subsided, and Bismarck became Prussian ambassador to the Confederation parliament in Frankfurt in 1851. As a counterrevolutionary he worked on the restoration of the old order. In 1859, he was sent to St. Petersburg as the ambassador, and three years later he became ambassador to France. It was Bismarck's loyalty to the Prussian monarchy that made William call on him as a last resort to solve the constitutional crisis. Bismarck became prime minister in 1862.

Bismarck now set out to solve the political crisis in his own way. He was determined to ram the controversial army reform bill through, with or without the consent of the parliament, whose abilities he did not judge very highly. His famous statement "It is not by parliamentary speeches and majority votes that the great questions of the day are decided—that was the great mistake of 1848 and 1849—but by blood and iron" horrified the liberal opposition, to whom Bismarck was the personification of the counterrevolution. But this did not bother Bismarck much. He calculated correctly that the Liberals would protest with little effect, while he pursued his political goals.

A more serious hurdle for the implementation of his political agenda, however, was Austria. Bismarck had no doubts that Germany was too small for both Prussia and Austria, but he still faced the problem of how to end Austria's involvement in German affairs. Bismarck privately favored an aggressive policy to oust Austria by marching "southwards with our entire army carrying frontier posts in our big packs," but he knew better than that. Before he openly attacked Austria, Bismarck used the old ally one last time in a conflict over the northern duchies of Schleswig and Holstein. The duchies had been ruled by the Danish crown as personal fiefs since the late Middle Ages, and a treaty from 1460 had demanded that the two territories remain undivided. The Congress of Vienna in 1815 had altered and further complicated their status. Holstein with its German-speaking population was allocated to the German Confederation, but both provinces remained possessions of the Danish crown without being part of the Danish nation-state. The details of the Schleswig-Holstein issue were in fact so confusing that, according to the British prime minister Lord Palmerston, only three people were able to understand them: "one was the Prince Consort who is dead, another one a German scholar who has gone mad, and the third one is me, and I have forgotten."

The status of Schleswig and Holstein remained a thorn in the side of both Danish and German nationalists. The Danish nationalist movement wanted Schleswig to become part of the Danish kingdom, while the German side stressed the indivisibility of the two provinces. In 1863, the Danish parliament sanctioned a constitution that annexed the duchy of Schleswig with its large Danish minority. Not surprisingly, this move outraged the German nationalists. Sentiments ran high, and heated words were exchanged. For political reasons, Bismarck put himself at the forefront of the mission to challenge Denmark over Schleswig and Holstein. He wanted to win favors with the smaller German states that sympathized with the fate of these territories, but he also wanted to prevent the establishment of an independent, liberal German state. Last but not least, the issue presented an occasion for common action with Austria.

When words could not solve the issue, war followed. In January 1864, Austrian and Prussian troops entered the duchy of Schleswig. The Danish defense presented no serious obstacle for the superior Austro-Prussian army, and the attack turned out exactly as Bismarck had anticipated. The first war of unification, as it was later called, ended in October 1864 with the defeat of Denmark. It had united the two rivals, Austria and Prussia, one last time. It also gave Bismarck the support of the Liberals who had hoped that after the war the territories would form an independent German state. Bismarck would make sure this was not the case. The peace agreement turned the two provinces into property of the Austrian and Prussian crowns, with Prussia administering Schleswig and Austria in charge of Holstein.

From the beginning, this arrangement was doomed to fail. Austria had no immediate interest in Schleswig-Holstein, and it proved difficult to administer a province so far away from its empire. Austria suggested the creation of a state combining the two provinces. Prussia, however, would not hear of it. It set about completing the next task: expelling Austria from Germany. Prussia put pressure on the other German states to renew their membership in the *Zollverein,* a free trade agreement that included all German states except Austria. Prussia was trying to revive the Confederation under Prussian domination. This was a bold step on Prussia's part, and Austria objected to it. In May 1866, the conflict escalated into war, this time between the two German powers.

The civil war between Austria and Prussia proved to be decisive for Germany's future. From the beginning, the Prussian military enjoyed a clear advantage. It swept through the German states that sided with Austria and confronted Austrian troops in Bohemia. The decisive battle at Königgrätz ended in the defeat of Austria. After peace was arranged, the North German Confederation (*Norddeutscher Bund*) was founded, and Prussia established its hegemony in all of northern Germany. The states that had sided with Austria in the war were now bound to Prussia economically and militarily. The German states south of the Main River were left on their own. Austria had no territorial losses other than Schleswig-Holstein; however, the defeat signaled much more than just a lost battle. It was the end of Austria's involvement in German affairs. It also decided whether Germany was to be large or small. The *Kleindeutsch* solution had won.

The North German Confederation accomplished almost everything Bismarck had set out to achieve. Austria was demoted, Prussian hegemony over a large territory was established, and the liberal opposition was muted. The constitutional conflict that had paralyzed Prussian politics since 1860 was finally resolved as well. The Liberals in the Prussian parliament passed legislation known as the Indemnity Bill that approved the government's policies since 1862 retroactively. With the endorsement of the bill, the Liberals gave up some of their dreams harbored during the revolutions, but the new Confederation brought economic changes that allowed Germany to embark on a rapid economic modernization. Even in the political realm advances were made. The Confederation had a parliament that was elected by universal male suffrage. The parliament's powers were limited, but it had some control over taxes and the budget. Last but not least, national unification seemed closer than it had ever been.

It would take one more war to overcome the south German states' resentment of a Prussian-led nation-state, and this third war of unification was to be fought against France. It started as a conflict over the succession to the Spanish throne. Without a native heir and in the need of stability, Spain offered the throne to Leopold von Hohenzollern-Sigmaringen, a nephew of William I. Napoleon III objected to a member of the Prussian royal family becoming king of Spain, a country that was close to his heart and ambition. He wanted Prussia not only to withdraw its candidate, but also to promise that the candidature would never be renewed. William gave in, but he did not promise anything for the future. The dispute seemed settled. William sent a telegram to Berlin informing Bismarck of the outcome. Bismarck decided to use this issue to arouse German national feelings, just as Napoleon III had stirred up emotions in France. Before releasing the telegram to the press, he changed a few words to dramatize France's demand and William's rejection of it. Bismarck's manipulation worked. The insulting tone of the altered telegram had the intended effect, and in an atmosphere of national outrage, France declared war. It was exactly what Bismarck had wanted: a war seemingly forced on Germany that would unite all Germans, including those in southern Germany, in a national mission against a common "hereditary" enemy. Even better, it came at a time when France was not at all prepared for a military conflict, while Prussia's military was ready to go to war.

The war between France and Germany involved more soldiers than any prior European conflict. Patriotism fed on nationalism, and both sides engaged in bitter fighting. The outcome of the war is well known: France was defeated, and with Napoleon III's abdication, the French Third Republic began. France lost two provinces, Alsace and the eastern portion of Lorraine, and was condemned to pay a large sum in reparations (5 billion francs) to its victorious neighbor. The German Empire was founded on January 18, 1871. It encompassed the territory of the North German Confederation and the southern German states. The founding ceremony took place in the Hall of Mirrors in Versailles as a sign of France's humiliation. For Prussia, the creation of the Second German Empire was a great triumph. Unification was achieved from above, under the leadership of the authoritarian and militarist Prussian state. The German Empire was a monarchy modeled after Prussia. The Prussian king became the German emperor, and the Prussian prime minister was chancellor of Germany.

German unification in 1871 settled the question of Germany's geographical dimensions—at least for the time being. The process of unifying Germans took much longer. During the 1870s and 1880s, a centralized and unified nation-state came into being. Germans from Schleswig to Bavaria now used a single currency, followed the same laws, and would eventually use the same symbols of national identity. In many ways, the outbreak of World War I completed the process of unification. On the eve of the war's outbreak, an enthusiastic Kaiser William II declared that there were no more differences between the people, no more political parties, religious beliefs, or other divisions. "Today we are all German brothers, and only German brothers," he proclaimed.

SELECTED BIBLIOGRAPHY

Blackbourn, David. *The Long Nineteenth Century.* Oxford: Oxford University Press, 1998. One of the best analyses of nineteenth-century Germany.

Bismarck, Otto von. *The Memoirs of Otto, Prince von Bismarck.* 2 vols. Translated by A. J. Butler. New York: Howard Fertig, 1966. Bismarck's memoirs have to be used with caution, but are nevertheless an important source.

Breuilly, John. *The Foundation of the First German Nation-State, 1800–1871.* New York: St. Martin's Press, 1996. Includes maps, a glossary, and a chronology. This small book is very useful for students.

Carr, William. *The Origins of the Wars of German Unification.* New York: Longman, 1991. A broad, more recent study of the origins of the wars, this volume integrates domestic and foreign policy.

Craig, Gordon. *The Battle of Königgrätz: Prussia's Victory over Austria, 1866.* Philadelphia and New York: Greenwood Publishing Group, 1964. Authoritative account of the war between Prussia and Austria.

———. *Germany 1866–1945.* Oxford: Oxford University Press, 1978. This standard work focuses on the political history of the period.

Gall, Lothar. *Bismarck: The White Revolutionary.* 2 vols. Translated by J. A. Underwood. London: Allen & Unwin, 1986. An important, more recent, critical biography.

Hamerow, Theodore. *The Social Foundations of German Unification 1858–1871.* 2 vols. Princeton, NJ: Princeton University Press, 1969–72. An influential and cogently presented two-volume study of the social institutions and political events of the unification period.

Howard, Michael. *The Franco-Prussian War: The German Invasion of France.* London: Rupert Hart-Davis, 1961. Definitive account of the war between France and Prussia.

Langewiesche, Dieter. *Liberalism in Germany.* Translated by Christiane Banerji. Princeton, NJ: Princeton University Press, 2000. Key study on German liberalism. Originally published in German in 1988.

Mommsen, Wolfgang J. *Imperial Germany, 1867–1918. Politics, Culture, and Society in an Authoritarian State.* Translated by Richard Deveson. New York: Arnold, 1995. Thirteen essays. Good introduction to historical debates on the legacy of imperial Germany.

Pflanze, Otto. *Bismarck and the Development of Germany: Vol. 1 The Period of Unification 1815–1871.* Princeton, NJ: Princeton University Press, 1963. Republished in 1990. This well-written biography is a major comprehensive work.

Schulze, Hagen. *The Course of German Nationalism: From Frederick the Great to Bismarck, 1763–1867.* Translated by Sarah Hanbury-Tenison. Cambridge: Cambridge University Press, 1991. Thought-provoking and accessible account of the forces that led to the foundation of a German nation-state.

Sheehan, James J. *German History 1770–1866.* Oxford: Clarendon Press, 1989. This survey of the period leading up to the unification offers a valuable alternative to the Prusso-centric interpretation. It includes the history of the Habsburg monarchy and focuses on economic, social, and cultural history.

———. *German Liberalism in the Nineteenth Century.* Chicago: University of Chicago Press, 1979. A comprehensive study of German liberalism before World War I.

Stern, Fritz. *Gold and Iron: Bismarck, Bleichröder, and the Building of the German Empire.* New York: Alfred A. Knopf, 1977. This study of the relationship between Bismarck and the banker Bleichröder provides insight into the development of German anti-Semitism.

Wehler, Hans-Ulrich. *The German Empire, 1871–1918.* Leamington Spa, England, U.K: Berg Publishers, 1985. A controversial interpretation of the period by a leading German historian.

Wetzel, David. *A Duel of Giants: Bismarck, Napoleon III, and the Origins of the Franco-Prussian War.* Madison: University of Wisconsin Press, 2001. Relying upon the most recent scholarship, this work analyzes the major actors of the conflict, their views, and relationships.

Windell, George. *The Catholics and German Unity, 1866–1871.* Minneapolis: University of Minnesota Press, 1954. A detailed study of the origins of political Catholicism.

3 —————————————————————

Industrialization, 1890–1910

INTRODUCTION

John Maynard Keynes, the British Nobel Prize winner in economics, once remarked that "the German Empire was built more truly on coal and iron than on blood and iron," as Otto von Bismarck, the empire's creator, had claimed. If one credits a modern system of rationalized production for generating the strength and wealth requisite for a nation's success, then Keynes's observation appears to be correct. Germany's steady economic growth that culminated in an astonishing expansion during the last decade of the nineteenth century and the first decade of the twentieth century brought impressive results. By the eve of World War I, Germany had left its French competitor far behind and had not only superseded Great Britain's output, but also was increasing the distance between itself and its island rival. Germany was the industrial king of Europe; in a global context, only the United States could match it.

Early nineteenth-century Germany bore little resemblance to this industrial powerhouse. At that time, agrarian concerns predominated. From the smallish landholdings in the west to the large Junker, or noble, estates in the east, agriculture ruled. What little economic activity there was beyond cultivation consisted of not much more than rudimentary trade and commerce and the occasional instance of cottage industry production. This stagnant picture began to change in the 1830s. For one thing, the transportation infrastructure began to improve. Upgraded roads, canals linking Germany's many rivers, steamboats plying these rivers, and, most importantly, the first railroads helped to transform the landscape. The

Germany's industrial output, especially its steel production, rose dramatically in the late nineteenth century. By 1914, Germany was Europe's industrial leader, having clearly surpassed its British rival. (Reproduced from the Collections of the Library of Congress.)

appearance of more modern facilities for iron and steel manufacturing in the Rhine River valley and for textile production in Saxony also contributed to Germany's economic growth. However, the most important development was the creation in 1834 of the *Zollverein,* or customs union. Up until then, each of the numerous German states had maintained its own customs regime. Now these customs barriers fell and a German "common market" emerged. Originally, the *Zollverein* included 18 states with a population of 23 million people and a territory of 162,000 square miles. The *Zollverein* proved so successful that every German state except Austria soon joined.

Economic growth continued during the early 1840s. By 1846, there were more than 1,200 miles of rail line, and for the first time Germany was building its own locomotives and rolling stock instead of importing these items from Great Britain. In the textile industry—one of the building blocks of industrialization—machines began to replace handlooms and spinning wheels. Cities grew, and the German class structure began to change. An industrial middle class (bourgeoisie) appeared, as did an industrial working class (proletariat). In 1848, the latter numbered approximately 600,000.

Economic setbacks at the end of the decade helped to ignite the Revolutions of 1848, but prosperity returned and industrialization picked up steam in the 1850s and 1860s. An ample supply of labor; an abundance of raw materials, especially coal; readily available capital; and a favorable governmental attitude fueled this expansion. Between 1850 and 1870, the German population grew from 35 million to 40 million, a 14 percent increase. In roughly the same period, the production of coal rose from 3.2 million metric tons to 29.4 million metric tons, and the production of pig iron jumped from 529,000 metric tons to 1.5 million metric tons. Most of the expansion took place in heavy industry—coal, pig iron, steel, and railroads. The textile sector continued to grow, and for the first time there appeared chemical and electrical producers, industries that were to become synonymous with Germany's spectacular industrial growth at the end of the century. This early stage of industrialization focused on Silesia and Saxony in the east, as well as the Ruhr region and the Rhineland, Westphalia, and the Saarland in western Germany.

German unification further stimulated industrialization. The 5 billion gold francs that France paid as an indemnity for losing the Franco-Prussian War greatly boosted the availability of capital for industrial expansion and speculation. Furthermore, the annexation of Alsace-Lorraine gave German industry easy access to the iron ore deposits of Lorraine. Iron ore is a crucial ingredient in the making of steel and, combined with the rich coal deposits of the Ruhr valley, it virtually guaranteed that Germany would emerge as a giant steel producer. However, in 1873 the bubble burst, and for the next 20 years industrialization proceeded in Germany at a slower pace.

Despite the uneven nature of its industrial development, Germany entered the 1890s considerably more industrialized than it had been 20 years earlier. Annual coal production jumped from 29 million metric tons in 1870 to 89 million metric tons in 1890, while pig iron production soared from 1.5 million metric tons to 4.6 million metric tons during the same time. By 1890, Germany was making 3.1 million metric tons of steel annually and was poised to overtake Great Britain as Europe's largest steel producer.

Banking and finance developments facilitated Germany's industrialization. In 1875, Germany created a central bank, the Reichsbank. Big private banks such as Darmstädter Bank, Dresdener Bank, Diskonto Gesellschaft, and Deutsche Bank supplied a steady stream of capital for industrial enterprises and worked closely with entrepreneurs. Often bankers sat on the boards of directors of the corporations they funded.

New industries set down firm foundations at this time. This was particularly true of the electrical and chemical industries. The German electrical industry can be traced to the work of Werner von Siemens, an engineer, businessman, and inventor who perfected the electric dynamo in 1866. His company, Siemens and Halske, made a wide variety of electrical equipment and brought the electric trolley to countless German towns and cities. Emil Rathenau emulated Siemens's success. Acquiring the German rights to Thomas Edison's electric light, in 1883 Rathenau formed the Allgemeine Elektrizitäts-Gesellschaft, or AEG, which has been compared to the American company General Electric. The German chemical industry's start can be attributed to the need for synthetic dyes. With the rapid expansion of the textile industry, Germany found itself lacking sufficient natural dyes. However, the German scientist August von Hofmann developed the process of making synthetic dyes from coal tar, and the German chemical industry was off and running.

Typical of German industrial success is the story of Krupp, the famous steel and munitions maker. Early in the nineteenth century, the Krupp family opened a small forge in the town of Essen. Enjoying a degree of success, the Krupp foundry expanded under Alfred, the son of the founder. Nevertheless, in 1846 Krupp employed all of 140 workers. However, Krupp took advantage of the railway boom to manufacture rails and locomotives, and later he expanded the business to supply armaments, especially artillery, to the new Reich's army. By 1914, Gustav Krupp was the richest man in Germany, and the Krupp factories, now spread throughout Germany, employed about 70,000 workers.

The pace of Germany's industrialization accelerated dramatically in the decades immediately preceding the outbreak of World War I. The production figures for the building blocks of industrialization—coal, pig iron, and steel—clearly indicate this. Coal production, which stood at 89 million metric tons in 1890, soared to 191 million metric tons in 1913; pig iron production jumped from 4.6 million metric tons in 1890 to almost 15 million metric tons in 1910; and steel output rose from 3.1 million metric tons in 1890 to 13.1 million metric tons in 1910, an astonishing increase of more than 400 percent. Thus, by 1910 Germany was producing more pig iron and more steel than Great Britain, and the gap separating the two countries was growing.

Developments in Germany's electrical and chemical industries were even more impressive. The number of workers employed in the former more than quadrupled between 1896 and 1906. By 1913, German firms controlled almost one-half of the global market in electrical equipment. The chemical industry saw the advance of firms that still remain giants in the field today—BASF, Bayer, Hoechst—and the production of these firms paralleled that of the coal, steel, and electrical industries. Between 1885 and 1913, the number of chemical workers grew from 78,000 to 282,000. The production of sulfuric acid swelled from 112,000 metric tons in 1878 to almost 1.5 million metric tons in 1907; the production of ammonia increased from 84,000 metric tons in 1897 to 287,000 metric tons in 1907; and the output of potash soared from 1 million metric tons in 1889 to 8 million metric tons in 1910.

During this era, German firms also initiated new business activities or substantially upgraded heretofore neglected ones. The German merchant marine, which had been negligible at the time of the empire's founding in 1871, enjoyed spectacular growth. The Hamburg-Amerika Line (HAPAG) expanded from a fleet of 22 steamers with a tonnage of 60,531 in 1886 to a fleet of 172 steamers with a tonnage of more than 1 million in 1913. HAPAG not only transported passengers on luxury liners from Europe to the Americas and Asia, but it also shipped commercial goods and industrial products. The North German Lloyd Company rivaled HAPAG. By 1913, it owned the second largest merchant fleet in the world, with more than 2,000 vessels and tonnage of more than 4 million. German ships traveled everywhere, and the German ports of Hamburg and Bremen were among the world's busiest. These German ships carried the fruits of Germany's industrial expansion. Between 1872 and 1913, the value of Germany's exports climbed from 2.5 billion marks to 10 billion marks annually; most of the increase occurred between 1900 and 1913, when the value of Germany's exports more than doubled. On the eve of World War I, Germany's share of world trade came very close to that of Great Britain.

Germany also became deeply involved in the export of capital. As late as the 1880s, Germany was a net importer of capital, with much of that money going to fuel its industrial expansion. However, by 1914 Germany had become so wealthy that it was now a net capital exporter, investing in such far-off locales as North and South America and Asia. By 1913, the value of German investments overseas was six times greater than the value of foreign investments in Germany. Moreover, the German mark had grown so strong that it started to challenge Great Britain's pound sterling as the world's most popular medium of exchange.

During the course of industrialization, the structure of Germany's business organizations changed significantly. Many German industrial firms devoted considerable time, energy, and capital to research and development. Unlike their British, American, and French counterparts, German companies employed a significant number of engineers and trained scientists, assigning them the task of developing new products or improving old ones. It is estimated that in 1900 the six largest German chemical firms employed about 650 scientists and engineers, as compared to perhaps 40 for the entire British chemical industry.

Another important feature of Germany's business structure was the cartel. Bearing a striking resemblance to a monopoly, the cartels came to dominate German industrial production. Some were vertical in nature, controlling every aspect of an item's production from the raw materials to the final product. Others were horizontal in nature, controlling the item itself in totality. Supporters of cartels—and there were many—claimed that they represented the "natural cooperative nature" of the Germanic peoples and pointed to the alleged existence of proto-cartels in Germany's preindustrial history. Perhaps as many as one dozen cartels existed during the 1870s; however, the number increased markedly as German industrialization accelerated. By the middle 1880s, there were close to 100 cartels, and by the first decade of the twentieth century, the number had jumped to several hundred, with no indication that the cartelization of Germany was complete.

Whereas at the turn of the century the United States broke up monopolies in the name of competition, Germany encouraged cartels in the name of efficiency. In fact, throughout the period of rapid industrialization the German government had stimulated growth. Why not? By 1914, Germany was clearly Europe's leading industrial power, and the gap between itself and its nearest competitor, Great Britain, was widening. Only the United States could rival Germany for industrial output.

INTERPRETIVE ESSAY
Eleanor L. Turk

Historians have routinely used the term "Industrial Revolution" to describe the economic modernization of England and Germany. The transformations of these two nations from rural agrarian societies to urbanized industrial powers were profound and dramatic, all the more so because each occurred in a relatively short period of time. Industrialization was a technological and economic process and can be clearly demonstrated by comparing production levels at the beginning and end of the period. It was also a social and political process, reflected through changes in the structure of society and the redistribution of political power. All this needs to be considered in order to understand the full dimensions of the German industrial revolution and its impact.

England is the model for the Industrial Revolution since it was the first to make the transition, starting in roughly 1780 and achieving modernization by 1850. In its compact island, village and town markets had been linked by roads since Roman times, and accommodating river harbors facilitated foreign trade. The rivers provided internal transportation for people and products and aided the building of an inland canal network. Water power also drove early mills. England's class structure located potential investment capital in the hands of the political decisionmakers, the landed hereditary aristocracy in the House of Lords, and the commercial urban gentry in the House of Commons. The gentry, especially, were economically motivated to increase their wealth through technical innovation and trade. They pushed England into the modern era by applying mechanization to the production of textiles and by the application of steam engines to transportation. The aristocracy, seeing potential profits, converted farmland to sheep-raising, which increased the supply of wool. This process of "enclosing" the former farmlands for sheep displaced the rural peasantry, the largest part of the population. Most were abruptly forced to migrate to the manufacturing centers in order to work. England was well provided with iron ore to help construct innovative looms and other machinery in its factories and with coal to generate the steam power to drive it. Mill towns sprang up in the Midlands close to these resources and grew to major urban complexes. Another very important factor for England was its control of colonies that were mandatory consumers of its goods. Despite the loss of its North American holdings, there were significant subject populations in Ireland and India and important trading posts in Africa which readily bought the new, less expensive English textiles and manufactured goods. The existing merchant fleet carried products to the European continent and the Americas and brought home the raw materials and agricultural products necessary to maintain the urban workforce.

This process of English economic development has become the model for gauging the modernization of other countries. In *The Stages of Economic Growth: A Non-Communist Manifesto,* the economist Walter Rostow offers a workable explanation. Rostow theorized that there were five stages for this economic development: (1) the traditional agrarian society; (2) a transitional stage when entrepreneurs worked to develop the transportation network and foundations for industry; (3) the takeoff, during which the workforce and productivity converted to mechanized industry; (4) the drive to maturity as the economy diversified; and (5) the achievement of high mass consumption. By 1850, England had reached the final stage and was the wealthiest and most powerful nation on earth.

The German industrial revolution was quite different. The Germans faced substantial challenges in their industrial transformation between 1850 and 1914. At the beginning of the nineteenth century, there was no single German nation. Instead, there were over 300 separate sovereign German states, small principalities, bishoprics, and free cities dominated by the major dynasties of imperial Austria and Bavaria in the south and Prussia and Saxony in the north. Napoleon forced most of the smaller states to surrender their independence and merge into larger ones (although the aristocracy retained titles, land, and privileges), an arrangement that was ratified by the Congress of Vienna following his defeat in 1815. As the major Germanic power, Austria was given the presidency of the new central European political entity, the German Confederation. While the Confederation represented the German states diplomatically, within it the hereditary rulers retained their sovereignty and local interests. Thus, even streamlined to 39 separate states, Germans were still divided by borders, tolls, governments, and mercantilistic competition. (Mercantilism was a policy of maximizing the state's wealth at the expense of competitor states, achieved by government control of all sectors of the economy, including the workforce. A prevailing principle was to purchase only raw materials abroad and sell only finished products, thus minimizing production costs and maximizing profits.) These divisions frequently separated potential German industries from their necessary raw materials; the resulting customs fees and transportation costs impeded significant capital formation and investment.

The social structure in most of the German states included the traditional hereditary aristocracy (relatively large in number since there had been so many monarchial states), an urban middle class, the *Mittelstand*, led by merchants and artisan guilds, and a peasantry. The peasantry, by far the largest component of the population, tended to be owners of small farms in the west, while at the beginning of the century there were still feudal serfs in lands east of the Elbe River. Political power was monarchial and, in most cases, unrestrained by legislatures. The local aristocracy exercised both political and judicial powers in the countryside. The exceptions were the self-governing "free" cities, major commercial centers such as Hamburg, Bremen, and Frankfurt, which had senates elected from among the leading merchants.

In Germany, the five stages of economic growth in the nineteenth century can be roughly dated. The traditional agrarian society lasted until about 1835. The transitional stage opened with the beginnings of transportation and trade networks in the 1830s. Of necessity, the German states had to modernize their political relations in order to maximize their economic potential. This was particularly important for Prussia, the second largest of the German states after Austria. Following the defeat of Napoleon, this northeastern German state had been given new territories in the Rhineland which were outside its traditional borders. In 1818, Prussia adopted a policy of free trade by eliminating domestic tariffs and tolls between its two regions. Ten years later, Prussia negotiated a limited commercial treaty with neighboring Hesse-Darmstadt which similarly dismantled trading barriers in the land between the Prussian districts. Other German states made their own agreements, and by 1830 there were two competing customs unions. Prussia took the diplomatic lead once more, seeking economic cooperation through diplomacy. The resulting *Zollverein* (customs union) treaty, which came into effect in 1834, included 18 of the German states and over 23 million of the 28,237,000 Germans (based on the territory of the later German empire). Significantly, it excluded Austria. Smaller German cities and states such as Schleswig, Holstein, Lauenburg, Nassau, Baden, and Frankfurt am Main later joined the organization. The *Zollverein* actually strengthened the role of state governments in commerce. Economic decisions within the German states were shared by the governments and the powerful artisan guilds that set standards of training, manufacture, and marketing. Nevertheless, the *Zollverein*'s free-trading zone provided the necessary platform for capital formation and investment in industry.

The Revolutions of 1848–49 interrupted German economic development. Following the overthrow of the conservative monarchy in France early in 1848, spontaneous liberal and nationalist movements across the German states called for a constitution to unify the nation and to provide for representative government. No doubt, the unifying impulse of the *Zollverein* contributed to the zeal of these movements. Intimidated by the force of these demonstrations, the monarchs permitted the convening of the Frankfurt Parliament to prepare a constitution. Representatives elected by hastily designed election laws began deliberations in May 1848. They were able to agree on almost every issue for a constitutional monarchy except the dimensions of the proposed new German state. Some, the Greater Germany faction (*Grossdeutsch*), wanted to include Austria despite its non-German minorities; others, the Small Germany faction (*Kleindeutsch*), wanted only exclusively German territories included. As this debate dragged on, the German monarchs recovered their courage and, in 1849, took military action to disperse the assembly. The revolution failed; the German Confederation, again headed by Austria, resumed control. Growth toward the transition stage was interrupted by the revolution, however, and the governments were deeply suspicious of the population at large.

Another social protest movement appeared in the textile-producing regions of Silesia in 1848. The production of linen had been an important cottage industry in the region, but less than 14 percent of the looms were actually owned by the weavers. Their uprising in 1848 was against their mistreatment by the loom owners. It reflected the growth of a working-class consciousness in Germany. Their economic distress, rather than political goals, helps explain the emergence of the radical socialism that found its voice in the writings of Karl Marx and Friedrich Engels.

Although the 1850s were years of political reaction, they provided the stability necessary for governments and major entrepreneurs to resume the drive toward industrialization. This is evident in the growth of railroad lines in Prussia, from about 500 miles of track in 1844 to 3,500 miles of track by 1860. The new lines, subsidized by large government investment, linked Berlin with the important coal fields and strategic border areas. In other German states private railroad companies began development, but after financial crises in the 1850s drove many of them out of business, governments became the mainstay for railroad line development. Significantly, the railroads provided long-distance transportation across the German states, reinforcing the economic unity of the *Zollverein*.

The final step in the transition period prior to the "takeoff" was also political. During the 1860s, Prussia sought to establish its hegemony over the other German states by eliminating the Austrian-controlled German Confederation. Led by Otto von Bismarck, Prussia first challenged Austrian leadership after the Danish War (1864), ostensibly fought to resolve dynastic issues in the Confederation's northern territories of Schleswig, Holstein, and Lauenburg. The conflict escalated into the Austro-Prussian War in 1866, in which Prussian forces soundly defeated the Austrians and ended the German Confederation. The outcome was the formation of the North German Confederation, led by Prussia, which encompassed the German states north of the Main River. Some of the German states joined this new Confederation by treaty; others, including Hanover, Hesse, Nassau, and Frankfurt, were simply annexed to Prussia. The three major southern states, Baden, Bavaria, and Württemberg, remained outside this new union but agreed to assist it if it were attacked. Bismarck next provoked France to do just that, and with surprising ease, Prussia thrashed France in the Franco-Prussian War (1870–71). Subsequently, Bismarck invited all the German rulers to a conference where they signed a treaty on January 18, 1871, agreeing to a unified German empire under the leadership of the king of Prussia as the German emperor. (The title was chosen to imply that the emperor was only the first among peer rulers, not the ruler "of Germany.")

Thus by adroit diplomacy and warfare, Bismarck had achieved the unification long desired by German nationalists and constitutionalists. Significantly, there was no popular input into the treaty or any referendum following it. Similarly, the agreement contained no measures like a bill of rights for the population at large. Nevertheless, the treaty became, de facto, the constitution of the new nation. The new German empire had a complex structure designed to give most of the power to the Prussian monarchy. The Prussian king, William I, was also the emperor; the Prussian minister president, Bismarck, was also the chancellor. Although the new legislature, the Reichstag, was based on the most liberal voting law written to date (all adult males over the age of 25), its actual powers were limited. All legislation had to be approved by the Federal Council, the Bundesrat, which consisted of appointed delegates from each of the states. Within the Bundesrat the size of each state's delegation was fixed, with Prussia having the largest number of votes. No measure could possibly be passed over its veto. The additional requirement that both the chancellor/minister-president and the emperor/king sign off on all legislation further strengthened Prussia's hand.

In the new imperial Bundesrat, four of the seven committees focused on economic responsibilities. The constitution was further characterized by its control (Section II) of the economy, reserving for the new national government the right to regulate trade and industry, including insurance;

customs duties, commerce and such taxes as are to be applied
    to the uses of the Empire;

weights and measures;...coinage; and the establishment of
    principles for the issue of funded and unfunded paper money;

general banking regulations;

patents for inventions;

protection of intellectual property;

the organization of a general system of protection for German
    trade in foreign countries;

railway matters...and the construction of land and waterways
    for the purposes of public defense and of general commerce;

rafting and navigation upon waterways, ...water dues.

Unification provided great impetus for the economy; the takeoff of Germany's industrial revolution was now possible. The decade of the 1870s became known as the *Gründerjahre,* or foundation period, of the German industrial economy. The German historian Koppel S. Pinson provides excellent data that clearly demonstrate the impact on the German economy of this new unified government supervision and investment. For example, Germany's production of pig iron rose from 1.6 million metric tons in 1871 to 14.8 million metric tons in 1910. Coal output grew from 29.4 million metric tons to 192 million metric tons in that same period. The great firms of Thyssen, Krupp, Borsig, and others led this industrial expansion. Much of the productivity went into building up railroads, an enormous merchant fleet, and military equipment. The development of economic diversification and mass consumption are clearly demonstrated by the growth in German foreign trade. In 1872, German exports, which were mainly agricultural products and raw materials, had a value of 2.5 billion marks. Imports of machinery and technology had a value of 3.5 billion marks. By 1910, Germany's foreign trade had undergone a fundamental shift. Exports, by then mainly finished goods and machinery, had attained a value of 7.5 billion marks; imports were mainly foodstuffs, with a value of 8.9 billion marks. On the eve of World War I, both exports and imports were over 10 billion marks.

German industrialization was as revolutionary as it was evolutionary. American students, using the example of the colonies' War for Independence (1775–83), usually identify revolution as a supremely political act in which one faction forcibly replaces another. This colonial perspective works well in North America, where there was no hereditary aristocracy and where an independent middle class fought to free itself from a foreign monarchy. (Class is determined by one's economic level in society and by the mobility to rise or fall, based on circumstances.) In other world regions, however, the governments were firmly in the hands of hereditary rulers and their aristocratic courtiers and bureaucracy, who, by tradition and law, owned most of the land and ruled from the top down. Since the Middle Ages, Europeans had inherited their social level from their parents. Constitutionally, this was identified as a status system, with the divisions known as Estates in France and *Stände* in Germany. The individual was born and died in either the knightly aristocracy, the Second Estate, or the peasant commoners, the Third Estate. (The First Estate was the clergy, which was not determined by property ownership.) Over the centuries, the military function of the aristocracy disappeared, yet they still retained their traditional privileges. Despite incremental social changes that allowed individual commoners to own property in the towns and that gave peasants opportunities to purchase land, the political structure still denied this growing *Mittelstand* political power. That remained firmly in the hands of the aristocracy. Thus, revolution in Europe meant a substantial challenge to the aristocracy's power monopoly by commoners previously excluded from decisionmaking. In England (1649) and France (1793), the internal conflict led to the beheading of sitting kings. It is no wonder the German monarchs were frightened in 1848.

The industrialization of Germany might simply be characterized as "progress" or "modernization" if it were not for the significant changes in the social structure and political empowerment of the commoners that accompanied it. Some may argue that the ideals of the French Revolution, carried to Germany by Napoleon, profoundly influenced German political practice in the nineteenth century. The reality was that local constitutions were issued by monarchial decree, and the national constitution was the product of treaties among the rulers. Although some monarchs permitted their states to have legislatures after 1815, most consisted of appointed advisors, and the major representation was of the aristocracy or the elites. It was the industrialization of Germany that gave commoners in the workforce the leverage they needed to take an active role in the political affairs of the nation. That was the revolutionary part of the process.

In the early decades of the nineteenth century, the German population consisted primarily of the peasantry. In 1807, Prussia had eliminated the legal constraints of feudal serfdom, but this did not appreciably improve the lot of the peasants. Unlike the American farmers, who could seek their fortunes by opening new lands on the frontiers, the German peasants had to buy land from their aristocratic masters. Their mortgages often extended to the next generation, and the lands were frequently marginal.

The Prussian aristocrats preferred to retain their land (and profits from it) through the use of dependent tenant farmers. These Junkers developed their vast holdings into large commercial grain farms, producing cash crops for the European export market. They were extremely prosperous throughout the first half of the century. Moreover, as the government entered more deeply into economic development, its bureaucracy expanded. Most of these positions, as well as the expanding officer corps, were open only to the aristocrats.

In the western German states, the peasantry had been acquiring land since the eighteenth century, but traditional inheritance laws made even this a problem. In the southwest, property had to be divided equally among heirs at the death of the landowner. Thus the individual pieces of property became increasingly small and fragmented, resulting in what was known as the *Zwergekonomie*, or "dwarf" economy. Many of the plots became too small be economically viable. In the northwest the land was to be passed intact to the oldest heir, thus disinheriting younger siblings and relegating them to the status of hired hands, or *Heuerleute*. In either case, what began to emerge was a growing number of landless paupers, dependent on day wages or charity.

Between 1808 and 1811, the Prussian cities were granted self-government, and some of the exclusive controls of the traditional guilds were eliminated. As the commercial *Mittelstand* in the towns became wealthier, however, they began sending their sons to the universities and technical schools scattered throughout Germany. Many of these educated men held important posts in teaching, city administration, law, and journalism. The artisans could seek out their own opportunities. While cities and towns thus opened up careers to the talents of the workers, they did not guarantee them work or a political voice. These individuals swelled the numbers available for new forms of work. The paupers and unemployed helped build the railroads and construct the canals for the *Zollverein*. The educated joined the new businesses; many engaged in research and development. As investment began to develop new forms of industry, they began the transition of German society from rural to urban.

The *Gründerjahre* in the 1870s marked the beginning of a significant population shift toward the industrializing cities. A few examples illustrate this change: Berlin in 1820 had fewer than 200,000 residents. In 1870, it had grown to 774,498 and by 1910 topped 2 million. Essen, in the mining region of the Ruhr valley, grew from a small town of 4,715 in 1820 to 99,887 in 1870 and 410,392 in 1910. In the east, Leipzig had only 37,376 in 1820, but 177,828 in 1870, and 644,644 in 1910. Germany was still 63.9 percent rural in 1871, but only 40 percent rural by 1910; by that date over 53 percent of the workers were occupied in industry, crafts, commerce, and communication. Many individuals also left Germany entirely, emigrating to find new opportunities in the United States, South America, and Australia. During the 1880s, the peak decade of German emigration, over 1.3 million left their homeland.

For the industrial workers, the standard of living deteriorated. In the 1880s, the majority of urban housing consisted of only one room for the worker and his dependents. Conditions in the older commercial cities were somewhat better than those in the new industrial cities: only 23 percent of dwellings in Frankfurt am Main, 28 percent in Hamburg, and 49 percent in Berlin were one-room dwellings. But in the newly industrialized cities one-room housing had reached crisis proportions, as in Dresden (55 percent), Breslau (62 percent), and Chemnitz (70 percent). Workers often lived in unheated tenements without plumbing. In Nürnberg by 1900, the number of individuals sharing one toilet ranged from 27 for the small apartments (below 270 square feet) to 13 for those with more than 538 square feet. Nor did increasing national prosperity offer the workers much relief. In 1905, it was estimated that the percentage of apartments with at least one heated room was only 20.45 percent in Hamburg, 24.84 percent in Leipzig, and 26.44 in Munich. Only Berlin, with 49.34 percent, seemed to offer more comfort for the worker. Throughout the final decades before World War I, the cost of living index rose while the level of wages in real terms remained relatively flat. In 1890, the cost of living index (1900 = 100) was at 98, while real wages were at 92. By 1910, the cost of living was at 120, while real wages were at 99. In 1914, although the economy had grown to 130 through the arms race and competition, workers' wages had only risen to 102.

The urbanized industrial workforce clearly lacked the protection that the former guilds had offered the artisans. While the Reichstag appeared to give workers a role in national politics, the reality was that the legislature gave them little actual political power. Legislation that might impinge on the prerogatives of the state governments or the aristocracy could be easily blocked in the Bundesrat or by the refusal of either the chancellor or the emperor to endorse it. The workers' real strength lay in their numbers, their literacy (by 1850 Prussia had only 20 percent illiteracy), and their determination to change the system. They did this by organizing into unions and political parties and by going out on strike to achieve their goals.

One of the most important legacies of Germany's industrial revolution is the development of political parties and pressure groups. Political organizations had been severely controlled ever since the German Confederation decreed in 1819 that it would not permit organized groups to discuss political affairs. During the 1848 revolutions, however, political factions emerged in the Frankfurt Parliament. After the restoration, governments legislated to control them as well. For example, in 1850 Prussia enacted an association law covering "organizations which intend to discuss political issues in public assemblies." It barred women and minors from political discussion, and it prohibited Prussians from collaborating with members of political groups outside the state. This *Verbindungsverbot* effectively prevented the formation of national political parties in Germany until early in the twentieth century.

The development of political parties and pressure groups reflects the impact of the industrial revolution in nineteenth-century Germany. At the Frankfurt Parliament in 1848, the factions could generally be divided into those that favored the status quo, those that wanted a constitutional monarchy, and those that wanted a republic. The conservatives dominated until 1859, at their core the great Junker landowners. A more liberal group of constitutionalists, who wanted unification as a boost to the economy, broke away from the conservatives to form the National Association. Two years later the Progressive Party (*Deutsche Fortschrittspartei*) came into being with a platform of uniting Germany under Prussian leadership. After unification, other German political parties began to organize. Ferdinand Lassalle, a socialist from Leipzig, founded the *Allgemeine Deutsche Arbeiterverein* (General German Workers' Association) in 1863 to help workers gain power through the ballot box. In Eisenach, August Bebel founded the Social Democratic Party, which adhered to Marxist revolutionary ideology. The two socialist organizations merged in 1875 as the Socialist Workers' Party. The Catholic Center Party (*Zentrum*) emerged in 1870, once the national Protestant majority threatened to overwhelm them. The last faction to form a major party was the Free Conservatives (*Deutsche Reichspartei*) in 1871, which represented the new industrial magnates. There were also numerous regional and ethnic parties competing at the state level.

In 1869, the new North German Confederation responded to these new voices by adopting an integrated approach to economic and political issues. It published the Industrial Code (*Gewerbeordnung*) of 1869, which confirmed to men and women workers alike the freedom to choose their occupation. It also authorized the formation of unions, which had previously been banned. Three types of unions emerged: the Free (unaligned with the companies) Trade Unions promoted by the socialists; the liberal Hirsch-Duncker Unions, which promoted worker education and self-help; and the more conservative Christian Trade Unions. Moreover, the unions used the press to promote their issues. In our era of broadcast media, it is difficult to comprehend the power of the press in Germany. By 1885, for example, when Germany had a population of approximately 46.8 million, there were 3,069 newspapers serving 1,554 locations; of those there were 224 cities with between 6 and 9 newspapers each. By 1914 (the population at more than 67 million), there were 4,221 newspapers in 2,321 towns, of which 265 had 6 to 9 newspapers each. By 1897, Berlin and Munich each had more than 20 newspapers, while 16 other cities had from 10 to 16 newspapers. The federal press law prevented censorship but permitted the prosecution of the "responsible editor" for articles deemed to be dangerous to public order. (At one time there were 16 "responsible editors" of the socialist newspaper *Vorwärts* in jail at the same time!)

This new organizational awareness and political literacy led to numerous political conflicts. Bismarck tried to dampen the Center Party in Prussia with laws to restrict the Catholic Church. This struggle between the church and the state was called the *Kulturkampf*. It only served to increase the importance of the Center Party across Germany. The socialist unions so worried the government that in 1878 Bismarck persuaded the Reichstag to pass anti-Socialist laws outlawing the party across the empire. These laws remained in force until 1890, but recognizing the attraction of socialism to the German workers, Bismarck, in 1881, attempted to preempt it by introducing a bold new social welfare program to the Reichstag. The first measure, enacted in 1883, set up health insurance with the costs split between worker and employer contributions. In 1884, the government mandated a compensation program for those injured on the job. In 1889, the program was completed with the enactment of old-age and invalid insurance. Although the purposes and methods were paternalistic, Germany's new social insurance was the most advanced in the world.

Despite the introduction of social welfare, the workers pressed demands for higher wages and an eight-hour workday. They backed these demands with strikes. There were major work stoppages by coal miners in the Ruhr (1889), dockworkers in Hamburg (1890), textile workers (1903), and steelworkers (1905). Many smaller strikes also disrupted other sectors of industry. There were 1,130 strikes between January 1889 and April 1890 alone. Thereafter, the incidence of strikes slowed to 1,233 in the next five years. But more efficient worker organization, as well as political agitation, brought the success rate of these strikes to 73.5 percent by 1896.

The anti-Socialist laws restricted the political activities of the Social Democrats for 12 years, until 1890. The one loophole open to them was the federal voting law, which permitted political campaigns by any citizens authorized to vote. Despite the ban, the Social Democrats grew from 351,952 voters in 1871 to 1,427,298 voters in 1890, the largest constituency for any party in the Reichstag. But because the government deliberately refused to redraw the voting districts to reflect the concentration of workers in the cities, it took the socialists another 10 years to become the largest party faction in the Reichstag. In 1907, it still took only 17,000 votes to elect a conservative, while a Social Democrat needed at least 70,000.

The socialist trade unions were similarly successful, emerging in 1891 with 278,000 members in 62 unions. By contrast, the Hirsch-Duncker movement had only 18 unions with a membership of 66,000. The Christian Trade Unions did not take hold until 1900, when their 23 unions had a total of 79,000 members.

The conservatives responded to this growing working-class strength by forming their own pressure groups. The Farmers' League (*Bund der Landwirte*) became a powerful voice for the Junkers. It argued for the introduction of tariffs once American grains hit the world market after the United States Civil War. Industrialists formed a number of trade associations, the most prominent of which was the Industrialists' League (*Bund der Industrieller*). It promoted control over the unions and argued for free trade in order to build global markets for industrial goods. The Colonial League (*Kolonialverein*) similarly pushed for expansion of German power overseas in the name of trade and nationalism. The Navy League (*Flottenverein*) urged the development of a strong modern navy. With government support, many of the industrial firms formed noncompetitive cartels to control costs of production and wages, while setting industry-wide prices to guarantee profits.

In 1888, after the deaths of his grandfather, William I, and his father, Frederick III, young William II came to the throne. He planned to establish his "personal regime" and wanted to win the trust of the workers. He disagreed with Bismarck's attempt, in 1890, to renew the anti-Socialist laws and unexpectedly accepted the great chancellor's petulant resignation. Extremely intelligent, yet without basic common sense, William II wanted to establish Germany's role as a global power. His accession also marked the "second industrial revolution" in Germany, the development of new industries based on oil, electricity, steel, and chemicals. These helped Germany produce new forms of weapons, higher speed transportation, and new commercial products.

The German industrial revolution reinforced the drive toward the unification of Germany in 1871. It caused profound economic and technological growth in less than half a century. While helping Germany become one of the most powerful nations on earth by the beginning of the twentieth century, it was not accompanied by a carefully nurtured political process for managing that power. Thus the traditional social divisions between the aristocratic and working classes led to constant social tension. The erratic policies of Kaiser William II further complicated these tensions and led to World War I. The tragic failure of the Weimar Republic (1919–33) and the Third Reich (1933–45) reflect that continuing political immaturity. The German people, however, retained their technological proficiency and, with Allied guidance, were instrumental in rebuilding the German government and economy after World War II. The peaceful reunification of the two German states in 1990 indicates that they gained true political maturity during the second half of the century.

SELECTED BIBLIOGRAPHY

Abrams, Lynn. *Workers' Culture in Imperial Germany.* New York: Routledge, 1991. A sympathetic view of the growth and spread of a working-class ethos.

Barkin, Kenneth D. *The Controversy over German Industrialization, 1890–1902.* Chicago: The University of Chicago Press, 1970. Although focusing on the struggle between industry and agriculture to control protectionist tariff policy, this study also shows how the new economic competition from Germany troubled Britain and other world powers.

Berghahn, Volker. *Imperial Germany, 1871–1914: Economy, Society, Culture, and Politics.* Oxford: Oxford University Press, 1994. A peerless study, Berghahn's volume traces the course of German industrialization and evaluates its impact on social, cultural, and political life.

Clapham, J. H. *Economic Development of France and Germany, 1815–1914.* Cambridge: Cambridge University Press, 1966. This excellent comparative study contrasts the dynamic growth of the German economy with the more stagnant economy of France.

Hamerow, Theodore S. *Restoration, Revolution, Reaction: Economics and Politics in Germany, 1815–1871.* Princeton, NJ: Princeton University Press, 1958. Although dated, this is still the best one-volume work on Germany's transition from a rural to an urban industrial state.

———. *The Social Foundations of German Unification, 1858–1871: Ideas and Institutions.* 2 vols. Princeton, NJ: Princeton University Press, 1969–72. A close examination of Germany's social conditions on the eve of unification.

Henderson, William Otto. *The Industrial Revolution on the Continent: Germany, France, Russia, 1800–1914.* London: Frank Cass and Co., 1961. An excellent comparative study of the modernization of three major world powers in the nineteenth century.

———. *Manufactories in Germany.* New York: Verlag Peter Lang, 1985. This examination of preindustrial (seventeenth and eighteenth centuries) manufacturing in six German states demonstrates that the porcelain, iron, textile, mining, and shipbuilding industries developed both productivity and technology and were the foundations of the later takeoff period.

————. *The Rise of German Industrial Power, 1834–1914.* Berkeley: University of California Press, 1975. The author's penetrating analysis helps to delineate the stages of economic growth.

Kelly, Alfred, ed. and trans. *The German Worker: Working-Class Autobiographies from the Age of Industrialization.* Berkeley: University of California Press, 1987. A fascinating collection of stories detailing the experiences of those who tended the machines in pre–World War I Germany.

Kitchen, Martin. *The Political Economy of Germany, 1815–1914.* London: Croom Helm, 1978. This volume provides an excellent starting point for understanding Germany's industrial revolution.

Lambi, Ivo N. *Free Trade and Protection in Germany, 1868–1879.* Weisbaden, Germany: F. Steiner, 1963. Although narrowly focused, this volume examines the crucial debate over the role of tariffs in promoting (or retarding) industrialization.

Lee, W. R., ed. *German Industry and German Industrialization.* New York: Routledge, 1991. Although the essays contained in this volume are rather scholarly, they offer good data and excellent bibliographies.

Milward, A. G., and S. B. Saul. *The Development of the Economies of Continental Europe, 1850–1914.* London: Allen and Unwin, 1977. This volume places Germany's spectacular industrial development in a European context.

Moses, John A. *Trade Unionism in Germany from Bismarck to Hitler.* Totowa, NJ: Barnes and Noble, 1982. A standard rendition of the rise of trade unions in an industrializing Germany.

Rostow, Walter. *The Stages of Economic Growth: A Non-Communist Manifesto.* Cambridge: Cambridge University Press, 1971. Rostow's classic offers a basic theoretical model for understanding the nature of modern industrialization.

Stolper, Gustav. *The Economic Development of Germany, 1870 to the Present.* Translated by Toni Stolper. New York: Harcourt Brace Jovanovich, 1967. Excellent overview of Germany's industrialization process.

4

The Pursuit of *Weltpolitik,* 1890–1914

INTRODUCTION

On March 18, 1890, the man most responsible for the creation of the modern German Empire passed from the scene. No, Otto von Bismarck had not died; rather, on that date William II, the German emperor, accepted Bismarck's letter of resignation. Although Bismarck was 75 years old, he remained vigorous and alert. His resignation came not as a result of old age, but as a consequence of increasing tension with his royal master. William II had ascended the throne in 1888, an avowed disciple of Bismarck. However, in a few short months these two headstrong and egotistical figures grew estranged. Bismarck was the man who reputedly said, "If there is music to be made, I and I alone shall make it." William, not content with simply occupying the throne, was determined to rule. Despite pronouncements of mutual admiration, a clash was inevitable.

In late nineteenth-century Europe, monarchs played a less significant role than they had earlier in the century. The British and Italian rulers were increasingly seen as figureheads, and France, a republic, had even gone so far as to do away with the monarchy. Only Russia retained the traditional autocratic form, and even there, rumblings of discontent could be heard. At first glance, Germany appeared to be another modern, progressive state, especially since it possessed a constitution that theoretically served as the supreme law of the land and had a Reichstag (parliament) elected by universal male suffrage. However, Bismarck, the author of the German constitution, had purposely produced a weak and ambiguous document that critics referred to as a sham constitution. The Reichstag also lacked

In pursuing *Weltpolitik*, Germany sought to achieve an ill-defined "place in the sun" for itself and increased influence in global affairs. In promoting *Weltpolitik* and the growth of a large German navy, Emperor William II (represented on the left) managed to antagonize Great Britain (on the right) needlessly. (Reproduced from the Collections of the Library of Congress.)

any real authority, serving instead as a toothless debating body. Where then did power lie in the German Empire? Thanks to Bismarck, it remained with the customary Prussian elite of centuries past, including the Junkers, or landed aristocrats, whose estates for the most part lay east of the Elbe River; the upper reaches of the bureaucracy; and the army's officer corps. At the top of this hierarchy stood the emperor. While theoretically constrained by the constitution and Reichstag, in practice the emperor enjoyed something approaching unlimited authority. This arrangement suited Bismarck as long as William I, whom he could control, reigned. However, with the arrival of William II the tables were turned on Bismarck, and the chancellor's handiwork ironically proved to be his undoing.

William II was born in 1859, the grandson of Great Britain's Queen Victoria on his maternal side and the grandson of Germany's Emperor William I on his paternal side. Although probably the most intelligent of Europe's monarchs at the turn of the twentieth century, William was also such a vain, neurotic bundle of nerves that he became a favorite topic for that century's latter psychohistorians. William was born with a withered left arm and spent much of his life overcompensating for this handicap. Not only did he enthusiastically engage in vigorous physical activity, but he also presented himself as completely self-assured on every possible matter and bragged without end. When the spirit moved him, William could be gracious and charming; however, most of the time he preferred to prattle on about his accomplishments, real and imagined.

William was an outstanding example of the triumph of style over substance. The bombastic young emperor surrounded himself with yes-men who saw it as their duty to inflate his ego. Never one to take advice, William demanded obedience, loyalty, and bonhomie. He was ostentatious and self-indulgent. No less a figure than Bismarck noted that the emperor wished to have a birthday party for himself every day. Nevertheless, at heart, William was a lonely, lazy, and cowardly figure who puffed himself up to no apparent purpose. Mercurial, loquacious, and shallow, William also possessed an unfailing knack for either creating problems or exacerbating existing ones.

William had poor relations with his father and abysmal ones with his mother. Despite the fact that he spent considerable time in Great Britain and spoke English as fluently as any British statesman did, William never seemed to grasp the workings of the British constitutional system. Instead, he passionately identified with Prussia's autocratic traditions. William was a romantic absolutist at heart and saw no value in modern political institutions such as constitutions or parliaments. Rather, he longed for an imaginary Germany of the past that featured knights in shining armor and a beloved king carrying out feats of heroism against a backdrop of childish sentimentality. In practice, these attitudes led William to scorn the Reichstag and to ignore the constitution. In particular, William allied himself with the army. The military was his "baby," and the emperor spent copious amounts of time consorting with its officers, designing its uniforms, and participating in its ceremonies—all activities that he loved.

It is said that upon Bismarck's departure William declared, "The course remains the same, full steam ahead." In fact, the course did not remain the same. Bismarck, as one might expect of a man of his age and upbringing, was a Eurocentric. For him, the world consisted of Europe and little else. His goal had been to make Prussia (and all that it represented) supreme in Germany and Germany supreme in Europe. William abandoned Bismarck's Eurocentrism and substituted a policy of *Weltpolitik.*

Weltpolitik literally means "world policy" or "global politics." In practice it signaled Germany's clumsy and ultimately destructive entry onto the stage of world politics. Citing its political importance, military strength, and economic vitality, Germany now demanded what it referred to as its rightful "place in the sun." While never clearly articulated, apparently this "place in the sun" meant that Germany now expected to be consulted about—and perhaps even deferred to on—every global issue, no matter how trivial. Moreover, in making this expectation known, Germany resorted to the tactics that Bismarck had employed so successfully—demanding, bullying, and threatening. In pursuing *Weltpolitik* in such a rude, insensitive, overbearing manner, Germany greatly harmed itself.

Not unexpectedly, the quest for a larger colonial empire figured prominently in *Weltpolitik.* For many years, Bismarck resisted appeals for Germany to build an overseas empire, regarding such overseas expansion as unattractive. However, in the mid-1880s he yielded to growing public cries for empire and unenthusiastically allowed Germany to establish protectorates over Southwest Africa, the Cameroons, East Africa, and Zanzibar. With *Weltpolitik,* the attitude of the German government changed markedly. Now Germany's claims to global importance positively required a colonial empire and the bigger the better.

In 1895, Germany joined Russia and France in forcing Japan to surrender some of the gains it had made during the recently concluded Sino-Japanese War. In 1898, Germany exploited a weakened China to expand its presence there. It signed a 99-year lease with China giving it control of the valuable Kiaochow region. In the same year, Germany took advantage of Spain's involvement in the Spanish-American War to buy Spain's South Pacific islands at a favorable price. In the following year it added to its South Pacific possessions when it claimed part of the Samoan Islands. When the Boxer Rebellion broke out in China in 1900, Germany spearheaded the international community's military response that crushed the Boxers.

Following the dictates of *Weltpolitik,* Germany also deeply involved itself in the Ottoman Empire. For a long time this empire had been in decline. Great Britain, France, Austria, and Russia had all evinced a selfish interest in the fate of the Ottoman lands. In fact, most observers credit the Ottoman ability to play these jackals against each other with preserving its independence. Neither Prussia nor Bismarck's Germany had shown even the slightest interest in the empire's fate. However, German economic penetration eventually led to political penetration. Starting from virtually zero, by 1910 Germany had come to supply the Ottoman Empire with 21 percent of its imports and owned 20 percent of its national debt. Its banks were also instrumental in financing the construction of Ottoman railways, especially the Berlin-to-Baghdad line, a route that upon completion would have linked the Persian Gulf with the North Sea. Reflecting Germany's expanded relationship with the Ottoman Empire, in 1898 William II paid a state visit during which he extravagantly announced that henceforth Germany would be the protector of the world's 300 million Moslems. In 1913, in response to an Ottoman request, Germany sent a military mission under General Otto Liman von Sanders to Constantinople for the express purpose of rebuilding the empire's shattered armies. To facilitate this objective, Liman von Sanders was named commander of Ottoman forces.

Probably the most important manifestation of *Weltpolitik* was the decision to build a huge fleet. Historically, Germany (and Prussia and the other preunification German states) had paid scant attention to naval matters. As late as the mid-1890s, Germany's fleet was only the seventh largest in the world. However, William, who loved sailing and reportedly was embarrassed by the existing German fleet's size and condition, needed little urging to become a convinced supporter of Germany's need for a large, modern naval force. In 1896, the emperor gave a speech declaring that the "German Reich had become a Weltreich." The following year, he appointed Admiral Alfred von Tirpitz secretary of state for naval affairs. With great energy and single-mindedness of purpose, Tirpitz turned to the task of creating the navy the emperor wanted. In 1898, Tirpitz pushed the first naval bill through a reluctant Reichstag. Additional naval bills (in 1900, 1906, 1907, and 1908) quickly followed, all providing huge amounts of money for naval construction and, ominously, provoking a full-scale naval arms race with Great Britain. Tirpitz was also something of a propaganda genius. In 1898, he established the *Flottenverein*, or Navy League, to lobby for the large fleet. Ten years later, the *Flottenverein* boasted more than 1 million members, including the most prominent figures in German society.

As disruptive as the policy of *Weltpolitik* was, the brusque, overbearing, and insensitive manner in which it was carried out proved to be even more unsettling. Insulting remarks and provocative behavior characterized *Weltpolitik*. A couple of examples will suffice to demonstrate the tone of *Weltpolitik*. Early in 1905, France—with the approval of Great Britain, Spain, and Italy—moved to strengthen its grip on Morocco, a nominally independent Moslem state in northwest Africa. Germany, which initially had ignored Mediterranean affairs since it had no interests there, now burst furiously onto the scene. Complaining loudly about being excluded from the decision-making process and declaring that such an important country could not passively absorb such a grievous insult, Germany dispatched William to Tangier, where he gave a speech supporting Moroccan independence. This unexpected challenge to France and its new ally, Great Britain, needlessly roiled the waters, but to keep the peace the competent but anti-German French foreign minister Theophile Delcassé resigned. Not content, Germany now turned this triumph into a Pyrrhic victory. Refusing to drop the matter, Germany demanded that an international conference be held to settle Moroccan affairs. In January 1906, Europe's statesmen assembled at Algeciras. Fully expecting the global community to join it in humiliating France, Germany suffered a major setback when the conference rejected its proposals out of hand. Only Austria-Hungary stood by an isolated Germany.

Germany could not leave the Moroccan issue alone. In 1911, as France gradually extended its sway over Morocco, the Moroccan cities of Fez and Rabat erupted in protest that necessitated the introduction of French troops. The appearance of the French army in Morocco violated the agreements reached at Algeciras. France acknowledged this and almost immediately opened negotiations with Germany for compensation to the latter. Germany, however, chose to make a grandstand play. At the start of July, it sent the gunboat *Panther* to the Moroccan port of Agadir. Ostensibly the *Panther* was sent to protect German interests there, but its voyage was really meant to embarrass and humiliate France. Moreover, Germany also demanded a huge chunk of France's Congo territory as compensation. A major international crisis ensued, which skillful diplomacy finally defused. Nevertheless, the two Moroccan crises cannot be considered isolated incidents; rather, they were the norm for German behavior under the policy of *Weltpolitik*.

INTERPRETIVE ESSAY
Charles F. Pennacchio

The German empire of 1890 was less than two decades old, having been born in 1871 through the combined processes of rapid industrialization, manipulative diplomacy, and calculated warfare. The leader of Germany's culminating drive to statehood was the Prussian nationalist Otto von Bismarck. Following successive military victories over Denmark (1864), Austria (1866), and France (1870), Bismarck, now chancellor of Germany, sought to consolidate his new nation's territorial gains, to forge—writ large—his dutiful commitment to Prussian autocratic rule, and to overcome Germany's political and diplomatic uncertainty in the aftermath of war with France. Remarkably, Bismarck's combination of defensive alliances, effective trade relations, and innovative statecraft enabled the new Germany to build close ties with Russia, Italy, and Austria-Hungary. However, by 1888 William I (Bismarck's patron from 1862) was dead, and his grandson, William II, had mounted the throne following his father's untimely passing after only a few months in power. What ensued was a quiet power struggle that culminated with William II pushing Bismarck aside and, with him, his balanced diplomacy of *Realpolitik*. William II then pursued a "New Course," a high-risk foreign and military policy that ultimately led to the Great War, or World War I (1914–18); the defeat of Germany; the collapse of Prussian-style rule; and the simultaneous rise of Weimar Germany (1919–33) and Hitler's National Socialist movement.

From 1871 to 1890, Bismarck had faced the dual difficulties of establishing a modern nation while also building a respectable presence—based on trade, statecraft, and self-restrained military might—in a European state system suddenly confronted with a German giant at its center. His complementary domestic and international responses revolved around a balance of strict autocratic rule, timely concessions and reforms, secretive diplomacy, economic might and productivity, and shrewd political maneuverings. In direct contrast, the years of Wilhelmine Germany (1890–1914) witnessed a systematic dismantling of Bismarckian diplomacy, the result of which was global war—World War I.

The Great War produced a conflict of such colossal proportions that it fundamentally changed the way Europeans viewed their polity. It altered the way they viewed European culture and civilization, and it destroyed much of their confidence, that brimming sense of ethnocentrism that was prevalent before the outbreak of World War I. In many respects, World War I marks the end of the nineteenth century and signals the beginning of two great conflicts in the twentieth century: World War II and the Cold War. The Great War, World War II, and the Cold War, collectively, represent a radical transformation in European history every bit as revolutionary as the French and Industrial Revolutions of the eighteenth and early nineteenth centuries.

The 1890 to 1914 prewar period is critical to our understanding of the causes of conflict and the standard by which we are to measure Germany's (and Europe's) dramatic shifts during and after World War I. No antebellum European state altered its relations with the outside world more abruptly, more aggressively, and more arrogantly than did Germany under William II. Simply put, not only did William II force Bismarck from power in 1890, he simultaneously and unilaterally jettisoned Bismarck's carefully constructed international state system.

Bismarck had created a European political order with Germany at its core. From 1871 to 1890, his system operated on the premise of German domination over the Continent—in military terms, in economic terms, but above all, in diplomatic terms. Germany's diplomatic hegemony on the Continent would guarantee peace and stability for 20 years, for the Europe of 1871 had recently endured a series of short, decisive wars. Remarkably, the Austro-Prussian War with Denmark in 1864, the Austro-Prussian War in 1866, and the Franco-Prussian War of 1871 had avoided the slippery slope of a European-wide conflict. Bismarck's subsequent policies of bilateral defense alliances and diplomatic isolation of France effectively precluded any temptation on the part of the French to seek military revenge against their German rivals.

In 1871, then, Europe witnessed the emergence of a new international system, with a new German state in the center and a newly unified Italy on the periphery. Moreover, Napoleon III's French empire had collapsed in the wake of its ignominious defeat at the Battle of Sedan. France's so-called Third Republic emerged out of the ashes of the Franco-Prussian debacle. One of the dominant questions across Europe, especially in Berlin, concerned the course of the Third Republic's foreign policy. How would the newly formed French government deal with a unified Germany following its humbling military defeat and the humiliating Treaty of Frankfort that required French reparations and the loss of Alsace and Lorraine?

Also of concern to Bismarck—and other European diplomats—was growing conflict in the Balkans. The Ottoman Empire, often called the "Sick Man of Europe," appeared extremely unstable in keeping control over lands and peoples that covered much of the Balkans. Many of the same problems appeared in the Austro-Hungarian Empire's portion of the

Balkans. Indeed, after their defeat by Prussia in 1866, the Hapsburg monarchy granted the Hungarians within the empire equal status in domestic affairs. Statesmen wondered if this would be a stable construct; would it stimulate more nationalist movements such as the one in Bohemia? Would the Hapsburg monarchy survive if the Ottoman Empire collapsed? Would the Hapsburg monarchy simply become the new "Sick Man of Europe"? If nationalist and ethnic tensions caused the Ottoman or Austrian empires to shrink or collapse, who would then fill the power vacuum?

Central to the fate of any kind of stable European order, to any sort of balance of power, was the role of the new German state. While Germany had become at last a unified state in 1871, the often-repeated question was: what role would the new Germany play? It was quite clear in 1871 that Germany had become a very powerful military force, easily the most powerful military establishment on the Continent. After 1871, the rates of industrial growth indicated that Germany was well on its way to becoming an industrial and economic colossus as well. It was the most populous—and fastest growing—state in central Western Europe, with an enormous and high-powered industrial establishment. Could the European state system absorb this new German state? Would it be an aggressive state? After all, its military had inflicted terrific defeats on major, potentially hostile, European powers. So would Prussian Germany continue its wars of conquest, as they were so often seen to be?

By 1890, Bismarck believed that he had advantageously positioned Germany despite the appearance of menacing storm clouds on the horizon. The situation in the Ottoman Empire—now disintegrating rapidly—clearly suggested that there was going to be very serious trouble in this area. Equally ominous from the point of view of European statesmen was that the very ethnic and national troubles that had been the source of the Ottoman decline—the Serbs, Bulgarians, Romanians, and Montenegrins all clamoring for independence from the Ottoman Empire—now confronted Austria. The Hapsburg monarchy also possessed the wide variety of ethnic groups, especially Slavic nations, that showed increasing signs of restlessness. When would Austria move to the front burner, in a sense, with these nationalities demanding independence from the Hapsburg monarchy as well?

The great problem that Bismarck had with both Austria-Hungary and Russia was that both alliances were secret. They were not commonly known even in diplomatic circles. So many in Germany began to feel, particularly after 1888, that this juggling act was just too difficult to maintain. In 1888, the old Kaiser, William I, died and was followed into power by his son Frederick, a man of the generation of 1848, the great darling of the German liberals, connected to Great Britain through his marriage to the daughter of Queen Victoria. But Frederick's reign lasted only 100 days, and he was followed into power by William II, his son, who was more than 50 years younger than Bismarck. Whereas Bismarck was a Prussian first and only after unification began to develop some larger notion of a new Germany, he was also traditional in the sense that he thought in European terms. But after William II assumed power, the relationship between the new Kaiser—a young, ambitious, and intemperate monarch—and the old chancellor quickly deteriorated. In 1890, William II forced Bismarck into retirement. The real question for Europe and the world was: could Bismarck's international state system (that had provided 20 years of stability) survive, and if not, what direction would German policy follow in the aftermath of his departure?

The 1871 to 1890 international state system, established largely by Otto von Bismarck, gradually fell apart after his dismissal in 1890. The Bismarckian system had rested on Germany's need for stability, Bismarck's determination to show his new nation's satisfaction with the post–Franco-Prussian War world, and Germany's need for time and space to develop itself into a coherent nation. As a result, Bismarck created a complicated set of alliances to protect Germany's security. For purposes of isolating a French nation that might seek revenge against Germany, Bismarck had established friendly relations with Great Britain, forged a close working relationship with the Austro-Hungarian Empire, and built intimate ties with tsarist Russia. However, after William II forced Bismarck to retire in 1890, he turned to a series of mostly weak-kneed foreign ministers and chancellors whose orientation was far more German than Bismarck's Prussian bias. William II pursued an aggressive foreign policy commonly called *Weltpolitik*, or world policy. During his reign (1888–1918), William II dismantled the Bismarckian alliance system, caused Germany's own isolation from previous allies, and divided Europe into two hostile camps that waged war from 1914 to 1918.

As Germany set off on a new course in foreign policy, political leaders and observers across Europe actively wondered whether the Kaiser's new international approach would, in fact, maintain the stability Bismarck had achieved for two decades or if his policies would elevate tensions already present in Europe. While it was known that William II's new age of German foreign policy, *Weltpolitik*, would radically reshape the diplomatic balance Bismarck had so carefully orchestrated since 1871, the fatal outcome of *Weltpolitik* was hardly predictable in 1890, or even in 1900.

As certain problems clearly surfaced in the Balkans in the 1890s, especially between Austria and Russia, William II and his advisors increasingly came to believe that Germany could no longer continue Bismarck's role as "honest broker." Instead of pursuing a policy of keeping Austrian and Russian interests in balance, Germany would have to choose between the two rivals. Part of the reason for this conclusion can be found in seemingly irreconcilable differences in the Balkan region itself. The multiethnic and hypernationalistic Balkan problem had become so intractable, so volatile, and so potentially explosive that the Kaiser's Germany felt compelled to side with the power (Austria) that would advance German interests the most.

Another reason for choosing between Vienna and Moscow was that Bismarck's agreements with both powers had been kept secret. What would happen, the Kaiser argued, if the actual terms of the different treaties went public? What would happen if the Russians were aware of the Austrian agreement and vice versa? This state of diplomatic secrecy could no longer continue. It simply was not possible to perpetuate the difficult juggling act that Bismarck had so skillfully carried out for so long—especially if the situation in the Balkans deteriorated further.

Moreover, William II and his foreign policy staff were not going to be limited to a continental policy. No longer would Bismarck's Prussian outlook drive Germany's international approach. Rather, the Kaiser's new *Weltpolitik* would follow a self-consciously *German* viewpoint—a bolder, more daring policy approach—one that decisively rejected his predecessor's more cautious approach. In order to achieve Germany's rightful "place in the sun" (*ein Platz an der Sonne*) in international relations, it needed to participate on the global stage, not simply in the European theater. The only way for an ambitious state to achieve world-class greatness was to follow a bold and unrelenting strategy in pursuit of global prosperity, global prestige, and global power.

While Bismarck had gone to great lengths to avoid colonial confrontations with England and France (and others), the Kaiser believed his nation required a break from such a cautious course. Yes, William II's aggressive foreign policy approach carried with it the risk of conflict over colonial policy, but Germany thought it a risk well worth taking. Even the Kaiser's frequent use of the phrase *"ein Platz an der Sonne"* personified his unfortunate habit of sounding even more confrontational than he actually intended in policy terms. To most Europeans, *ein Platz an der Sonne* seemed to smack of a German sense of entitlement. In fact, after initially uttering this statement without much clarification, William II gave a diplomatically disastrous interview to the London-based *Daily Telegraph* with the Boer War in South Africa serving as a backdrop.

While trying to cultivate better relations between Great Britain and Germany, the Kaiser inadvertently drove a deeper wedge between the two powers. In particular, he bluntly and condescendingly described how the Germans had devised a military plan that helped the British exit the conflict relatively unscathed. Even though the story was factually correct, it stirred up resentment in Great Britain and resounded throughout all the European capitals. In addition, William II used the politically counterproductive term "the yellow peril" to describe the Chinese at a time of rising tension between Beijing and numerous European nations. Similar to his backhanded treatment of the English in the South African context, the Kaiser chilled the diplomatic climate between Berlin and other European capitals.

In explaining Germany's *Weltpolitik* objectives in the early 1890s, William II spoke bluntly of what he felt Germany was entitled to, namely, colonial conquests similar to those achieved by other global powers. However, what he seemed incapable of acknowledging was that Germany had already grabbed a significant share of overseas territory during the latter period of Bismarck's tenure. Therefore, given his diplomatic blunders, antagonistic comments, and seeming denial of Germany's considerable land holdings in Africa and Asia, the Kaiser's declaration of *Weltpolitik* appeared to many to be irrationally provocative. By contrast, one of the foundations of Bismarckian foreign policy had been the need to be predictable in the eyes of other state actors. In other words, Bismarck had operated on the principle that one's real and potential opponents must be able to anticipate, within reason, the course and actions of the leading state actor in question. However, with William II leading German foreign policy, outside observers increasingly saw Berlin as erratic, bombastic, and aggressively expansionistic.

Kaiser William II's *Weltpolitik* rested on critical assumptions that would prove fatal to its practitioner. The first failed belief was that republican France and tsarist Russia would never create a cross-continental, cross-ideological alliance. Were such an alliance to materialize, Germany would be at risk. Germany's location in central Europe meant that it faced potential military disaster were it forced to fight a two-front war. Consequently, a cardinal principle of Bismarck's diplomacy was to isolate France while maintaining cordial relations with Russia.

Second, while Bismarck had effectively isolated France through a series of bilateral defensive alliances with Italy, Russia, and Austria, William II allowed all but that with the crumbling Austrian Empire to lapse. What this meant was that Italy and especially Russia could explore more diplomatic options—with each other, with France, and with others—away from more exclusive ties with Berlin.

Third, the Kaiser subscribed to the faulty assumption that seemingly unbridgeable colonial and ideological differences between Great Britain and Russia precluded their forming a closer relationship. Specifically, because Persia (Iran) was a source of frequent conflict between Russia and Great Britain, it seemed from Berlin's perspective that the two nations could never overcome their differences.

Fourth, William II and his advisors arrogantly believed that Germany was a far more valuable ally to Russia, Austria, and Great Britain than any of these countries might be to Germany. Based on yet another false assumption—the indispensable place of Germany in the European alliance system—William II engaged in a series of striking diplomatic moves that radically transformed the international system and greatly exacerbated tensions within Europe and across the world.

One of the Kaiser's critical diplomatic shifts involved his rejection of Bismarck's previously friendly relations with Russia. Specifically, despite strenuous pleas from Moscow, William II and his advisors allowed Bismarck's Reinsurance Treaty with Russia to lapse in 1890 at the time for its renewal. Because the Russians desperately craved Berlin's financial support for their rapid drive toward industrialization, the tsar's representatives argued the case to continue floating their bonds in Germany. When the Kaiser said no, French financiers quickly opened their own markets to Russian bonds and provided additional capital for the tsar's industrial campaign. Still, for the next two years the Russians unsuccessfully continued to press their case for renewed economic ties with the Germans.

By 1892, German-Russian relations had chilled considerably; by 1894, Franco-Russian talks yielded a formal military agreement. This dramatic and unexpected turnabout represented a serious setback not only for Bismarck's diplomatic balancing act of the 1870s and 1880s, but also for William II's *Weltpolitik* calculations. The startling merger of republican France's and authoritarian Russia's economic and military interests dealt a major blow to proud Germany's assumption that it would never face a two-front war. War with France in the west, yes; but war with Russia in the east? Impossible! Now, suddenly, the impossible looked entirely possible—at least to the rational policymakers outside William II's inner circle. As for the Kaiser himself, his state of denial—again, built around the unrealistic assumptions of *Weltpolitik*—allowed him to embrace the idea that Germany remained invulnerable to Russian power.

Relations between Berlin and London also took a turn for the worse with Germany's adoption of *Weltpolitik*. Great Britain saw several threats emanating from Germany in the late nineteenth century: dramatic increases in industrial growth, stepped-up military research and production, and territorial and commercial global expansionism. Projections that the Germans could well overtake British industrial output in virtually all areas of heavy industry and commercial trade by the turn of the century alarmed London. So fearful were the British that Parliament contemplated a heretical economic measure—placing tariffs on imported commodities from Germany. In the end, however, the free-trade-minded government simply labeled all such imports "Made in Germany." But even this backfired since British citizens primarily purchased goods based on their quality, not on their nation of origin.

Beyond the intensifying economic competition between Germany and Great Britain there also simmered an imperial rivalry that played out in Africa, Asia, and the Middle East. Over time, London grew increasingly anxious about German movements in the Ottoman Empire and beyond. In particular, the Germans publicly discussed a Berlin-to-Baghdad railroad project as a means to reach into the Middle East. The British saw this German proposal as a potentially hostile penetration of a region considered vital to its security. Making matters worse, William II visited Palestine, where he arrogantly claimed to speak for all Moslems living in this area dominated by British and French economic and military interests.

Adding further tension to the Anglo-German rivalry, Berlin failed to cooperate with the British in South Africa during both the Jameson Raid of 1895 and the Boer War of 1899–1902. At a critical diplomatic moment in the Jameson Raid controversy (involving British settlers moving into the Transvaal), William II fired off a congratulatory telegram to President Paul Krueger of the Boer Republic of Transvaal to applaud his victory over the British. When the Kaiser's message went public, British leaders boiled over with fury. With the experience of the Jameson Raid fresh in mind, Great Britain turned to Germany a few years later for backing in the Boer War. Berlin's refusal followed the Kaiser's extraordinary belief that his British counterparts depended more on German support than the other way around.

More damaging still to Anglo-German relations was a naval arms race—following the precepts of the Kaiser's *Weltpolitik*—that pitted the two powers against one another at the turn of the century. German naval leader Admiral Alfred von Tirpitz's so-called "Risk Fleet Theory" challenged British preeminence on the high seas like no other country in centuries. While Tirpitz believed there was no way for Germany to equal the strength of London's navy, he bent every effort to develop a naval fleet powerful enough to deter British thoughts of war should a crisis arise between the two nations. Tirpitz theorized that Great Britain would not risk doing battle with Germany because of the incalculable destruction its own naval forces would suffer. The prospect of huge losses would be enough to deter Great Britain. Risk or no risk, Tirpitz's theory begins with the assumption that confrontation and conflict between Germany and Great Britain are inevitable.

Beginning in 1898, Germany launched a naval buildup that got Great Britain's immediate attention. In 1900, the German Reichstag enacted new legislation that accelerated fleet production dramatically. By 1904–5, in direct response to Germany's naval expansion, London introduced its own new battleship design, the Dreadnought; the first was launched in 1906. Berlin then countered with its version of this larger, quicker, and more powerful ship. The Anglo-German naval arms race, already well underway, suddenly and alarmingly picked up speed. Experts concurred that the Dreadnought itself would revolutionize naval warfare, much as the Dreadnought competition dramatically raised the stakes between Berlin and London and captured the attention of leaders and readers across Europe and around the world. Despite British King Edward VII's strong advice to his nephew that Germany halt its own Dreadnought program, William II ordered the government and industrialists to proceed apace with the Dreadnought. Anglo-German relations sank precipitously.

Fed by diplomatic, economic, imperial, military, and personality considerations, Great Britain dramatically improved its relationship with France. The resultant Entente Cordiale was thought unimaginable by most observers just a few short years earlier. As a starting point, Paris and London agreed to work more closely on colonial questions that affected both and to identify a common ground for addressing the perceived threat inherent in Germany's *Weltpolitik*.

For the British, the Entente Cordiale represented a rather informal working relationship for discussing and potentially pursuing areas of mutual interest. For the French, however, the Entente Cordiale was a firm pact that tied London and Paris together over issues of military security. While France had climbed out of the diplomatic box Bismarck had previously placed them in and successfully established strong military and economic ties with Russia, Paris sought to enhance its security through a closer alliance with Great Britain. The Germans themselves aided the process of France's rapprochement with its former British rival through a series of missteps involving a crisis in Morocco. The Kaiser's Germany had so antagonized French and British interests in North Africa that it effectively brought the one-time enemies in London and Paris together in opposition to the seemingly more threatening Germans.

In addition, German aggression and adventurism prompted the Russians and British—also historic rivals—to come together in common purpose. In

1907, following its humiliating defeat by Japan in the Russo-Japanese War of 1904–5, the Russians agreed to an entente with Great Britain. Putting aside their differences over Persia, the two powers developed a nascent diplomatic triangle that would evolve into the Triple Entente of Russia, France, and Great Britain. Between 1890 and 1914, Germany had traded its Bismarckian placement at the center of European politics (with France strategically isolated) for a position of facing a two-front war with France in the west and Russia in the east. At the same time, Britain hovered ominously across the English Channel.

Threatened by potential encirclement, the Kaiser directed his military to consider Germany's options should a worst-case scenario unfold. Germany's chief of staff, General Alfred von Schlieffen, forged a response in 1905 that, appropriately enough, acquired the name Schlieffen Plan. In the event of war, Schlieffen imagined a lightning-quick German mobilization, a rapid movement through Belgium (with or without the consent of Brussels), and an overwhelming drive into northern France to capture Paris. After defeating France, the German army would wheel around to the east to take on the cumbersome Russian military. The Germans calculated that the huge Russian army, dispersed across an even larger land mass and handicapped with poor communication and transportation systems, would need many weeks to mobilize.

The Schlieffen Plan—a direct outgrowth of Germany's failed *Weltpolitik*—had many flaws. For one, all of Europe (including Germany itself after unifying in 1871) had stood up for Belgian neutrality, dating originally to 1839. Perhaps even more importantly, if a crisis arose in the Balkans, particularly one between Austria and Russia, Germany's first step would be to attack France through Belgium. Thus, the Schlieffen Plan made certain that if war began in the Balkans it would mushroom into a continental war of vast proportions. Consequently, on the eve of the Great War, Europe found itself divided into two militarized camps: on one side France, Russia, and Great Britain and on the other side Germany and Austria. Germany's policy of *Weltpolitik* played no small part in producing a fractured, tense, and belligerent continent that slid into World War I. That conflict grew into a global conflagration causing the deaths of some 10 million citizens and soldiers, the psychological devastation of millions more, and the ruination of the European continent.

SELECTED BIBLIOGRAPHY

Anderson, P. R. *The Background of Anti-English Feeling in Germany, 1890–1902.* New York: Octagon, 1969. Traces domestic politics, nationalist propaganda, and public opinion in both driving and manifesting German Anglophobia prior to World War I.

Balfour, Michael. *The Kaiser and His Times.* New York: Norton, 1972. Highly readable biography of William II with a moderately pro-English bias.

Berghahn, V. R. *Germany and the Approach of War in 1914.* London: Macmillan, 1973. Explores the confluence of imperial ambitions and the movement to uphold Germany's authoritarian political system.

Blackbourn, David. *The Long Nineteenth Century: A History of Germany, 1780–1918.* New York: Oxford University Press, 1998. Focuses on class conflict and the uses of political power in explaining prewar tensions and instability.

Blackbourn, David, and Geoff Ely. *The Peculiarities of German History: Bourgeois Society and Politics in Nineteenth-Century Germany.* Oxford: Oxford University Press, 1984. Argues that German aggression is to be understood both in terms of national character and international patterns of behavior.

Calleo, David P. *The German Problem Reconsidered: Germany and the World Order, 1870 to the Present.* Cambridge: Cambridge University Press, 1978. Points to domestic and foreign policy, as well as political culture, as defining a German mass following of authoritarian rule.

Craig, Gordon A. *From Bismarck to Adenauer: Aspects of German Statecraft.* Rev. ed. New York: Harper & Row, 1965. This survey of German foreign policy leadership zeroes in on the persistently weak diplomats who orchestrated William II's wishes in *Weltpolitik.*

Fink, C., Isabel V. Hull, and MacGregor Knox, eds. *German Nationalism and the European Response, 1890–1945.* Norman: University of Oklahoma Press, 1985. Centers on the interplay of nationalism across borders and domestic political motivations within nations.

Fischer, Fritz. *War of Illusions: German Politics from 1911 to 1914.* Translated by Marian Jackson. New York: Norton, 1975. In this and several other controversial studies, the author argues persuasively that Germany's *Weltpolitik* bears the major responsibility for the coming of World War I.

Geiss, Imanuel. *German Foreign Policy, 1871–1914.* London: Routledge and Kegan Paul, 1976. Considers an array of factors that produced an increasingly aggressive German foreign policy.

Gordon, M. "Domestic Conflict and the Origins of the First World War." *Journal of Modern History* 46 (1974): 191–226. Emphasizes convergence of nationalistic politics in Germany and Great Britain in explaining the rise of war.

Hobsbawm, Eric. *The Age of Empire, 1875–1914.* New York: Pantheon Books, 1987. Connects larger political, economic, and cultural currents of the age with special focus on class conflict.

Hull, Isabel V. *The Entourage of Kaiser William II.* Cambridge: Cambridge University Press, 1982. Discusses in depth the often-overlooked roles of monarchy and personality in bringing on the Great War.

Joll, James. *The Origins of the First World War.* New York: Longman, 1992. Considers the role of nationalism, politics, military planning, big business, and empire building with deft balance.

Kennedy, Paul M. *The Rise of the Anglo-German Antagonism, 1860–1914.* London: Allen & Unwin, 1980. Explores the growing conflict between Great Britain (an established world power) and Germany (an expansionist power seeking its "place in the sun").

Massie, Robert K. *Dreadnought: Britain, Germany, and the Coming of the Great War.* New York: Random House, 1991. Centers on the naval rivalry between Great Britain and Germany following Queen Victoria's death in 1901 as one of the leading causes of war.

Mommsen, W. J. "Domestic Factors in German Foreign Policy before 1914." *Central European History* 6 (1973): 3–43. Focuses on the primacy of national politics in driving German activity overseas.

Tuchman, Barbara W. *The Proud Tower: A Portrait of the World before the War: 1890–1914.* New York: Macmillan, 1966. Provides the economic, social, political, and technological context for the dynamic and anxious prewar period.

Williamson, Samuel R., Jr. *Austria-Hungary and the Origins of the First World War.* New York: St. Martin's Press, 1990. Argues that it was Austria-Hungary, not Germany, that initiated the military steps that brought on World War I.

5

World War I, 1914–1918

INTRODUCTION

On June 28, 1914, Archduke Franz Ferdinand, heir to the Austro-Hungarian crown, was assassinated in the remote Bosnian town of Sarajevo. Although at that time political assassination was not uncommon—in the previous 35 years the Russian tsar, the Austrian empress, and two U.S. presidents had been assassinated—the archduke's murder set in motion a chain of events that led directly to the outbreak of World War I in early August. His killing served to ignite a powder keg that had been building for several decades. Germany contributed significantly to this unhealthy atmosphere that allowed a political murder to escalate into global warfare.

To begin with, Germany's annexation of Alsace-Lorraine from France at the conclusion of the Franco-Prussian War (1870–71) permanently soured Franco-German relations. More importantly, *realpolitik*, the methodology Bismarck employed to defeat France and to bring about the unification of Germany, undermined peace. *Realpolitik*, or what might be called "hardball politics," enshrines the notion that the end justifies the means. Lying, cheating, bullying, and threatening are all inherent in *realpolitik*. In the case of Bismarck's use of *realpolitik*, the old adage that "nothing succeeds like success" applies. By virtue of his success, the Iron Chancellor so popularized *realpolitik* that an entire generation of European statesmen who followed Bismarck copied his example. However, these imitators lacked Bismarck's skill, especially his sense of timing and brinksmanship, or what could be achieved without provoking a cataclysmic response. The result was a Europe filled with duplicitous, belligerent, headstrong, yet

During World War I, Emperor William II effectively ceded authority to his military commanders, Paul von Hindenburg (seen here to the left of the Kaiser) and Erich Ludendorff (on the right). The protracted struggle proved fatal for the German empire, and in 1918 William II abdicated and fled into exile in Holland. (Reproduced from the Collections of the Library of Congress.)

basically clueless statesmen who either could not or would not act effectively to keep the peace.

If Germany provided an unhappy model for statesmanship, the country also found itself enmeshed in developments over which it had little control, but which significantly increased tension with its neighbors. During the last decades of the nineteenth century, Germany had industrialized at a breathtaking pace. Thanks to its more modern industrial infrastructure, cheaper labor costs, and aggressive marketing, at the start of the twentieth century Germany was rapidly eclipsing Great Britain as Europe's leading industrial power. While this success pleased many in Germany, Great Britain was distressed. Nor was Great Britain—or most of the Continent for that matter—pleased with Germany's behavior in the realm of colonial expansion. At the turn of the twentieth century, European imperialism was at its height. It was tacitly understood that no Great Power was really a "great" power unless it had a large and growing global empire. However, because it was not unified until 1871, Germany arrived late to the imperial scramble to gobble up the globe. Consequently, little or no land of any value was available for the taking when German overseas expansion moved into high gear in the 1890s. Greatly resenting this, Germany tended to act like a spoiled child, demanding its "place in the sun" and inciting several crises over colonial issues.

It can be argued that economic and imperial disagreements were inherent in the natural course of events at that time and that Germany's role was no different than that of any other major European state; however, the same cannot be said of several other developments. The accession of William II (1888) and the dismissal of Bismarck (1890) marked a watershed in German history. In a semiautocratic state such as the German Empire, the ruler exercises considerable power, and William II was hardly a model of rational, prudent stability. Although he was highly intelligent, charming, and curious, William was also mercurial, romantic, bellicose, and insecure. He was a spellbinding speaker, but all too often what he had to say angered or confounded others. In other words, William II was the proverbial walking time bomb.

A couple of examples should suffice to demonstrate the difficulties that William created for himself and Germany. During the events leading up to the Boer War (1899–1902), the bitter struggle between Great Britain and the Boers (Dutch settlers in South Africa), Cecil Rhodes, prime minister of Great Britain's Cape Colony, surreptitiously tried to overthrow the Boer Republic of the Transvaal led by Paul Kruger. When this attempt failed, William sent the "Kruger Telegram" in which he publicly congratulated the Boers for their triumph "without having to call for support of friendly powers." It was universally understood that Germany was that "friendly power"; Great Britain most certainly was not amused. Several years later, in 1908, William gave an interview to London's *Daily Telegraph* in which he declared that German public opinion was anti-British, took credit for providing Britain with a war plan to defeat the Boers, and brushed off German naval expansion as being directed against Japan. Great Britain's lack of amusement dissolved into howls of outrage.

The German policy of *Weltpolitik* and the construction of a huge navy that accompanied it further unsettled observers. *Weltpolitik,* or world policy, clearly represented a shift away from Bismarck's close focus on European matters. However, Bismarck's successors never clearly defined what they meant by *Weltpolitik* and what they hoped to accomplish with this policy. The resulting ambiguity and confusion disturbed Europe, especially in light of Germany's obvious economic and military strength. Certainly one aspect of *Weltpolitik* was Germany's decision to build a large, modern fleet. When questioned about the need for such a fleet, Germany's inability to respond clearly and reasonably set off alarm bells, especially in London, which suspected that Germany would use this fleet to challenge Britain's traditional domination of the high seas.

As tensions grew, Europe's Great Powers began to ally with each other, grouping themselves into two hostile alliances by the eve of World War I. Great Britain, France, and Russia formed the Triple Entente, while Germany joined with Austria-Hungary and Italy to create the Triple Alliance.

As the crisis over the archduke's assassination intensified, Germany unequivocally supported Austria-Hungary in its decision to intimidate Serbia, the small Balkan country that had spawned the murderers. In particular, in early July 1914, Berlin extended to Vienna what has become known as the "Blank Check," which promised German support for whatever Austria-Hungary chose to do. Recent research indicates that important segments of the German military and government did not look unfavorably upon the prospect of conflict.

Europe rapidly slid into war, and by early August, troops were on the move everywhere as Germany declared war on Russia on August 1 and on France on August 3. In preparation for just such a contingency, a decade or so earlier the German army's general staff under General Alfred von Schlieffen had drawn up a strategic battle plan. Knowing that Germany would probably have to fight on two fronts and believing that modern warfare could not drag on interminably, Schlieffen designed a plan that called for Germany to hold the line in the east against Russia while concentrating the bulk of its prodigious forces in the west against France. With the outbreak of war, the German army was to fall upon France and defeat it quickly and then utilize its superb rail network to move its forces to the east in order to engage a slow-moving and now isolated Russia.

The Schlieffen Plan almost succeeded. However, the Russians mobilized more quickly than thought possible, and when they invaded East Prussia, a shaken Helmuth von Moltke, the German army's chief of staff, transferred units from France to the eastern front. This move created gaps in the German lines that the French—supported by a small British contingent—exploited to stop the German offensive at the first Battle of the Marne in early September 1914. With the failure of the Schlieffen Plan, the western front soon became mired in trench warfare, or a monumental war of attrition.

Ironically, at the very time that the Schlieffen Plan was failing, Germany achieved a singular victory over Russia. Early in September, at the dual battles of Tannenberg and the Masurian Lakes, Germany crushed two Russian armies. The German victory not only preserved the integrity of East Prussia and set the stage for Germany's conquest of most of Russian Poland in 1915, but it also brought to the fore two generals, Paul von Hindenburg and Erich Ludendorff, who would become de facto military dictators of Germany before the war's end.

During 1915, the merciless meat grinder of trench warfare defined the western front. Evenly matched, the two sides slugged it out with an appalling loss of men and no perceptible change in the ongoing stalemate. One of the war's many low points came in 1915 when the Germans introduced poison gas to repel a British offensive near Ypres. In the east, Germany continued to pound its Russian adversary and occupied significant chunks of territory; however, its Austro-Hungarian ally showed clear signs of terminal weakness.

In the following year, Germany concentrated its efforts on the western front. In February, General Erich von Falkenhayn, chief of the general staff, launched a massive offensive against the French fortress of Verdun with the intention of bleeding France white. As expected, the French rose to the bait; soon, however, Germany also found itself in a "must-win" situation and committed many more troops than it had anticipated. When the battle finally wound down in June, little territory had changed hands, but 281,000 Germans and 315,000 French lay dead. One month later, the British launched an offensive on the Somme River that also ended in a draw in October, at a cost of 420,000 British and 450,000 Germans. The year 1916 was also notable for the war's one and only conventional naval battle of any significance. On May 31, the German and British fleets clashed in the North Sea at the Battle of Jutland. Although technically a draw, after the battle the German fleet withdrew to its berth at Kiel and never again ventured out to challenge the British.

When the war began in 1914, political disagreements, which had been on the rise in prewar Germany, came to a halt. Instead the *Burgfriede,* a political truce for the duration of the conflict, came into effect. As most Germans expected the war to be of short duration and joined the wave of patriotism that swept the country, the *Burgfriede* enjoyed initial popularity. However, the war dragged on, casualties skyrocketed, and a tight British naval blockade began to strangle Germany. Divisions started to appear within the German body politic, but the fact that power was rapidly moving away from the civilians, including the emperor and his advisors, and into the hands of the military rendered them insignificant. By mid-1916, for all intents and purposes, Germany had evolved into a military dictatorship dominated by Ludendorff, who tended to control events from the wings, and Hindenburg, who represented the triumph of style over substance. Increasingly, the military ignored the civilians while it imposed a tight censorship designed to keep the German population in the dark about the true nature of the war's course.

Events took a dramatic turn in 1917. On February 1, Germany commenced unrestricted submarine warfare, or the policy of sinking any and all vessels destined for its enemies' shores. The German military knew such a step would bring the United States into the war. Moreover, the arrival of the United States, with its virtually unlimited supplies of money, men, and war materiel, would inevitably tip the balance conclusively in favor of the Allies. Nevertheless, Germany took the risk. Its naval experts assured the general staff that the submarine campaign would starve Great Britain from the war well before the United States could make its presence felt. With Britain gone, the reasoning went, France would sue for peace; the war in the west would be over; and Germany could then reach some sort of amicable agreement with the United States. As Germany anticipated, the United States declared war on April 6, 1917.

Although Germany came close, it failed to bring Great Britain to its knees, and by summer 1917 it was becoming apparent that the campaign to starve Great Britain into submission had miscarried. Nevertheless, a stroke of great fortune in the east overshadowed Germany's failure in the west. In March 1917, reeling under the responsibilities inherent in fighting a modern war, the antiquated Russian Empire collapsed. A few months later, the Bolsheviks, or Communists, took power and opened peace negotiations. Germany drove a very hard bargain, and had the March 1918 Treaty of Brest-Litovsk that ended fighting in the east endured, Germany would have been undisputed master of that region.

Despite its triumph in the east, Germany's military leaders knew that the situation in the west was precarious. There, the war of attrition had seriously weakened Germany, and the prospect of U.S. forces arriving in France was alarming. Moreover, the British blockade now caused great hardship within Germany. Consequently, Ludendorff and Hindenburg decided on an all-or-nothing roll of the dice. Marshalling all its available resources, on March 21, 1918, Germany launched a gigantic offensive on the western front. The objective of this offensive was to break through and defeat the French and British before the Americans could arrive in full force. Once again Germany came close to success. By June 1918, its armies once more stood on the banks of the Marne River outside of Paris. However, as was the case in August 1914, the German attack stalled. With American troops now pouring into France, Germany was done.

By September, with the German army in retreat, the military leadership told a shocked William II that Germany had lost the war. Thereafter, the end to the fighting came fairly quickly. William II abdicated; the empire collapsed to be replaced by a republic; and on November 11, 1918, the shooting stopped. In the negotiations that followed, a formal treaty ending Germany's participation in World War I was signed on June 28, 1919, in the Palace of Versailles' Hall of Mirrors. While the Treaty of Versailles' provisions are too numerous to mention, several stand out: Germany's borders were redrawn to reflect a loss of territory in the west, the east, and the north; Germany was saddled with a huge but unspecified reparations bill; Germany's army was greatly reduced in size and armaments; Germany surrendered all her colonies; and Germany accepted blame for starting the war.

INTERPRETIVE ESSAY
John K. Cox

World War I, or the Great War as it is often called, both slowed and skewed Germany's development as a nation. The war was a disaster for nearly every country that fought in it. The conflict resulted in over 10 million battlefield-related deaths, discredited many traditional ideologies, drastically increased the technological deadliness of warfare, and paved the way for communist and fascist takeovers of key European countries. Although our minds today have been conditioned by the Cold War (1945–91) and subsequent struggles related to globalization and terrorism, the fact of the matter is that the Great War seems to have had precious little to do with competing ideologies or political systems. Indeed, although national pride and supposed cultural superiority were at issue and even though many people held to Social Darwinist ideas about the inexorable competition and conflict between different people or "races," the war derived from a struggle for power and not ideas.

In the case of Germany, the war was an enormous and exhausting event. It is important to remember that over 2 million German soldiers would die in this war, along with over 600,000 civilians—out of a population of 64 million. Eventually, over 13 million German men—an astoundingly high figure—would be put into uniform.

Like other Europeans, most Germans went to war happily in the summer of 1914, expecting a short and victorious conflict that would vindicate their growing nationalism and imperialism. Today, pictures of cheering urban crowds sending young soldiers on their way are famous, even though they were often staged. As popular as the war might have been in the cities, it was greeted with less enthusiasm in the countryside, where the harvest was just beginning and the manpower would be sorely missed. Popular support aside, it is true that opposition parties in parliament closed ranks with the government in the name of patriotism, and poets waxed almost surrealistically nationalistic.

When war was declared, nearly all segments of German society lined up behind their government in what was called the *Burgfrieden* (castle peace), a medieval historical term indicating that domestic disputes would be put on hold as long as the country faced a grave external threat. The Reichstag immediately passed a massive new military budget, and fiscal policies and budgets were changed a dozen more times during the war to support the huge operating expenses and debts.

Germany's immediate objective in 1914 was, of course, to knock France out of the war quickly and then focus on Russia. Specifically, the Germans planned on violating both Belgian and Dutch neutrality to encircle Paris from the north and west, while holding the British at bay and keeping the majority of the French army (which was expected to attack eastward immediately) engaged in Alsace-Lorraine and central Germany. This plan, known as the Schlieffen Plan, failed for a variety of reasons. Some pertained to matters that the General Staff should have paid attention to when updating the plan, such as improvements in both the French and Russian armies and a greater need to protect the increasingly important coal- and steel-producing areas in central Germany. But at the last minute, Field Marshal Helmuth von Moltke, Chief of the General Staff, chose not to move through Holland, thus creating a traffic jam in Belgium, which was more heroically defended than he had anticipated. Worst of all, Moltke decided to transfer troops to the Eastern Front to stem the surprisingly quick Russian advance.

Naturally, it is difficult to summarize a war this extensive and this long. However, the salient fact of the war was the same for all participants: the incredible carnage resulting from huge armies, powered by nationalism and led by traditional-minded officers, advancing into the teeth of murderous new military technology. The widespread use of the machine gun, poison gas, flamethrower, barbed wire, airplane, long-range artillery, submarine, and tank made this carnage possible. Nobody really won the great battles of attrition, such as Verdun and the Somme on the Western Front, because there were no breakthroughs; both armies, entrenched across broad fronts and bolstered by a wide array of artillery batteries, lost men—killed or wounded—by the hundreds of thousands. The inability to exploit breakthroughs or to throw the enemy off balance characterized the fighting on all the European fronts to a considerable degree, though nowhere was the field as static and blood-soaked as in France and Belgium.

In 1916, the Russian military under General Alexis Brusilov was the first to make some progress toward the development of new tactics to create breakthroughs under existing combat conditions. These tactics featured attempts to force narrow breakthroughs by surprise, using small numbers of elite forces and only very brief preliminary shelling. The Germans copied and expanded on these tactics on the Western Front, and by the end of the war, the Allies were also in a position to use large numbers of tanks to create and exploit fluidity in the battle lines. During the course of the war, the Germans coined the word *Materialschlacht* (battle of material goods or products) to express the nature of "total war" on both the home front and the attrition-driven battlefields. However, the Germans were unable to win or to alter significantly the style of warfare, and this proved fatal for their ambitions. Germany found itself threatened due to its geographic position, lack of strong allies, and government's loss of popular support.

The argument is easily made that engaging in a two-front war was a major mistake for Germany in the first place, especially when its ally was the declining Habsburg Empire. However, one should not lose sight of another early but fundamental German miscalculation: the belief that somehow Great Britain would not come to France's aid. By focusing on the lack of an explicit treaty relationship between those two countries, the Germans ignored the fundamental community of interest and recent history of cooperation between London and Paris. In addition, the Kaiser would not—and his chancellors could not—reassert the primacy of the civilian political leadership over the military. Furthermore, a culture of arrogance and overconfidence, based on nationalism and the outdated

Schlieffen Plan, prevailed in Germany's military and diplomacy. For instance, the campaign of naval construction to overtake the British fleet was wildly expensive and ultimately quite unsuccessful. These problems collectively made it impossible for Germany to break up the alliance that encircled it and clear the way for its continuing evolution into a world power. It is interesting to note that some German leaders also viewed the war as a chance to distract or suppress domestic discontent. The old Bismarckian goal of having foreign policy serve the objective of protecting the fledgling German national state had long been superceded by these more inward-looking designs.

Discussions of tactics and strategy belong to what has been called the "old" military history; nowadays there is also a great deal of scholarly interest in the "new" military history concerned directly with the soldiers' experiences in the trenches. While there are comparatively few readily available sources on German daily life and combat, it seems clear that ultimately German soldiers suffered more from lack of supplies and rest than their Allied foes; still, they seldom mutinied or deserted despite the carnage and the lack of victories. In 1918, however, German troops began surrendering in large numbers and falling ill due to exhaustion and malnutrition. In addition, there were two small but significant naval mutinies.

One of the most controversial topics in the study of World War I has been the behavior of German troops toward civilians during the initial invasion of Belgium and France in 1914. Reports of German atrocities emerged quickly and were widely and luridly publicized by the Allies in an effort to drum up support for the war. German leaders and many historians long denied or downplayed these reports, but it has now been established that the Germans killed about 6,500 civilians and destroyed 20,000 buildings. The German army reacted with hysterical brutality to its own fears of potential guerrilla resistance to the Schlieffen Plan. Moreover, violence was directed at civilians on other fronts as well. German attacks on Russians in 1915, Austrian attacks on Serbs in 1914–15, and disastrous Ottoman measures against Armenians throughout the conflict demonstrate yet another way in which the Great War laid the foundation for World War II.

Because most belligerents declared total victory and territorial aggrandizement to be their goals, when studying World War I historians traditionally have paid little attention to nongovernmental groups and organizations. Large-scale peace movements were limited to the British Empire and the United States, and there were few overtures meant to end the fighting. Additionally, the Catholic Church in Europe was split down the middle. European socialist political parties and labor movements, traditionally a counterweight to aggressive nationalism, abandoned their internationalism in 1914, and their members firmly lined up behind their individual national flags. Some socialists did hold an important meeting in September 1915 at Zimmerwald, Switzerland, where one faction ended up condemning the war as a capitalist enterprise in which workers were being hoodwinked by nationalism to do the dirty work of ruling elites. However, a significant group, including Russia's future leader Vladimir Lenin, ended up rather ironically supporting the war. Lenin reckoned—rightly, at least for his own country, as it turned out—that the war would provide a decisive opportunity for revolutionaries and the discontented masses to seize power in war-ravaged lands across Europe.

The pronouncements of U.S. president Woodrow Wilson did offer some hope to Germans looking to end the war they seemed to have lost by the summer of 1918. Wilson called for the creation of a League of Nations and for a democratic government in Germany. After the death of the Austrian emperor Franz Joseph in late 1916, a Belgian relative of the Habsburgs had contacted Vienna with a peace proposal, but such moves were the exception. The main thrust of diplomacy was simply to win over new allies, usually by enticing them with disputed chunks of territory (often called *irredenta*, or unredeemed lands). One of the most famous examples of such crass coalition building was the Allies' successful wooing of Italy with promises of Alpine and Adriatic territory to be taken from Austria. Another was Germany's proposition to Mexico, in which the possibility of regaining the southwestern United States was held out as a reward for possible anti-American action. The Allies also managed to win over Greece and Romania after the war started, while the Central Powers added the Ottoman Empire and Bulgaria to their ranks.

Germany's chancellor for much of the war was Theobald von Bethmann-Hollweg, who had assumed office in 1909. Usually portrayed as a colorless bureaucrat and political lightweight, Bethmann was ambivalent about the start of the war (though not dead-set against it). However, he already had been outmaneuvered by the country's leading military man and the Kaiser's favorite, Chief of the General Staff Helmuth von Moltke. Bethmann was forced to resign in July 1917. The next two chancellors, Georg Michaelis and Count Georg von Hertling, were very much under the thumb of the military shadow state created by Generals Paul von Hindenburg and Erich Ludendorff. The unpleasant but urgent task of ending hostilities, once the generals had suddenly informed the Kaiser that victory was impossible, fell to the final war chancellor, Prince Max of Baden. However, he handed over power to the Reichstag after the Kaiser abdicated on November 9, 1918 and fled to Holland. Thus, it was the parliament, led by such opposition figures as Friedrich Ebert and Matthias Erzberger, that accepted the cease-fire of November 11, 1918. With the decks now cleared, negotiations for a peace settlement could begin, as could the construction of a new German government and, indeed, a new German state.

Von Moltke himself ultimately fared even more poorly than his rival Bethmann. The nephew of a more famous namesake who had orchestrated Germany's smashing defeat of France in 1871 and laid the foundation for what would later become known as the Schlieffen Plan, the younger von Moltke held the powerful position of chief of the general staff from 1906 to 1914. After his failure to knock France out of the war early, he was replaced by Erich von Falkenhayn. This leader, too, was unable to resolve the massive and bloody deadlock on the Western Front. Falkenhayn was also held responsible for the so-called *Kindermord,* or rash sacrifice, of young, green German troops against British and Belgian forces at the Battle of Langemarck in the fall of 1914, for the huge failure at Verdun, and for the failed strategy of attrition in general. He was replaced in mid-1916 by Hindenburg, who had charted considerable success on the Eastern Front and seemed to have the "golden touch" necessary to pull off a victory, however Pyrrhic it might be.

The ascent of Hindenburg and his colleague and collaborator Ludendorff was of tremendous significance for Germany politically as well as militarily. The two men, with the former as supreme commander and the latter technically as his first quartermaster general, reshaped and recharged the country's military effort. They greatly strengthened government control over the economy by increasing planning of all types. They also tightened Germany's control over its occupied territories (most of Belgium, much of France and Poland, and eventually Romania) by instituting forced labor programs to bring workers to Germany for use in factories and agriculture. Their Hindenburg Program provided for a sharp increase in war industry production, while a specific part of it, the controversial Auxiliary Service Law, mobilized much of the rest of society for the war effort by drastically increasing the number of men and boys eligible for the draft, closing universities, and limiting the rights of individual workers.

Neither man had much understanding of or patience with politics, but they nonetheless wielded—with decidedly authoritarian instincts—a great deal of political power during the war. However, it was on their watch that the Reichstag finally began to reclaim its oppositional role, in part because President Wilson called for the establishment of a democratic Germany with which the Allies would then be prepared to deal somewhat

more leniently. The virtual military dictatorship over Germany also ultimately had the effect of encouraging Reichstag leaders to question the
government's unending accounts of battlefield success and to consider
ending the war with a negotiated peace and no annexations, instead of
holding out for the total victory that most Germans expected in 1914.

Concern over Hindenburg and Ludendorff's policies and interest in the
success of moderate and leftist groups in Russia in overthrowing the tsar,
caused the Social Democratic Party (SPD) to split in April 1917. The newly
formed Independent Social Democrats were much more vocal in criticiz-
ing the war than the regular SPD. Further to the left there emerged a group
called the Spartacus League, which later formed the nucleus of the German Communist Party under the leadership of Rosa Luxemburg and Karl
Liebknecht.

In purely military terms, Ludendorff made what were probably Germany's two most disastrous military mistakes of the war after 1914. In
1917, he foolishly pushed for the resumption of unrestricted submarine
warfare against the United States. This colossal blunder brought the
United States quickly into the Allied coalition. He also prolonged the war
in the east in order to force the already defeated Russians to make greater
territorial concessions, at a time when German troops were desperately
needed in the west for the last-gasp offensive before the arrival of American forces turned the tide.

The beginning of the end of the war for Germany came in September
1918 when Ludendorff and Hindenburg abruptly decided that continued
military action would be unfruitful. Facing defeat, they reasoned with
great cunning that it would be better for a civilian government to shoulder
the burden of making peace with the Allies before the German army was
completely destroyed or met with a shattering humiliation. At that point,
they empowered the Reichstag to begin peace negotiations.

There exists a common view that World War I occasioned great changes
in the status of women in Germany and, indeed, in the rest of Europe and
even North America. This conclusion is important but must be carefully
limited. Certainly, in general one can say that many women across Europe
moved temporarily into factory jobs and other positions left empty when
millions of men went off to fight, but it should be remembered that many,
if not most, of these women had already been employed outside the home,
thus limiting the social impact of this "new" employment pattern. Also,
most women were pushed out of these industrial jobs right after the war
to make room for returning veterans—a trend supported by governments
and unions as well. In addition, the cultural impact of women's new roles
was circumscribed by the tendency of war to emphasize masculine virtues

both in public and private: the courage and physical strength of male fighters, supported by women as nurses and mothers, along with the objectification of women for reasons of sentimentality or sexual fantasy. The German government used tax and housing policy to reinforce pronatalism, or the emphasis on the production of babies as women's greatest contribution to the war effort. There were also restrictions on birth control, adultery, prostitution, and sexual relationships between Germans and foreign workers that were disproportionately targeted at women, reinforcing the conclusion that the war's modernizing effect on women was indeed limited.

Finally, work in munitions factories and other war industries was often extremely dirty and hard. The unattractive nature of the work combined with the need to take care of their children, aged relatives, and homes and the fairly generous financial support from the German government limited women's desire to pursue new types of work. By 1917, the war and the Allied blockade had such a devastating effect on the German economy that there was little to buy, so monetary incentives to move women into factory jobs were ineffective.

Of course, economic conditions on the home front impacted everyone, not just women. During the course of the war, food costs in Germany rose over 300 percent. Wages rose too, but real buying power declined considerably due to inflation and shortages, especially of meat, eggs, sugar, vegetable oil, and butter. Workers' frustration was increasingly expressed through strikes—some of them very large—which were especially worrisome to the government when they occurred, as they frequently did, in war-related industries such as mining, metallurgy, and chemicals. Public demonstrations were also frequent, and they included large numbers of women. By mid-1918, these activities and growing unrest in the armed forces convinced the German military that it could not fight a losing war for much longer.

It is hard to summarize neatly the net effects of the war on German society. The position of the middle class declined somewhat, reducing a social force that would soon be key to the success of the country's new democracy. The role of the government in the economy grew tremendously, as did the importance of cartels and big business. But labor unions also won some additional collective rights, and the voting system was updated to be more representative. Certainly the presence after the war of militaristic and nationalistic right-wing paramilitary groups such as the infamous *Freikorps* was a destabilizing force in politics and in society at large.

That there was little opposition to World War I at its beginning is beyond doubt, although enthusiasm for the war was not as universal as historians once believed. More than 100,000 young German men quickly volunteered to fight, and there was a tremendous deluge of patriotic (if not jingoistic) verse and speeches. Take, for example, a letter from Walter Roy, a medical student who died at the front in 1915. In writing home Roy said, "Only one thing is real now—the war! And the only thing that inspires and uplifts one is love for the German Fatherland and the desire to fight and risk all for Emperor and Empire." Nationalist excesses were not limited to young soldiers. The famous scholar Werner Sombart published a long critique of the current situation in 1914, portraying it as a titanic struggle between "salesmen" or "shopkeepers" of the West and the modern-day "heroes" of Germany. Even more telling was the manifesto of October 1914, in which 93 famous German intellectuals praised German nationalism and the brutal invasion of Belgium.

Not all German cultural figures endorsed the war effort. Novelist Hermann Hesse publicly corresponded with the famous French writer Romain Rolland on the necessity of separating military conflict from cultural denigration and destruction. Both men asserted that European culture was one unified, supranational edifice. This is, of course, a very popular assertion today, but during World War I it forced both men to seek refuge in Switzerland. A German journal known as *Die Aktion* (Action) was also a highly respected, if low-profile, center for artists and writers appalled by the conflict.

Historian Robert Wohl has demonstrated that the youth of Europe at the start of the war had a distinct feeling of unity and nationalism. Perhaps it is true that for this group the certainties of religion and traditional culture were being eroded by modern, urban, industrial life; nevertheless, Europe's youth found optimism and hope in the idea of the nation and in the promise of technology. This sanguine view was aided by the fact that Europe had not seen a major, disastrous war for several generations. The traumas of the Great War magnified many times over the distinct identity of this generation, and this would have a major effect on their political views by the 1930s. Many veterans, from Germany and other lands, came to support pacifism or leftist causes as a result of the carnage of the war and their alienation from their nationalist governments. Others eventually veered into right-wing politics, and with their sense of national mission further strengthened and militarized by the postwar settlements and the Great Depression, they formed the matrix from which fascism and Nazism would emerge.

Despite reinforcing traditional views in a number of ways, the Great War ultimately provided a decisive push to cultural modernism around the world. Among German and Austrian painters, for instance, it is only necessary to mention Georg Grosz and Egon Schiele, whose work focused primarily on negative aspects of the war. Additionally, the works of Max Beckmann, Otto Dix, and Max Liebermann are representative of important new trends in art. Film was also a new cultural phenomenon that received a great boost during the war. The number of German film production companies and cinemas grew impressively during the war, as the government first opened a film office (Bufa) and then founded its own production company (Ufa) to make patriotic features and news segments. After the war, German film quickly developed further into a world leader.

Several classic works of literature partially set the mood for the postwar period. The most famous one, of course, is Erich Maria Remarque's *All Quiet on the Western Front* (1929). Remarque's book has parallels in the work of France's Henri Barbusse (*Under Fire*) and Great Britain's Richard Aldington (*Death of a Hero*). There are several reasons for the importance of Remarque's simple novel about young German draftees. For one thing, the German soldiers are not shown as bloodthirsty beasts, but as fragile and normal young men. Moreover, the war is not glamorized as something heroic but is constantly revealed to be savage and pointless. The cultural historian Modris Eksteins has pointed out a third invaluable feature of the book: even more than capturing the experience of the trenches, the novel showed "how the war had destroyed the ties, psychological, moral, and real, between the generation at front and the society at home." Thus, Remarque has made a point of depicting the postwar alienation that destroyed those men whose bodies were spared by the bullets and gas.

This negative evaluation of the war did not go uncontested in Germany. For example, the novels and essays of Ernst Jünger stressed not only the noble nature of Germany's cause in the war, but also the salutary effects of the war itself on individuals. The man-made hell of the war, here described by Jünger after the Battle of the Somme in 1916, was in turn making tougher men: "After this battle the German soldier wore the steel helmet, and in his features there were chiseled the lines of an energy stretched to the utmost pitch, lines that future generations will perhaps find as fascinating and imposing as those of many heads of classical or Renaissance times."

Such attitudes were obviously much more popular with Hitler and the Nazis than anything that Remarque had to say, but glorification of the war was not a German phenomenon alone. The work of the consciously "politically incorrect" (but gifted) author Henri Montherlant played the same role in postwar France. Nonetheless, it is accurate to state that the vast majority of postwar literature emphasized the suffering and stupidity of the war rather than its supposed benefits. The German authors Arnold Zweig, Siegfried Kracauer, Theodore Plievier, Ludwig Renn, Georg Kaiser, Edlef Köppen, Ernst Toller, Fritz von Unruh, Werner Beumelburg, Leonhard Frank, and Hans Chlumberg wrote fascinating novels and plays about the most varied military aspects of the war and clearly conveyed to their audience the brutality of the war as the participants saw it and waged it.

The Great War meant drastically different things for each of its participants. For Germany, the war was an unmitigated disaster, resulting in a humiliating and bloody defeat; the collapse of its government amidst agitation from the left and right; the loss of foreign colonies and European territories; and peace treaty provisions that forced the country to accept guilt for the war, pay astronomical reparations, and severely limit the size of its military in the future. Although World War II would prove to be an even greater disaster for Germans and their homeland, it is impossible to dismiss the seminal importance of World War I.

The carnage and scope of the war, the appearance of high-tech weaponry, and the level of military and home-front mobilization combined to make this war unlike any before it. By October 1918, public and military morale in both Germany and Austria-Hungary was crumbling, as it had nearly done a year earlier in France. The great artist Kaethe Kollwitz, who lost her son Peter in the notoriously bloody fighting in France in 1914, wrote in her journal at that time: "There has been enough of dying! Let not another man fall!...'Seed for the planting must not be ground.' " Although Germany was in many ways turned upside down by this war, much of prewar authoritarian, nationalistic, bellicose German society remained in many ways unchanged. In 1931, Carl Zuckmayer wrote a devastating satire of Prussian militarism, which remains famous to this day. Zuckmayer's *Der Hauptmann von Köpenick* (*The Captain of Köpenick*) was, after all, not just an indictment of the German past but an ominous indication of the rise of Nazism.

For the Romanov dynasty of Russia, the Ottomans of Turkey, and the Habsburgs of Austria-Hungary, the war meant the collapse of their empires. Germany's Hohenzollern dynasty vanished as well. The Ottoman and Habsburg Empires disappeared altogether into a plethora of successor states and victors' colonies. Russia ended up in the throes of a Bolshevik revolution and civil war that resulted in the new Soviet state of Lenin and, soon thereafter, Stalin. Although Germany neither disappeared outright nor was launched immediately on the path of revolution, the Great War so radicalized its political atmosphere that the Nazi revolution was rendered possible. The truism that World War I ended Europe's era of faith in progress, rationality, and technical advancement finds no more convincing validation than in the case of Germany.

SELECTED BIBLIOGRAPHY

Beckett, Ian F. W. *The Great War, 1914–1918.* New York: Longman, 2001. This is arguably the best history of World War I in print today. Comprehensive, interesting, and modern. Includes valuable information on the home fronts, neutral countries, the effects of the war, and ways in which the war has been represented and commemorated since 1918.

Bessel, Richard. *Germany after the First World War.* New York: Oxford University Press, 1993. A social history stressing how the psychological costs of the war and the huge dimensions of German defeat poisoned the politics of the Weimar Republic.

Chickering, Roger. *Imperial Germany and the Great War, 1914–1918.* New York: Cambridge University Press, 1998. An indispensable work. Well-written and up-to-date study with extensive coverage of social, cultural, and political as well as military history.

Cross, Tim, ed. *The Lost Voices of World War I: An International Anthology of Writers, Poets, and Playwrights.* Iowa City: University of Iowa Press, 1988. An excellent source for German authors who wrote on war themes, especially poets.

Daniel, Ute. *The War from Within: German Working-Class Women in the First World War.* New York: Berg, 1997. Important analysis of economic conditions and political activism.

Fischer, Fritz. *Germany's Aims in the First World War.* New York: Norton, 1968. One take on the seemingly endless debate about the degree to which Germany was responsible for the outbreak of the war.

Glover, Jon, and Jon Silkin, eds. *The Penguin Book of First World War Prose.* New York: Viking, 1989. Contains selections from many key authors, including Rosa Luxemburg, Ernst Gläser, Arnold Zweig, Ludwig Renn, and Erich Maria Remarque.

Grayzel, Susan. *Women and the First World War.* New York: Longman, 2002. An excellent monograph, short but comprehensive, covering all the major belligerents. Very useful bibliography.

Gudmundsson, Bruce. *Stormtroop Tactics: Innovation in the German Army, 1914–1918.* Westport, CT: Praeger, 1995. A partial rebuttal to the traditional idea that tactics in World War I were totally stagnant.

Herwig, Holger. *The First World War: Germany and Austria-Hungary, 1914–1918.* London: Arnold, 1997. A very detailed military history that is also clear and interesting.

Horne, John, and Alan Kramer. *German Atrocities 1914: A History of Denial.* New Haven, CT: Yale University Press, 2001. A well-documented study asserting that the German military did commit many avoidable war crimes in World War I.

Jelavich, Peter. "German Culture in the Great War." In *European Culture in the Great War: The Arts, Entertainment, and Propaganda, 1914–1918,* edited by Aviel Roshwald and Richard Stites, pp. 32–57. New York: Cambridge University Press, 1999. Excellent survey.

Keegan, John. *The First World War.* New York: Knopf, 1999. A classic work by a world-famous scholar.

Kocka, Jürgen. *Facing Total War: German Society, 1914–1918.* Translated by Barbara Weinberger. Cambridge, MA: Harvard University Press, 1984. An important social history.

Lafore, Laurence. *The Long Fuse: An Interpretation of the Origins of World War I.* 2nd ed. Long Grove, IL: Waveland Press, 1997. A clear standard account, long in use in colleges and universities. Focuses on imperialism, alliances, and militarism.

Linder, Ann P. *Princes of the Trenches: Narrating the German Experience of the First World War.* Columbia, SC: Camden House, 1996. A fascinating study of German wartime writing of both the left and the right.

Nagel, Fritz. *Fritz: The World War I Memoir of a German Lieutenant.* Rev. ed. Huntington, WV: Blue Acorn Press, 1995. Nuts-and-bolts account of the war by a German soldier who later emigrated to the United States.

Schmitt, Bernadotte E., and Harold C. Vedeler. *The World in the Crucible, 1914–1919.* New York: Harper, 1984. Extensive survey of all aspects of the war.

Showalter, Dennis E. *Tannenberg: Clash of Empires, 1914.* Dulles, VA: Brassey's, 2004. A leading study of one of Germany's major open-field victories in the Great War.

Strachan, Hew, ed. *The Oxford Illustrated History of the First World War.* New York: Oxford University Press, 2000. Gripping and thought-provoking with lots of information and photographs about life and death in the trenches.

Vincent, C. Paul. *The Politics of Hunger: The Allied Blockade of Germany, 1915–1919.* Athens: Ohio University Press, 1986. Detailed study of an often overlooked but notorious strategy used by the Allies.

Whalen, Robert Weldon. *Bitter Wounds: German Victims of the Great War, 1914–1939.* Ithaca, NY: Cornell University Press, 1984. How the war brutalized and then politically mobilized people of differing ideological persuasions.

Winter, Jay, and Jean-Louis Robert, eds. *Capital Cities at War: Paris, London, Berlin, 1914–1919.* New York: Cambridge University Press, 1994. A detailed social history of daily life. An important contribution to the wider study of total war that goes well beyond just men on the battlefield.

Witkop, Philipp, ed. *German Students' War Letters.* Philadelphia: University of Pennsylvania Press, 2002. Presents young German soldiers as patriotic and even nationalistic, but far from the aggressive monsters that Allied propaganda made them out to be.

Wohl, Robert. *The Generation of 1914.* Cambridge, MA: Harvard University Press, 1979. A complex but time-honored study of a cross section of European young people in 1914.

6

The Collapse of the Weimar Republic, 1929–1933

INTRODUCTION

The ill-fated Weimar Republic was an accident born of necessity. In the waning days of World War I, civil authority in imperial Germany collapsed. The reluctant leaders of Germany's Social Democratic Party (SPD) stepped into the ensuing vacuum. Although the most popular political party in Germany, the SPD had been unable to make up its mind as to whether it wanted to be a revolutionary force marching to the beat of Karl Marx or whether it preferred a more evolutionary route to socialism as advocated by Eduard Bernstein. Reflecting the party's schizophrenia, its leadership settled for the strident rhetoric of Marx and the revisionist practices of Bernstein.

The leaders of the SPD in 1918 were Friedrich Ebert and Philipp Scheidemann, two very moderate men who had supported Germany's entry into the war and its subsequent war effort despite their commitment to socialism. Stunned by the collapse of traditional authority and fearful that more radical socialists led by Rosa Luxemburg and Karl Liebknecht might try to establish a new regime in Germany that would emulate the Bolshevik (Communist) experiment then unfolding in Russia, the leaders of the SPD took over the reins of government. Then, on November 9, 1918, Scheidemann unexpectedly announced the creation of a German Republic.

Key to both the immediate success and the long-term failure of the republic was the following day's agreement between the SPD leadership and the head of the army, General Wilhelm Groener. Groener pledged to

Because of a number of factors, the Weimar Republic lived a very precarious life. In 1923, runaway inflation threatened its very existence. Here, a Berlin woman burns worthless paper money in order to start the morning fire. (Reproduced from the Collections of the Library of Congress.)

support the republic in its efforts to maintain law and order, in return for which the civilians committed themselves to block Germany's Marxist radicals and, perhaps more importantly, to allow the army's traditional command structure to remain untouched. In other words, the army was to become something resembling a state within the state, beyond the reach of civilian authority.

Despite this agreement, the republic's initial days proved quite precarious. In addition to the massive dislocation caused by the war and the disbelief of the German people upon learning of their defeat, German communists mounted a direct challenge to the republic's authority. Early in January 1919, the Spartacist Revolt broke out in Berlin. The Spartacists comprised the bulk of the newly founded Communist Party of Germany led by Luxemburg and Liebknecht. They regarded the SPD's republic as a decidedly nonrevolutionary sellout to the interests of the bourgeoisie, the Junkers, and the officer corps, and they took to the streets to overthrow it in favor of a Soviet-style regime. With this step, the left in German politics permanently fractured. Gustav Noske, the SPD's minister of defense, realized the predicament that the Spartacists had created; however, he took responsibility for protecting the republic with the words, "Someone must become the bloodhound! I can not evade the responsibility." Noske called upon the generals, who were more than happy to attack the radicals. During a week of street fighting in Berlin, the Spartacists were brutally crushed, and both Luxemburg and Liebknecht were murdered.

Amazingly enough, in the midst of this turmoil successful elections for a constituent assembly took place on January 19. Because conditions in Berlin remained unsettled, the new assembly met at Weimar, hence the name Weimar Republic by which the new German state was universally known. Ebert was elected president, and Scheidemann became prime minister of what would be called the Weimar Coalition, a combination of the SPD, the Catholic Center Party, and the left-liberal Democratic Party that dominated Weimar politics throughout the 1920s. The task of drafting a new constitution for Germany fell to Hugo Preuss, a prominent legal scholar and a determined supporter of the republic. Pruess's liberal constitution included some of the best features of the British, French, and American systems including universal adult suffrage, proportional representation, a bicameral legislature, a supreme court, and a full contingent of civil liberties and human rights. Fatally, as it turned out, the constitution also included Article 48 that in times of domestic distress gave to the largely ceremonial Weimar president the right to suspend the constitution and to rule by decree.

Shortly before the constituent assembly accepted the constitution, the Weimar Republic faced yet another crisis. By early June, the peace talks in

Paris to wrap up World War I had neared completion. The Weimar Republic's leaders had been keenly disappointed that their representatives had not been allowed to take part in the negotiations as equals, but they were utterly astounded and outraged when the Allies presented to them what would become the Treaty of Versailles. Furthermore, the Allies ordered Germany to sign it or else. The initial German inclination was to tell the Allies to drop dead; however, Groener explained to Ebert that were hostilities to resume Germany would face certain defeat. With the most profound misgivings imaginable, representatives of the new republic signed the Treaty of Versailles on June 28, 1919.

Neither the completion of the constitution nor the official end of the war brought a halt to the Weimar Republic's tribulations. In fact, in March 1920, there was yet another attempt to destroy the republic. Unlike the Spartacist Revolt, this threat came from the political right. A band of disgruntled officers led by General Walther von Lüttwitz, the Berlin commander, teamed up with several prominent disaffected civilians, including Dr. Wolfgang Kapp, to overthrow the republic. The conspirators succeeded in seizing Berlin and forcing the government to flee to Dresden. However, the rebels proved to be an incompetent, indecisive, divided bunch. Most importantly, however, the rebellion—named the Kapp Putsch—failed because the workers of Berlin responded with a very effective general strike that shut down the city. In a few days, the Kapp Putsch had fizzled, and the Weimar Republic was restored. Ominously, however, the army had not come to the republic's rescue. Rather, General Hans von Seeckt, who became commander of the *Reichswehr,* informed Ebert that officers of the army would never fire upon fellow officers, even if this meant the end of the republic.

A precarious economic situation further discredited the republic. Because imperial Germany had relied upon borrowed funds and an inflated currency rather than taxes to finance the war, from its inception the Weimar Republic found itself saddled with a huge debt. Moreover, the republic was too unsure of itself to levy taxes on the rich and powerful. The Allied demand for reparations added to the problem. Normally, reparations consisted of monies owed by the loser of a war to the winner of a war for damages which the former had caused. However, because the war left the European allies as broke as Germany, they had redefined the term reparations to mean monies owed by the loser of a war to the winner of a war for the entire cost of the war! Finally, the war itself had ruined not only Germany's, but also Europe's economy. Markets had been lost, machinery was now worn out and obsolete, capital for economic renewal was nonexistent, and millions of returning soldiers could not find work.

For several years, the Weimar Republic failed to address these serious problems in a satisfactory manner.

If this were not enough, the republic's leaders faced several other major issues, including general hostility toward the entire concept of a republic. Obviously, Germany's numerous communists and their sympathizers had no use for the republic, nor did the political right. The Junkers, officer corps, monarchists, and industrialists who had dominated Germany since unification despised the republic. Although they were too weak to retain power in November 1918, these archconservatives quickly regained their nerve and now raised a steady drumbeat of calumny against the republic. For example, they successfully propagated the *Dolchstoss*, or "Stab in the Back" myth, which maintained that Germany's glorious, invincible armed forces were on the verge of victory in World War I until "stabbed in the back" by traitors at home, including communists, Jews, socialists, and liberals. For these virulent opponents of democracy, the Weimar Republic's founders would forever remain the "November criminals." The republic's supporters failed to counter these lies, thereby allowing the republic's mortal enemies a free hand in shaping public opinion. Is it any wonder that contemporary observers sometimes described Weimar Germany as a "republic without republicans"?

Much to almost everyone's surprise, Weimar Germany's fortunes turned around starting in 1924. The previous year had been a disaster, beginning with a Franco-Belgian occupation of Germany's industrial Ruhr River valley and ending with a hyperinflation that totally destroyed the value of the mark. However, by the middle of 1924, the Dawes Plan, an American-led scheme to regularize German reparations payments, was in place, and Germany's postwar economic recovery finally began. With prosperity's return, hatred of the republic abated, and dangerous fringe groups such as Adolf Hitler's Nazis found themselves marginalized. Germany's international image also recovered. In September 1926, Germany joined the League of Nations, and its foreign minister, Gustav Stresemann, pursued a policy of fulfillment that called for Germany to play a constructive international role in order to mitigate or even erase the harsh terms of the Treaty of Versailles. The Weimar Republic's heyday also witnessed a remarkable cultural flowering. German music, theatre, literature, painting, philosophy, architecture, and design flourished; however, popular culture frequently descended to appalling depths that alienated and dismayed many Germans.

The onset of the Weimar Republic's demise came rather suddenly and unexpectedly. In early October 1929, Stresemann, the republic's most able politician, died. Even more catastrophically for Germany, the collapse of

Wall Street later in the month touched off a global depression that ultimately destroyed the republic. Because Germany was so dependent upon
loans from U.S. financial houses, when the stock market collapsed and
financial panic in the United States ensued, Germany saw its source of
capital dry up, and in fact, many loans were called in. Financial panic soon
became economic panic, and countries slapped exorbitant duties on
imports in order to protect domestic producers. This step contributed to
the collapse of global trade, an especially hard blow for Germany since it
produced much for the export market. Consequently, German unemployment figures skyrocketed. From about 900,000 unemployed in the summer of 1929, the figure rose to 3 million unemployed in late 1930. There
was no relief in sight, and unemployment continued to rise until in early
1932 more than 6 million Germans lacked jobs.

In the wake of this unmitigated disaster, something akin to paralysis
gripped the republic's leadership. Feeble efforts to stem the tide of economic disaster proved totally inadequate. In March 1930, Hermann
Müller's SPD-led government resigned to be replaced by Heinrich Brüning, a colorless politician from the right wing of the Center Party whose
commitment to democracy was tepid at best. Brüning governed in collaboration with President Paul von Hindenburg—elderly, senile, and no supporter of the republic. Together they made liberal use of Article 48 of the
constitution that provided for rule by executive decree. The future for
democracy in Germany grew more ominous in the later months of 1932
when Brüning resigned and his replacements—first Franz von Papen and
then General Kurt von Schleicher—clearly displayed their contempt for
the republic.

Meanwhile, Germany's economic condition remained perilous. Many
Germans found themselves in desperate straits, and not surprisingly,
these desperate people sought radical solutions. Parties representing the
political extremes made substantial electoral gains. In conflict with each
other on almost every other issue, the extremist parties agreed on the need
to destroy the republic. In three national elections between September
1930 and November 1932, the German Communist Party (KPD) almost
doubled its vote total to just under 6 million and became the third largest
party in the Reichstag. Even more stunning were the gains of the National
Socialists, or Nazis, who increased their vote total by a factor of 15 to just
a shade under 12 million! The Nazis emerged as the most popular party in
Germany with about 100 more deputies in the Reichstag than their nearest
competitor, the SPD. As leader of the republic's largest political party,
Adolf Hitler assumed the chancellorship of Germany on January 30, 1933,
a development that ended Germany's experiment with democracy.

INTERPRETIVE ESSAY
Gregory F. Schroeder

In January 1919, just two months after the end of the Great War, Germany held elections for a National Assembly that would write a constitution for a new republican state. These elections represented a victory for three parties most closely associated with reform of Germany's imperial political system: the Social Democrats (SPD), the liberal German Democratic Party (DDP), and the Catholic Center Party. Together, these parties gained 76 percent of the votes and formed a government that came to be known as the Weimar Coalition. This seemed a clear expression of Germans' desire for parliamentary democracy founded on a strong constitution, and even in the midst of postwar chaos and suffering, the results offered promise for democracy in Germany. Eleven years later, in March 1930, Germany's political system made a clear break with parliamentary democracy and moved in the direction of what have come to be called "presidential regimes"; the chancellors of these governments gained their positions through appointment by the president and not through the normal parliamentary process of building coalitions. In January 1933, Adolf Hitler, leader of the National Socialist German Workers' Party (NSDAP), was appointed chancellor, and within two months he had gained dictatorial powers that would allow him to destroy any remnants of democracy in Germany. How does one explain the dramatic shift from the democratic promise of 1919 to the threshold of dictatorship in 1933? How does one explain the collapse of Germany's first republican state?

The Weimar Republic (1918–33) has been the subject of decades-long and rich scholarly debate because the experiences of the republic were central to the developments in twentieth-century German history. Interestingly, the Weimar Republic often receives attention not for its own sake, but rather because its failure ushered in the Nazis' Third Reich. In fact, the collapse of the Weimar Republic and the rise of National Socialism are so closely linked that one cannot be discussed thoroughly without making reference to the other. The linkage of these two themes is especially close when one considers the period 1929–33, when the republic experienced what would be its final crises, and the National Socialist movement came to be viewed more and more as a solution to these crises. Despite this close connection, however, one should avoid viewing the Weimar Republic as merely a prelude to the inevitable emergence of the Third Reich; such an approach obscures the experiences of German society during the Weimar years and oversimplifies a very complex story. This essay will offer an explanation for the collapse of the republic in the final years of 1929–33, but in order to do so, it will be necessary to consider developments prior to 1929.

The history of the Weimar Republic is commonly divided into three phases: the foundation and early crises from 1918 to 1924, a period of relative stability from 1924 to 1929, and a period of renewed crisis and collapse in 1929–33. Individual authors may adjust the dates of the beginning or end of these phases depending upon their interpretations, but the basic three-part division is widely accepted.

Weimar's fate cannot be attributed to a single factor such as the existence of Article 48 in the constitution, Hitler's personal charisma and his determination to seize power, or the shattering experience of the economic crises. The German historian Eberhard Kolb has formulated seven categories of factors that contributed to the collapse of the Weimar Republic: the institutional framework of the Weimar political system; economic developments and their repercussions for political and social life; the "peculiarities of German political culture"; developments in German social classes and their impact on the political system; ideological factors; mass psychology; and the personalities of those wielding political power. Individual interpretations of the Weimar experience will necessarily emphasize these factors in differing measures, but at the very least they must acknowledge the complexity of the array if they are to be convincing.

Kolb's categories are daunting in their breadth, but they can be regrouped into a more workable configuration for the purposes of this essay: (1) the legacy of war and defeat, (2) the rejection of the parliamentary system and the society associated with the republic, and (3) the convergence of several threats to the republic during the crisis of the Great Depression. As will be demonstrated, the boundaries between these three categories were not always clear, and it is often impossible to separate them.

Any discussion of the Weimar Republic must take into account the enormous and catastrophic impact of the Great War (1914–18). First of all, the Weimar Republic itself resulted directly from Germany's military collapse, not from a successful domestic campaign to create a new political system. In an effort to gain better terms with the Allies, the leadership of the empire made last-minute political reforms and turned power over to the Social Democrats in October and November 1918. The surprising and unexpected manner in which the empire ended and the new state began had important psychological and political consequences. For many Germans, the establishment of the new regime seemed a humiliation and its continued existence an unwelcome reminder of defeat. Even those who wanted the new democratic government felt that it had been tarnished by the circumstances of its creation. The republic's enemies on the political right would eventually distort historical explanations to argue that the Social Democrats and other "unpatriotic" forces "stabbed" Germany in the back and ushered in military defeat, but such arguments ignored the facts of the empire's military demise.

The association between defeat and republic was certainly negative, but the war's legacy did not end there because the outgoing political and military leaders of the empire left behind a number of political, economic, social, and international challenges that their successors now had to face. Most obviously, the new republic was forced to deal with the Allies regarding the armistice and, ultimately, the peace treaty itself. The terms of the Versailles Treaty—territorial losses, military limitations, astronomical reparations, and a declaration of "war guilt"—were shocking and offensive to Germans across the political spectrum, including the new leaders. Unfortunately, the government had no choice but to accept the terms because the Allies threatened to renew military operations in the event of German refusal. Despite this fact, the new republic was blamed for signing the treaty; it bore responsibility for a war begun by an entirely different set of politicians in a German Empire that no longer existed. Politically, the war's aftermath dealt the republic a heavy blow.

The war left economic and social consequences as well, and these were felt long after 1918. Two specific examples—inflation and war victims—deserve special attention. During the war, the German government financed its operations through borrowing and inflationary policies. The decision to pay for war in this way had detrimental effects during the war itself, but it also set in motion a longer-term trend that culminated in the devastating hyperinflation of 1923. The scholar Gerald Feldman refers to the inflation as a "decade-long affair" and thereby clearly links the economic difficulties of the early Weimar years with the policy decisions made during the empire. The war left behind more than economic problems, however; it produced millions of war victims, both invalid soldiers and survivors of killed soldiers, who required financial support to make up for diminished ability to work or the loss of a breadwinner altogether. As the authority Richard Bessel demonstrates, war victims expected the state to meet their needs not merely as a social welfare obligation, but also as a moral obligation to those who had sacrificed so much for the nation. Benefit payments for these people constituted a very great part of the state expenditure. It is important to note that these issues converged in devastating ways. During the inflation, financial commitments to war victims were especially burdensome for state budgets, even as the payments lost real value and then came under consideration for cutbacks during times of budget reduction. Regardless of the fiscal constraints, war victims were angry over support levels they deemed insufficient. This inability to satisfy the demands of war victims posed a dangerous threat to the legitimacy of the state.

Finally, the war did much to shape Germany's place in the postwar international system as well. Defeat and the Treaty of Versailles transformed Weimar Germany into an outcast state of sorts. Germany was excluded from the newly created League of Nations, and its relations with its neighbors were very strained. Tensions were especially evident between France and Germany, for example in 1923, when the two clashed over the issue of reparations payments and France occupied the Ruhr area. In the early 1920s, Weimar Germany found more diplomatic and military cooperation with another pariah state, the Soviet Union, than it did with powers in western and central Europe. At the same time, however, Weimar Germany became increasingly dependent on the United States as a source of loans. This dependence would prove very detrimental during the Great Depression when U.S. banks called in loans early and thereby withdrew capital from a struggling German economy.

Although this discussion has covered only a few topics, it should be clear that the war contributed greatly to both the creation of the Weimar Republic and the numerous problems the new state faced over the course of its existence. The second category of factors under consideration in this essay, the rejection of the parliamentary system and its society, presented many more threats. One of the facts of life for the Weimar Republic was its more or less continuous struggle to win supporters and defend against opponents. Some segments of German society opposed the republic from the start, whereas others tolerated but did not love it. Some were staunch supporters, and others were willing to support the republic until it was unable to meet their needs. Throughout its 14 years, the republic struggled to gain legitimacy in the eyes of German society.

Parties and people on the extreme left and right of Weimar's political spectrum were committed opponents of the republic, and for the most part, their opposition spanned the entire life of the regime. The early years of the republic were characterized by a civil war mentality, as demonstrated by the numerous episodes of political violence. The Spartacists and Communists on the left attempted to overthrow the republic, which they believed to be insufficiently revolutionary. In response, the government, led by the Social Democrats, resorted to cooperating with the military to put down rebellion by force; the government was desperate to preserve order, prevent a radicalization on the Bolshevik model, and ensure the survival of the new democratic state. These clashes spawned great bitterness among the Communists, who viewed the SPD as traitors and the new state as an enemy. The Communists maintained this bitterness throughout the 1920s, and in the early 1930s, they attacked the Social Democrats even more viciously than they did the National Socialists. The Kapp and Hitler putsch attempts, in 1920 and 1923 respectively, and several political assassinations demonstrated that the political right, too, despised the fledgling regime and was willing to use force for political purposes. These various acts represented direct attacks on the Weimar political system, but they contributed to the weakening of the republic in another, more lasting way: they initiated a trend toward the increasing use of public violence for political aims. Over the course of the 1920s, various political groupings, including the Communists, Socialists, National Socialists, and veterans' organizations, established their own paramilitary organizations to battle each other in the streets. These clashes were especially violent in the early 1930s, and election campaigns often provided the spark for fighting. This development had a corrosive effect on the parliamentary system of Weimar because it shifted political conflict from the realm of democratic debate to open violence.

Politicians on the political right and even officials and servants of the state itself personally rejected the republic, sometimes very publicly so. They had come of age and achieved their professional status under the empire, and while they tolerated the new order, they were also ill-disposed toward it. This mentality can be found, for example, in judges who dealt leniently with right-wing violators convicted of crimes against the republic, even as they treated leftists harshly. Military officers as a rule disliked the parliamentary system and hoped to return to the monarchy. The German National People's Party (DNVP), heir to the conservatives of the imperial era, was an especially important antirepublican force that refused to form coalitions with the Social Democrats. It became more strident in the late 1920s, when party moderates were marginalized and Alfred Hugenberg became party leader. The official party platform in 1931, for example, openly called for the reconstitution of the monarchical empire. In 1929 and 1931, the DNVP joined with the National Socialists and other groups to attack the Young Plan and create a so-called National Opposition. Important leaders in the Catholic Center Party, too, which repeatedly participated in coalition governments in the Weimar years, were monarchists at heart. Even the second president of the republic, Paul von Hindenburg, was at best ambivalent toward the postimperial state. He served out of a sense of duty and wished to act legally, but he considered his true master to be the Kaiser. In his last years, he became increasingly susceptible to the views of his narrow circle of antirepublican advisors.

In addition to the effect of Weimar's outright opponents and reluctant servants, however, one must consider cases in which actual or potential supporters of the republic were undermined and even led to abandon hope in the parliamentary system. The liberal parties of the middle classes and the state's social welfare system offer two such cases. Historians have examined the party system of the Weimar Republic closely and focused much of their attention on the middle-class liberals, the German Democratic Party (DDP) and the German People's Party (DVP), who might have been expected to support the new democratic state. Unfortunately for Weimar, repeated crises—war, inflation, and the currency reform (1924) implemented to remedy the inflation—undermined the economic stability of the middle classes and, importantly, destroyed their faith in the ability of the new government to protect their interests. These Germans responded not by coalescing around liberal principles and strengthening liberal political parties, but rather by seeking help from smaller interest group parties dedicated to single issues. This contributed to the fragmentation of the larger political picture in Weimar Germany and made normal parliamentary cooperation difficult, if not impossible. In the late 1920s and early 1930s, the liberal parties lost many voters to more radical parties, including the National Socialists.

The welfare policies of the Weimar Republic should, theoretically, have been able to win wide support for the new political system, but in this case, too, the facts of life in Germany undercut this potential source of support. In the early years of the republic, the government worked hard to establish public welfare programs under the direct control of the municipalities and the state; this represented a shift from the earlier, widespread model of private welfare groups, many of which were administered by religious organizations even if they received financial support from the state. Although this newly asserted state responsibility was welcomed by many, it angered those committed to a more traditional understanding of social welfare. In the years of relative stability (1924–29), the republic worked hard to build the "Weimar welfare state" so often associated with the era. The state financed public housing and public works, and in 1927, the government passed major legislation to expand unemployment insurance to millions of people. These were remarkable achievements, but they required commitments that could not be sustained in times of grave economic crisis. The inflation of the early 1920s was one such crisis, and the Great Depression of 1929 was another. The republic's inability to meet all expectations cost it—fairly or not—the support of many of its citizens.

Another potential basis for support of the republic was its foreign policy after 1924, which did much to reconcile Germany with its wartime enemies. Convinced that open resistance to the provisions of the Treaty of
Versailles, especially the sections on reparations, would lead Germany
nowhere, Foreign Minister Gustav Stresemann embarked upon a policy
known as "fulfillment." Its basic tenet was cooperation with the Allies in
the hope that Germany would benefit from the international goodwill.
The concrete results of this approach were several. The Locarno Treaty of
1925 confirmed postwar borders in the west, but it also foresaw early
evacuation of occupation troops in Germany and Germany's entry into
the League of Nations. Overall, Locarno promoted a spirit of international
cooperation and improved Germany's international position. In 1926,
Germany in fact gained membership in the League of Nations, an important step toward its readmittance into the international community, and in
1930, French troops evacuated their zone of occupation along the Rhine
five years ahead of schedule. In 1924 and 1929, Germany reached important agreements on reparations in the Dawes Plan and Young Plan respectively. These agreements recalculated reparations payments and linked
these payments to Germany's ability to pay. After Stresemann's death in
1929 and as the effects of the Great Depression were being felt in Germany,
the government was able to gain first a moratorium on reparations payments (1931) and then the cancellation of payments altogether (1932).
Despite these achievements, significant segments of German society were
dissatisfied and even furious with Weimar's foreign policy. The nationalists, especially the National Socialists and the DNVP, relentlessly attacked
the government for acquiescing to the reparations negotiations and for
submitting Germany to continued national humiliation.

The preceding examples concerning opponents and disappointed
potential supporters of the republic are essential to an understanding of
the republic's collapse, but the Weimar system was also threatened by the
rejection of modernity. Although modernity is a complicated concept, for
the present purposes it may be defined as the set of developments that
transformed Germany in the nineteenth and twentieth centuries: industrialization, urbanization, secularization, the development of mass politics,
the incremental emancipation of women, and experimentation in the arts.
It is important to understand that a consideration of modernity places
Weimar into the broader context of European history and experiences
over many decades. The Weimar Republic did not initiate any of the
developments listed here, but it did come to represent their convergence.
That is to say, Weimar Germany was viewed by many to be the product
and symbol of modernity.

Weimar's modernity was alien to the many Germans whose cultural, social, and religious values were more traditional. A comparison of "modernist" and "traditionalist" responses to Weimar society will demonstrate the basis of this alienation. Supporters of Weimar society—those who accepted or even embraced the modern elements of the new Germany—could point to many promising and fascinating developments. Women were able to vote and hold elected office. The state took an active interest in welfare policies and developed substantial programs to safeguard the population. Cultural expressions were vibrant and exciting and revolutionary, whether one considered the paintings of the so-called New Objectivity or the architecture of the Bauhaus school. The traditionalists viewed these developments very differently. They did not agree with the new roles and opportunities for women, whom they believed were better suited for the sphere of the family or strictly maternal tasks performed for the public. They were angry at the huge state expenditure for social programs. They felt attacked by modern art and building designs and responded by characterizing these as "cultural Bolshevism," thereby associating them with the communist Soviet Union. Furthermore, the traditionalists were often at home in smaller towns, where religious and community values defined daily life to a large extent. They associated the Weimar state with urbanism, godlessness, and immorality. There were, therefore, many reasons why traditionalists felt uncomfortable with the world of Weimar Germany, and this discomfort, if not outright alienation, made them much less inclined to support the republic and even provoked their resistance.

The preceding discussion of the first two sets of factors demonstrates that the Weimar Republic faced very great difficulties. Nevertheless, if it were to collapse, another blow would have to be delivered. This blow came with the Great Depression, which hit Germany in late 1929 and early 1930. In the midst of this renewed economic crisis, the various weaknesses and challenges described previously converged in disastrous fashion. Before Germany emerged from the Depression, parliamentary government had been abandoned, and the very republic itself was destroyed.

The end of parliamentary government and the Depression were very closely linked, and the specific point of connection was unemployment in Germany. Even before the Great Depression struck Germany, the members of Hermann Müller's coalition government (SPD, DVP, DDP, and Center) had been at odds over the cost of the welfare state, especially the cost of the unemployment insurance instituted in 1927. The SPD wanted to increase payments to benefit the unemployed, whereas the DVP and Center argued that support should be decreased to relieve the state's budget. The numbers of unemployed increased dramatically in the early months of the Depression, and the question became all the more pressing by early 1930. The members of the coalition were unable to reach agreement, however, and the government resigned in March 1930. In its place, President Hindenburg appointed Heinrich Brüning of the Center to serve as chancellor. When the Reichstag rejected Brüning's proposals to make drastic budget cuts, the chancellor forced them through with the backing of the president, who was empowered by Article 48 of the constitution to rule by decree. When the Reichstag challenged this maneuver, the president dissolved it in accordance with the provisions of Article 25 of the constitution.

At this point, it is necessary to discuss Weimar's constitution and the personalities of the men in charge of the republic's future in 1930, because with the appointment of Brüning the Weimar Republic entered a phase in which antirepublican forces used provisions in the constitution to weaken and eventually destroy the republic itself. Article 48 was inserted into the constitution with the intention that it be used in extraordinary circumstances to protect the republic. This is not surprising when one recalls that the constitution was written during a period of near civil war in Germany and that the communists had attempted to overthrow the regime early in 1919. The first president, Friedrich Ebert, used Article 48 several times in the early 1920s, but he always did so in defense of the republic. The authors of the constitution did not foresee or discounted the possibility that someone might use Article 48 against the republic. This is what happened in 1930, and it is impossible to deny or minimize the impact of the specific persons involved.

President Hindenburg himself, although very wary of openly breaking with the constitution, was personally unsympathetic to the parliamentary system of Weimar and disinclined to deal with the Social Democrats. The first presidential chancellor, Heinrich Brüning, was a committed monarchist and nationalist whose memoirs stated that he hoped to use the crisis of the Great Depression to extricate Germany from the reparations obligations and to reintroduce the monarchy. Prior to Brüning's appointment, the president and the soon-to-be chancellor agreed that the next government would be rightist in its political orientation and exclude the SPD, despite the fact that the SPD was the largest party in the Reichstag. This agreement constituted a clear and calculated move toward authoritarian rule. Furthermore, Hindenburg's circle of advisors consisted of men who, for their part, rejected the republic. Franz von Papen and Kurt von Schleicher, the second and third presidential chancellors respectively, advised Hindenburg in the direction of more authoritarian alternatives to the republic. During the period of the presidential regimes, the chancellors repeatedly made use of emergency powers and dissolved the Reichstag more than once. During Brüning's tenure, for example, the number of laws passed by the Reichstag decreased, but the number of emergency decrees increased dramatically. Rather than resort to the emergency powers of the constitution as extraordinary tools, as had been the case under Ebert, the presidential chancellors employed them regularly.

Although Brüning's appointment in 1930 led directly to the destruction of parliamentary government, the fate of the republic had yet to be determined. The presidential chancellors sought to establish an authoritarian regime, but to do this they needed a strong popular basis in German society. The policies of the Brüning, Papen, and Schleicher governments, however, did not win this support, and traditional right-wing political parties such as the DNVP continued to lose supporters. The authoritarians of the president's circle had to look elsewhere for mass political support, and Hitler's National Socialists offered a real but unappealing option.

Before the Great Depression, the National Socialists were not a major party in the Weimar political spectrum. Adolf Hitler served an abbreviated term in prison for his role in the putsch attempt of November 1923, and after his release in 1924, he worked to revitalize and reorganize the party. These efforts did not result immediately in electoral victories—the party received only 2.6 percent of the vote in the 1928 Reichstag elections—but they did build a very strong basis for expansion in the future. After 1928, the Nazi party devoted enormous energy to the tasks of voter registration, election propaganda, and incessant political meetings. Nazi propaganda was nationalist, antirepublican, anti-Marxist (which in practical terms meant anti–Social Democracy), and anti-Semitic (although this aspect was not so prominent in the party's campaign efforts of the late 1920s and early 1930s). The party worked to attract Germans across the political spectrum, and although the interests of farmers, workers, and the urban middle classes were different, the party promised something for everyone, regardless of the inherent contradictions among these promises. It attacked the "Weimar system" and its failure to solve Germany's problems. The party became, in effect, a *Volkspartei,* or "people's party," meaning that it drew on support from various groups in German society, not simply one class, one region, or one religion. Despite the fact that the National Socialists shared many sentiments with the more traditional authoritarians, Hindenburg and his advisors rejected Hitler's movement because they considered it too crass and too radical.

In the Reichstag elections of September 1930, which were necessitated by the dissolution of the Reichstag earlier that summer, the National

Socialists gained a surprising 18.3 percent of the vote. Chancellor Brüning's hopes for a Reichstag more to his liking were destroyed. In subsequent elections, the National Socialists increased their strength: 37.3 percent in July 1932 and 33.1 percent in November 1932. The National Socialists became increasingly strident in their demand for political power; specifically, Hitler demanded the chancellorship. Although Hindenburg disliked Hitler and had refused to appoint him in 1932, the continued failure of presidential chancellors persuaded the president and his advisors to reconsider Hitler in January 1933. They believed that they would be able to form a coalition with Hitler, take advantage of his mass support for their own political plans, and contain the National Socialist leader. On January 30, 1933, Hindenburg appointed Adolf Hitler as the fourth presidential chancellor. Hitler came to power, therefore, not as the result of a functioning parliamentary system but rather as the result of a presidential decision based on the now normal use of emergency powers. He began immediately to destroy the remnants of the republic and to establish the structures of the Third Reich.

This essay carries the title "The Collapse of the Weimar Republic, 1929–1933," but it should be clear that the collapse was not confined to a mere four-year period. Rather it resulted from the interaction and convergence of many factors, some of which predated the republic itself. It should also be clear that although the demise of Weimar was connected to the rise of National Socialism, interpretations of the era must be careful to distinguish between the two developments. Perhaps it is fair to say that the emergence of National Socialism was one symptom of Weimar's weakness, whereas Weimar's very weakness and collapse were the preconditions for the establishment of the Third Reich. Finally, it remains to be stated that the republic was certainly vulnerable by 1929–30, but its ultimate demise was the result of a specific set of antirepublican responses to crisis, not the inevitable and only possible outcome for that crisis situation.

SELECTED BIBLIOGRAPHY

Allen, William Sheridan. *The Nazi Seizure of Power: The Experience of a Single German Town 1922–1945.* Rev. ed. New York: Watts, 1984. The first half of this classic study examines the contributions of the Depression, local electoral politics, and political violence to the emergence of the National Socialists at the local level.

Baranowski, Shelley. *The Sanctity of Rural Life: Nobility, Protestantism, and Nazism in Weimar Prussia.* New York: Oxford University Press, 1995. Examines the social structures, religious values, and economic situation in the Prussian province of Pomerania to reveal an antirepublican frame of mind increasingly at odds with the Weimar system, which it associated with urbanism, moral decline, irreligiosity, and antirural economic policies.

Bessel, Richard. *Germany after the First World War.* New York: Clarendon Press of Oxford University Press, 1993. Provides an excellent discussion of the social, economic, and moral impact of the war on German society in the period roughly 1914–24.

Bessel, Richard, and E. J. Feutchwanger, eds. *Social and Political Development in Weimar Germany.* Totowa, NJ: Barnes & Noble, 1981. Contains 10 essays covering a wide spectrum of issues: revolution, inflation, party politics, social classes, women, agriculture, and foreign policy.

Bookbinder, Paul. *Weimar Germany: The Republic of the Reasonable.* New York: Manchester University Press, 1996. A good overview of the Weimar Republic with a set of selected documents and a brief bibliographic essay.

Bracher, Karl Dietrich. *The German Dictatorship: The Origins, Structure, and Effects of National Socialism.* Translated by Jean Steinberg. New York: Praeger, 1970. This classic study offers a vigorous defense of parliamentary options after 1929 and focuses blame for destruction of the republican government on the small, authoritarian circle of advisors around Hindenburg.

Breitman, Richard. *German Socialism and Weimar Democracy.* Chapel Hill: University of North Carolina Press, 1981. Focuses on the leadership of the Social Democrats at the Reich level to argue that the various crises of the Weimar years pushed the SPD onto the defensive and hindered successful interparty collaboration.

Diehl, James M. *Paramilitary Politics in Weimar Germany.* Bloomington: Indiana University Press, 1977. Examines the development of paramilitary groups across the political spectrum to demonstrate how political violence became a normal part of Weimar society.

Dorpalen, Andreas. *Hindenburg and the Weimar Republic.* Princeton, NJ: Princeton University Press, 1964. This biography argues that although many Germans repeatedly looked to Hindenburg to provide stability and order in times of crisis, his inherent desire to abstain from political controversy and his natural lethargy prevented him from active engagement and generally led him to accept passively the decisions of his nominal subordinates.

Feldman, Gerald D. *The Great Disorder: Politics, Economics, and Society in the German Inflation, 1914–1924.* New York: Oxford University Press, 1993. This massive and detailed study of the inflation from its origins in the Great War to stabilization in 1924 will likely intimidate many, but its sources and scope make it a new standard on the topic.

Fritsche, Peter. *Germans into Nazis.* Cambridge, MA: Harvard University Press, 1998. Focuses on several "moments" between 1914 and 1933 when Germans exuberantly expressed their patriotism to argue that Nazism became possible because of middle-class, nationalist desires.

Gay, Peter. *Weimar Culture: The Insider as Outsider.* New York: Harper & Row, 1968. Extended essay on the "Weimar spirit" in art, literature, and thought: experimentation, cosmopolitanism, challenge against received values, and efforts to create new meaning and provide new direction.

Hong, Young-Sun. *Welfare, Modernity, and the Weimar State, 1919–1933*. Princeton, NJ: Princeton University Press, 1998. Examines the conflict among several approaches to social welfare—Christian (both Protestant and Catholic), Progressive, and Social Democratic—to reveal how fundamental differences weakened the position of the parliamentary republic as an agent of social welfare.

Jones, Larry Eugene. *German Liberalism and the Dissolution of the Weimar Party System, 1918–1933*. Chapel Hill: University of North Carolina Press, 1988. Examines the failure of the German Democratic Party (DDP) and German Peoples' Party (DVP) to develop a unified, effective representation of their predominately middle-class base during the crises of the Weimar years.

Kaes, Anton, Martin Jay, and Edward Dimendberg, eds. *The Weimar Republic Sourcebook*. Chapel Hill: University of North Carolina Press, 1994. A remarkable collection of primary sources covering a wide range of topics such as politics and ideology, art and culture, social groups and classes, and everyday life.

Kershaw, Ian. *Hitler, 1889–1936: Hubris*. New York: Norton, 1999. An outstanding study that demonstrates vividly just how close Hitler was to political failure in late 1932 and early 1933 before he and his movement were handed power by the president.

———, ed. *Weimar: Why Did German Democracy Fail?* New York: St. Martin's, 1990. Four essays and a series of related comments representing a spectrum of interpretations concerning economic policy options in the Brüning years.

Kolb, Eberhard. *The Weimar Republic*. Translated by P. S. Falla. London: Unwin Hyman, 1988. Provides both a useful historical overview of Weimar and a detailed historiographical discussion of major themes and questions.

Mommsen, Hans. *The Rise and Fall of Weimar Democracy*. Translated by Elborg Forster and Larry Eugene Jones. Chapel Hill: University of North Carolina Press, 1996. Argues that Weimar did not fail because of deficiencies in democracy but rather that it was destroyed by its political enemies on the conservative, antirepublican right.

Patch, William L., Jr. *Heinrich Brüning and the Dissolution of the Weimar Republic*. New York: Cambridge University Press, 1998. A revisionist interpretation of Brüning that argues, against Brüning's own account in his memoirs, that the chancellor worked to defend parliamentary democracy and had much less room to maneuver than his critics have acknowledged.

Peukert, Detlev J. K. *The Weimar Republic: The Crisis of Classical Modernity*. Translated by Richard Deveson. New York: Hill & Wang, 1992. This study views the history of Weimar in the longer context of modernization, reaching back into the nineteenth century, and argues that the political system of the republic lacked the legitimacy necessary to survive crises associated with modernization.

Reagin, Nancy R. *A German Women's Movement: Class and Gender in Hanover, 1880–1933*. The last several chapters of this study demonstrate how the increasingly nationalistic women's movement, with a long local history in Hanover, was traumatized by war and revolution and ultimately developed stances in opposition to the political and moral system of the republic.

Sneeringer, Julia. *Winning Women's Vote: Propaganda and Politics in Weimar Germany.* Chapel Hill: University of North Carolina, 2002. Despite their fundamental differences, the parties as a whole routinely courted Germany's newly enfranchised women through "essentially feminine" topics such as welfare, family, culture, and religion.

Weitz, Eric D. *Creating German Communism, 1890–1990: From Popular Protests to Socialist State.* Princeton, NJ: Princeton University Press, 1997. Contains five chapters on the communist political and social world during the Weimar years and carefully documents the fundamental confrontations between the German Communists and Weimar's political, social, and economic order.

7

The Hitler Experience, 1933–1945

INTRODUCTION

On January 30, 1933, the Weimar Republic, Germany's attempt at democracy, died. On that day Adolf Hitler, a mortal enemy of the republic, took office as chancellor and immediately began to transform Germany into a Nazi dictatorship. Hitler was born on April 20, 1889, in Braunau am Inn, Austria, the son of a minor customs official. Abused by his father and coddled by his mother, Hitler was orphaned as a teenager and drifted to Vienna where he failed in his bid to enter the Academy of Graphic Arts. Hitler ended up living on the fringe where he readily absorbed the various strains of anti-Semitism that coursed through Vienna. Eventually, he relocated to Munich, where in 1914 he entered the German army. Up to now a ne'er-do-well, drifting misfit, Hitler found a home in the army. He served honorably on the western front, rose to the rank of corporal, and was decorated for bravery. He also fell victim to a poison gas attack that left his vocal chords permanently damaged, thereby giving his voice an eerie resonance.

With Germany's defeat in 1918, Hitler returned to Munich where he maintained contact with elements of what remained of the German army. The army assigned him to scout out right-wing organizations that had sprung up in the wake of the empire's collapse in order to determine which should receive money from a secret fund. In fulfilling his mission, Hitler stumbled upon and later joined the German Workers' Party, a tiny radical group founded in 1919 by Anton Drexler, a Munich lathe operator.

Adolf Hitler, with Heinrich Himmler on the left and Viktor Lutze on the right, walks between the ranks during the 1934 Nazi Party Day at Nürnberg. The Nazis frequently staged spectacular ceremonies in order to generate popular support and to cow their enemies. (Reproduced from the Collections of the Library of Congress.)

In a short time Hitler elbowed Drexler aside and made the party his own. In 1920, the party renamed itself the National Socialist German Workers' Party (NSDAP), or Nazi Party.

Due in large measure to Hitler's exceptional rhetorical skills, he and his Nazis stood out among the many "lunatic fringe" groups that thrived in postwar Bavaria. In November 1923, Hitler gained national notoriety when he led a failed attempt to overthrow the Bavarian authorities. This "Beer Hall Putsch"—given that name because its planning allegedly occurred in the back rooms of Munich's beer halls—had also enlisted the support of the well-known former general Erich Ludendorff, one of Germany's wartime leaders. In the aftermath of the failed putsch, Hitler was convicted of treason but sentenced to only five years imprisonment, of which he served less than one year. While incarcerated, Hitler wrote *Mein Kampf*, a rambling quasi-autobiography filled with his observations, pronouncements, and plans for the future that became the Nazis' Bible.

Upon his release from Landsberg Fortress, Hitler revived the Nazi Party. This was not such an easy task since the return of prosperity to Germany greatly lessened the attraction of the radical groups. In fact, most of the post–World War I radical groups now faded from the scene; the Nazis were unusual in their perseverance. Nevertheless, one could hardly accuse the Nazis of enjoying widespread popularity; in the German parliamentary elections of 1928, the Nazi Party garnered only 810,000 votes of the more than 30 million votes cast, or about 2.6 percent.

However, two years later in the 1930 elections the Nazis polled 6,400,000 votes, or more than 18 percent of the total cast. What accounts for this spectacular increase? The answer, quite simply, was the onset of the Great Depression, which destroyed the German economy. In Germany the level of unemployment went through the roof, and the Weimar Republic seemed powerless to reverse the economic collapse. As a consequence, increasingly desperate people sought radical solutions. While the Communists saw an 85 percent jump in their vote total, the Nazis were the chief beneficiaries. In the July 1932 elections, the Nazis received fully 37 percent of the vote and became the largest party in the Reichstag, or parliament, by almost 100 seats. Although their vote total dropped a bit in a subsequent 1932 election, at the start of 1933 the Nazis remained by far the most popular political party in the country.

The political chicanery surrounding the Weimar Republic's last days presents a sordid and complex story. In summary, a number of "respectable" German conservatives, including representatives of the army, big business, the aristocracy, and the bureaucracy, who were committed to destroying the republic in a sanitary fashion, fought among themselves for control of

the state. As personal ambitions undermined their cause, these conservatives concluded that Hitler was their man. They reasoned that the
"Bohemian corporal's" great popularity and unquestioned rhetorical
skills would make him an effective "front man," while they called the
shots from behind the scenes. Accordingly, they persuaded the elderly
and easily befuddled German president, Paul von Hindenburg, another
World War I hero who had no use for the republic, to appoint Hitler chancellor on January 30, 1933.

Hitler, however, had no intention of being anyone's puppet. On the contrary, he moved rapidly not only to destroy the republic, but also to subordinate the conservatives who had elevated him to power. On February
27, the Reichstag building burned. Although the cause of the fire has never
been determined conclusively, Hitler blamed it on the Communists and
on February 28 issued "For the Protection of People and State," a decree
that suspended civil liberties. Arrests of Hitler's political opponents began
almost immediately, and Heinrich Himmler, the Nazi head of the Munich
police, established Germany's first concentration camp at Dachau. One
month later, after an election campaign marked by widespread violence
and intimidation that netted Hitler and his antidemocratic conservative
allies a majority in the Reichstag, the Nazis rammed through the Enabling
Act that allowed Hitler to rule by decree for the next four years. The
Enabling Act finished off the Weimar Republic and cleared the way for
Hitler to establish his personal rule.

Hitler's assault on Germany's institutions now moved into high gear.
On May 2, Germany's independent labor unions were outlawed. In their
place the Nazis established the German Labor Front, a national body that
brought all labor under its sway and thereby guaranteed that no strikes or
other labor unrest would upset Nazi Germany. In June and July, Hitler
turned Germany into a one-party state by effectively outlawing all political parties other than NSDAP. In order to whip up popular support for his
regime, Hitler created the Reich Ministry for Public Enlightenment and
Propaganda, headed by Joseph Paul Goebbels, a master manipulator of
public opinion. One of Goebbels's first acts was to organize the public
burning of "unGerman" books in Berlin and various university towns and
cities. The Nazis also purged the administration, judiciary, and educa-
tional establishment. Across the board, Nazis replaced non-Nazis in positions of authority and prestige. The universities were Nazified, and the
traditional judicial system was superseded by the Nazis' "People's
Courts" that heard accusations of treason against the regime.

In his drive to bring all Germany under Nazi control, Hitler did not
overlook his bête noire, Germany's Jews. Although numbering a little less

than 1 percent of a total population of about 60 million, Hitler blamed the Jews for all of Germany's ills—real or imagined. On April 1, 1933, the Nazis initiated a boycott of all Jewish shops. Over the course of the next months, the Nazis took steps to expel Jews from every aspect of official German life. Jews were dismissed from the various administrative units, forced out of schools and universities, and further marginalized economically. A climax of sorts in Hitler's anti-Semitic campaign occurred with the promulgation of the Nürnberg Laws on September 15, 1935. These laws provided a legal basis for further discrimination against German Jewry. They defined a Jew as anyone who had at least one Jewish grandparent. Under the Nürnberg Laws, Jews lost their German citizenship and, consequently, were reduced to a second-class status. Jews were forbidden to marry non-Jews. Emigration for Germany's Jews became more difficult as the Nazis forced the would-be emigrants to surrender everything except the proverbial shirts on their backs.

In 1934, Hitler tightened his control over both Germany and NSDAP. On June 30, he engineered the "Night of the Long Knives," a blood purge of the party's leadership as well as non-Nazi allies and enemies who had displeased him. In particular, he struck at Nazis who possessed the potential to challenge him, such as Gregor Strasser, who evinced an interest in the socialist aspect of National Socialism, and at the SA (*Sturmabteilungen*), the brown-shirted Nazi militia led by Hitler's friend Ernst Röhm. The conservatives who had originally placed Hitler in power were also targeted. A few weeks after the Night of the Long Knives, President Hindenburg died. Hitler quickly took advantage of the old commander's death. After giving Hindenburg a funeral befitting a Norse god, Hitler combined the offices of chancellor and president in himself. Taking a page from Italian fascist dictator Benito Mussolini, Hitler named himself Führer, or unquestioned leader. He also required the army to swear a personal oath of allegiance.

Hitler gave Nazified Germany a new name; henceforth, it was to be known as the Third Reich. Hitler promised that it would last for one thousand years. To ensure that the Third Reich would not wither away in his lifetime, Hitler employed carrot-and-stick tactics to keep the German people docile. Undoubtedly, the most important arrow in his quiver was a host of coercive organizations. Although the Night of the Long Knives eliminated the SA leadership, its rank and file remained loyal to Hitler. SA thugs provided a visible public presence for the Nazi leadership when they were not busy terrorizing ordinary Germans, especially the Jews. Supplanting the rather undisciplined SA as Hitler's coercive body of choice was the SS, or *Schutzstaffel*. The SS was originally established in 1925 as Hitler's personal guard. In 1929, Himmler took command of the SS and within three years had expanded it from 250 men to more than 50,000! After the Night of the Long Knives, the SS gradually came to control either directly or indirectly all aspects of the Third Reich's security, from the concentration camps to internal intelligence to the ordinary police. One of the most effective branches of the SS was the Gestapo, the Third Reich's secret police who acted as the eyes and ears of the state. Germany abounded with jails, prisons, torture chambers, execution rooms, and concentration camps. A casual comment, an offhand joke, a furtive glance—any of these could spell disaster.

Despite the terror tactics that characterized the Third Reich, Hitler and the Nazis enjoyed genuine popularity during the regime's early years. In particular, ordinary Germans credited the Nazis for putting them back to work. When Hitler came to power, Germany found itself mired in the worst stages of the Depression with an unemployment rate of 40 percent. Hitler quickly launched a series of major public works projects including construction of the *Autobahnen*. He spent even more capital on a massive rearmament program. Although wages were not particularly high, jobs became plentiful. The Nazi organization Strength Through Joy provided extras such as vacations and summer camps for workers' children. By 1936, Germany was back at work, and the unemployment rate had dropped significantly.

Hitler also earned points with virtually all Germans by systematically destroying the Treaty of Versailles. Germans universally despised the treaty, seeing it as a symbol for all that was wrong with the world. The Weimar Republic had first chosen to weaken the treaty through a policy of passive noncompliance. When that produced a negative result, the Republic under Gustav Stresemann switched to a more fruitful plan of undermining the treaty through compliance. Hitler decided to attack the treaty in a head-on manner. Throughout the 1930s, he hammered away at the treaty, to the great delight of the Germans.

Nor should one discount the role propaganda played in generating support for the Nazi dictatorship. Joseph Goebbels, Hitler's "marketing" genius, produced spectacles that were both entertaining and creative. Combining the latest in mass psychology with techniques pioneered by Madison Avenue and Russia's Communist revolutionaries, Goebbels turned Germany into a Nazi circus. All cultural, intellectual, athletic, social, and environmental activity fell under the purview of the Nazis. The Nazis also made major strides in the spiritual sphere, gaining control of a significant portion of the Lutheran Church and entering into a formal agreement with the Roman Catholic Church that was not unfavorable for the Nazis. Hitler himself played an important role, making excellent use of modern communications, especially the radio. His emotional broadcast speeches rivaled the more restrained "fireside chats" of Franklin D. Roosevelt in their ability to reach the hearts of their audience.

In 1938, Hitler completed his dictatorship when he brought the German army fully under his control. Despite Nazi inroads, he remained wary of the army, an institution that had been a virtual state within the state under the Weimar Republic, and he had been circumspect in his dealings with it. However, he now felt strong enough to subordinate it to his wishes. Hitler engineered the ouster of the army's two leading generals, Werner von Blomberg and Werner von Fritsch, by falsely making them appear to be morally derelict. Then, in the name of recovering the army's lost honor, he effectively took control of Germany's military forces.

As Hitler emasculated the German army, he once again moved aggressively against Germany's remaining Jews. In retaliation for the assassination in Paris of a German embassy official by a disgruntled Jew, Hitler unleashed his bullyboys. In the *Reichskristallnacht* (the Night of the Shattered Glass) of November 9, 1938, Nazi thugs destroyed hundreds of Jewish shops, set fire to most of Germany's synagogues, and murdered approximately 100 Jews while beating countless others. To add insult to injury, Hitler forced the Jews to pay for the damage done by the Nazis.

Such was the condition of Germany when it entered World War II on September 1, 1939. During the course of the war, little changed save an intensification of the barbarous brutality that proved to be the dominant characteristic of Hitler's Third Reich.

INTERPRETIVE ESSAY
George P. Blum

The history of National Socialist Germany—the Third Reich—has thus far been largely viewed as the history of a unique occurrence in the development of modern Germany. With growing distance from its dreadful path and the recent rebirth of Europe after the collapse of the communist systems, it is possible to assess this era in the context of the unfolding of Germany's history in the twentieth century. To understand how Adolf Hitler and National Socialism could hold such a strong appeal among the German populace after he was appointed chancellor and retain much support throughout most of World War II, it is important to examine Hitler regime's development as it evolved rather than from the perspective of its destructive ends. The voters who cast their ballots for the National Socialists before and during 1933 did not envisage a regime that would practice terror, bring genocide, and launch a catastrophic war; rather, they looked to the National Socialists to save them from poverty, provide employment, restore national greatness, and revive national unity.

The NSDAP or National Socialist German Workers' Party—often just called the Nazi party—emerged from the post–World War I political turmoil in the early 1920s as Adolf Hitler's creation. It depended entirely on his oratorical talent, demagogic skill, and charisma for its development as a political force. His message contained raw ideas and ideologies that appealed to significant segments of the public. The designation National Socialism stood in contrast to "international socialism" and was expected to resonate among workers with nationalistic sentiments. It also captivated young people drawn from the middle and upper classes who had idealistic notions of a "popular" or "national" community going back to nineteenth-century Romanticism. Hitler's utopian idea of national community (*Volksgemeinschaft*) appeared to ensure the kind of society that would overcome the class tension of modern industrial life and unite all social classes in a new community that would lead to a racially pure entity, that is, the Aryan Greater German Reich. Nation and race reinforced each other and the racist anti-Semitic aspect of this ideology gave Germans a mission in world politics. Hitler applied the Social Darwinist principle of the survival of the fittest to the realm of international relations, in which the racial character of nations determined their existence and claim to survival and dominance.

It was the worldwide economic crisis of 1929–33, the Great Depression, that provided the environment in which the Nazi political fortunes improved dramatically. In 1930, parliamentary government in Germany was replaced by presidential government under which the Reich president, Paul von Hindenburg, enacted measures proposed by the chancellor by emergency decree, that is, without consulting the Reichstag. In the two parliamentary elections of 1932, the National Socialists became the largest party in the multiparty Reichstag, and Hitler, as its leader, insisted on being named chancellor. Hindenburg, the aging and tired field marshal of World War I, twice rejected the boisterous Nazi leader—he called him "the Bohemian corporal"—as unsuitable for the chancellorship. But weary of the responsibility for undemocratic emergency decree government and reassured by his archconservative colleagues that the coalition cabinet contained enough trustworthy ministers that would control Hitler, he was persuaded to appoint the Nazi leader chancellor on January 30, 1933.

Hitler's followers always hailed his appointment to the chancellorship as "the seizure of power" and the beginning of the restoration of Germany. But the political takeover occurred under basically constitutional circumstances, and the Nazi leader's acquisition of full dictatorial power was a process that extended over 18 months. There were very few voices raised in alarm when Hitler was sworn in, and the Nazis staged loud triumphal celebrations with hours of street parades. One dissenter was General Erich Ludendorff, who had marched with Hitler in 1923. But now, 10 years later, he charged in a letter to his wartime associate Hindenburg that he had placed the "German fatherland" in the hands of "one of the greatest demagogues of all time" who would plunge it "into the abyss and bring our nation to inconceivable misery." World War II and Auschwitz were not even on the horizon at this time, and those few who had bothered to read Hitler's *Mein Kampf* did not take his political and imperial fantasies very seriously. The leading non-Nazi member of the coalition government, Franz von Papen, who had helped negotiate Hitler's appointment, boasted that in two months he and his fellow cabinet conservatives would have pushed Hitler into a corner. He could not have been more wrong.

The Nazi leader's early objective was to destroy the Weimar Republic quickly and lay the foundation for his dictatorship. Within two days of his inauguration, he embarked on a dynamic Reichstag election campaign—he contended it would be the last—which cleverly exploited the nation's longing for unity and recovery. On February 4, he persuaded Hindenburg to issue a decree that gave his government the power to forbid political meetings and ban newspapers. At the end of the month the destruction by fire of the Reichstag building, which the Nazis claimed heralded a Communist uprising but was evidently set single-handedly by a wandering Dutch workman, led to a new decree that suspended basic civil rights guaranteed by the Weimar constitution.

Even with high-powered Nazi electoral mobilization, violence, and civil rights restrictions, the last multiparty Reichstag election on March 5 gave Hitler's party only 43.9 percent of the vote and required an alliance with the Nationalists to achieve a majority in the Reichstag. To free himself of parliamentary restraint, Hitler prevailed upon the newly convened Reichstag to pass the Enabling Act on March 23. It transferred full legislative and executive powers to the cabinet for four years, allowing Hitler to rule by decree. With its adoption, parliamentary democracy had been destroyed by essentially legal means. The ministerial cabinet rarely met after 1934, and the Reichstag was reduced to a one-party parliament that was periodically convened until 1942 to provide a stage for Hitler's programmatic pronouncements.

Through a policy of *Gleichschaltung* (ideological coordination), the Nazi leader proceeded to bring state governments, bureaucracies, trade unions, and political parties into line with the National Socialist regime. *Reichsstatthalter*, or Reich state governors, were centrally appointed and also served as *Gauleiter*, or regional party leaders, placed directly under Hitler in the latter capacity. They could issue laws on their own. The civil service was purged of democrats, liberals, and especially Jews, and positions were filled with Nazis. Trade unions were dissolved and replaced by the Labor Front, which included all working Germans. The Communist Party was banned in March, and the Social Democrats were banned in June. The Nationalists, the Liberal parties, and the Catholic Center Party voluntarily disbanded several weeks later, leaving the Nazis as the only political party in Germany.

The regime succeeded in gaining control of the state and political instruments of power but faced a more arduous task with the military, whose leadership tried to preserve the army's autonomy. Many high officers viewed with suspicion the party's paramilitary force, the SA (*Sturmabteilungen* or Storm Troopers), who pressed for more reforms of social and state institutions. Army leaders were especially troubled by the aspiration of the SA Chief Ernst Röhm to turn his 2.5 million SA troops into a new people's army, which would eventually absorb the *Reichswehr* (name of the Reich Armed Forces until 1935, when they were renamed *Wehrmacht*). Hitler was not in sympathy with Röhm's radical reform ideas and understood the importance of the regular army to his plan for German rearmament and war. Hindenburg, who was tied to the military, also brusquely demanded that Hitler deal with the Röhm challenge.

To appease the army leadership and eliminate a dangerous rival, Hitler carried out a murderous purge of the SA chief of staff and his associates during the "Night of the Long Knives" in late June 1934 with the help of the elitist SS (*Schutzstaffel* or Protection Squad), led by Heinrich Himmler. Through his action he assured the German army that it would remain the nation's sole bearer of arms. He also gained the generals' acquiescence in combining the offices of the Reich presidency and chancellorship when Hindenburg died in August 1934. Hitler assumed the title of *"Führer und Reichskanzler,"* and from that time, soldiers swore their oath of allegiance not to the state or constitution but to Adolf Hitler. However, it was only in early 1938 that the Nazi dictator gained direct control of the military by taking over for himself the supreme command of the *Wehrmacht.*

The Third Reich exemplified a Nazi *Führerstaat*, which was a complex one-man dictatorship over state administration, army, big business, and industry. It was a system of competing centers of power, often ill-defined chains of command, and rivaling authorities, requiring either by design or default the frequent intervention of the dictator.

In the Hitler regime, the party or its affiliated organizations, such as the elite SS—which carried out police, state security, intelligence, and in World War II also military functions—commanded a prominent and powerful place. The feared Gestapo, or secret police, and the concentration camps were all under the aegis of the SS. Under the leadership of Heinrich Himmler and his lieutenant Reinhard Heydrich, the SS, with its many formations, became a veritable state in itself and, in many ways, became synonymous with the National Socialist system.

Hitler's rule did not sustain itself by achieving control of the instruments of government, force, and terror alone. It also strove to gain control over the minds of the people. A major objective was to realize a national consensus and community in which every member of the society internalized the aims of Nazi ideology. Liberal, democratic, and socialist intellectuals and political opponents were silenced in Germany through censorship, enforced outer or inner emigration, persecution, or confinement to concentration camps. Newspapers, publications, radio, and films were controlled by the Reich Ministry for Public Enlightenment and Propaganda under Joseph Paul Goebbels, who tried to keep the German populace attuned to Nazi aims and psychologically receptive to the regime's messages. Nazi organizations encompassing most members of the society, from youth, workers, and professionals to women, were to expose as many people as possible to the ideas of the regime.

From the beginning of National Socialism, the Jews were singled out as the racial enemies of the Aryan Germanic race. Hitler's periodic anti-Semitic tirades, sometimes subdued for tactical reasons, set the climate for anti-Jewish actions after the Nazi takeover. The overall object of these actions between 1933 and 1938 was to force Germany's Jews to leave the country. Although Goebbels instigated a short-lived boycott of Jewish businesses on April 1, 1933, more far-reaching was the removal of the Jews, as non-Aryans, from civil service, university positions, cultural entertainment, and journalism that soon followed. At the Nürnberg party rally in 1935, Hitler announced the notorious Nürnberg Laws, which forbade marriages and sexual encounters between Germans and Jews and deprived Jews of their German citizenship. In the years that followed, Jews were progressively barred from universities, schools, restaurants, hospitals, and most public facilities. Starting in 1938, Jewish businesses were taken from their owners through systematic "Aryanization" by the Nazi authorities. There was no significant protest from the German population against any of these actions. In fact, many Germans approved the separation of the Jews from the society and the economy. On November 9–10, 1938, known as the *Reichskristallnacht* (Night of the Shattered Glass), Goebbels instigated massive violence, with the acquiescence of Hitler, against large numbers of Jews. Nonlocal SA men in and out of uniform, members of the SS, and other Nazi activists set fire to or destroyed close to 200 synagogues and wrecked over 8,500 Jewish businesses and private dwellings. More than 90 Jews were killed and close to 30,000 Jewish men were thrown into concentration camps. Though many Germans regretted the wanton destruction of property at the time of the 1938 pogrom, they kept their disgust private. Only a few isolated church pastors and priests spoke out in public protest. This horrid event was the prelude to the eventual deportation of German and other European Jews into eastern European ghettoes and their murder that began during World War II in 1940.

While Germans turned their backs on the Jews, Hitler enjoyed remarkable popularity among the great majority of the German people, lasting until the middle years of the war. Nazi propaganda furbished his image as a heroic leader who would reawaken Germany and restore the nation's greatness. This Hitler myth was magnified by Goebbels's proficiently guided political and cultural activities that aimed to generate a national consensus based on Hitler's idea of *Volksgemeinschaft* or national community. Periodic Nazi memorial days with mass parades, political documentaries like *Triumph of the Will,* and annual party rallies at Nürnberg celebrated the grandeur of the awakened nation and the community that united all ranks and social classes.

However, Hitler's popularity was not based on dramatic mass mobilization alone; he was given credit for the success of many state policies. It seemed that every social group benefited in some way from National Socialist measures or programs. Job creation programs like the construction of bridges, canals, public buildings, and four-lane superhighways, the famous *Autobahnen,* impressed blue-collar workers and gave many of them jobs at last. Expanding industrial production and intensified rearmament also reduced unemployment, as did especially the voluntary and then compulsory half-year labor service for males between 18 and 24 and the military conscription starting in 1935. The number of unemployed fell from 6.2 million in 1932 to 4.5 million by the end of 1933, 2.6 million in 1934, and 1 million in 1936. By 1939, there was a shortage of labor. In the eyes of much of the public, Hitler's success in wiping out unemployment was his most notable socioeconomic achievement. There was also some improvement in workers' benefits, including vacations. The Nazi Strength Through Joy recreation program, an arm of the Labor Front that offered events from concerts to sports and featured short trips and package tours, became especially popular. Big department stores were required to pay higher taxes, easing the competition for some retail merchants. Farmers benefited from protective tariffs, domestic price supports, and protection against foreclosures. Industrialists no longer had to contend with workers' participation in decision making and with labor unions over wages. The increasing number of government contracts, particularly in the armaments industry, assured them of order and prosperity.

The approval of the Hitler regime by the majority of Germans was further bolstered by the Führer's successes in economic policies and especially in foreign affairs. But the broad public failed to understand the implications of Hitler's economic policies and their relation to his plans for war. Only a few days after his appointment to the chancellorship, he stated in complete candor at a meeting of high-level military commanders that his policy would be "conquest of new *Lebensraum* (living space) in the East and its ruthless Germanization."

Hitler realized that Germany's recovery from the Depression was a prerequisite for the achievement of a strong economic base and rearmament. He enacted pragmatic policies that poured larger and larger funds into public works projects. Subsidies were granted to private construction firms to renovate old buildings and construct new housing. There were tax breaks for industrial expansion. Rearmament began in earnest in 1934 when the military budget grew to 4.1 billion *Reichmarks;* by 1939, it had ballooned to 30 billion *Reichmarks.* Both the economic recovery program and the rearmament required massive deficit spending, which quite soon created a very unfavorable balance of payments because of lack of foreign exchange for raw material imports to support rearmament. Greater state control was imposed, and in 1936, the Four Year Plan was instituted in order to enhance Germany's economic self-sufficiency, or autarky. Hitler declared that the German army must be ready for war in four years, and he intended to solve most of Germany's economic problems by conquest.

Many scholars believe that Nazi foreign policy objectives were outlined in Hitler's *Mein Kampf* in the 1920s. They called for the destruction of the Versailles settlement, the conquest and colonization of Eastern Europe for German *Lebensraum,* and the domination and exploitation of racial inferiors. In the implementation, however, Hitler demonstrated singular opportunism in the means and timing of his actions and remarkable skill in exploiting the weaknesses of the democracies. In October 1933, he took advantage of Anglo-French differences and walked out of the disarmament conference and the League of Nations, all the while professing his desire for peace. By concluding a 10-year nonaggression pact with Poland, one of Germany's traditional adversaries, in early 1934, Hitler surprised the world and caused a major breach in the French alliance system in Eastern Europe. His effort to reach an alliance with Britain starting in 1933 resulted only in a naval convention in June 1935, limiting the German navy to 35 percent of the Royal Navy. However, France was outraged for only several months earlier it, together with Britain and Italy, had protested Hitler's announcement of German military conscription and rearmament in violation of the Treaty of Versailles.

In March 1936, against the advice of his military leaders, the emboldened Nazi dictator remilitarized the Rhineland in violation of several postwar treaties. But France, lacking the support of Britain, took no effective military countermeasures, and Hitler scored an impressive victory. He came away convinced that France and Britain were weak nations unwilling to defend the old order. Now Italy aligned with Germany, forming the Rome-Berlin Axis. All of these successes raised the prestige of the Nazi leader and the Reich at home and abroad, and Hitler announced that Germany was again a major European power, in fact, even a world power. As he became ever more confident, his speeches in 1937 took on a more bellicose tone. In November he convened a secret conference of his military and diplomatic chiefs and outlined plans for conquest of "living space" in Eastern Europe to be accomplished by 1943–45 and the annexation of Austria and Czechoslovakia even earlier. Most historians agree that the ideas that Hitler developed did not constitute a ready-made blueprint for Nazi aggression but gave him the chance to test his ideas on some of his military and diplomatic leaders and impress upon them the urgency of war preparation. When several of them raised grave reservations about the diplomatic and military risks of his plans, Hitler soon removed the doubters and replaced them with pliable subordinates. In the engineered reshuffling of the military leadership, the Führer assumed supreme command of the *Wehrmacht*.

In March 1938, Hitler's army marched into Austria, while Britain and France offered little but platitudes of objection. Italy, too, stood aside. The majority of Germans and Austrians greeted the annexation of Austria with jubilation, seeing the nineteenth-century liberal dream of a Greater German Reich fulfilled. Only a minority of Austrian Jews, liberals, committed Catholics, and socialists who were rounded up and arrested experienced the nightmare of this reality. With Germany's strategic position in central Europe improved by the *Anschluss,* or union with Austria, Hitler now eyed the economic resources of Czechoslovakia and demanded the Sudetenland, a largely German-speaking border region. War was averted at the last moment by the hastily convened Munich Conference in September

1938. Its participants, Germany, Italy, Britain, and France, forced Czecho-slovakia to cede the Sudeten territory to Germany.

After Munich, Hitler was convinced he could redraw the boundaries of Eastern Europe without British or French interference. In March 1939, his troops occupied the rump Czechoslovak state, and he began to press Poland for concessions on Danzig and the Polish Corridor. The Polish government refused. The British prime minister Neville Chamberlain, after years of appeasement, at last denounced Hitler for breaking his word, and Britain, backed by France, now guaranteed the territorial integrity of Poland. Chamberlain also attempted to revive the old pre–World War I British-Russian *entente*. Hitler hoped to isolate Poland, but if he failed, he was prepared to risk fighting Britain and France. The key to the coming conflict lay in Moscow where, in the summer of 1939, both the Western powers and Germany competed to negotiate an agree-ment with the Soviet Union. Somewhat reluctantly, Hitler and Stalin car-ried on secret negotiations for weeks. On August 23, the world was stunned when the Nazi-Soviet Nonaggression Pact was announced. In a secret protocol Hitler and Stalin divided Eastern Europe into two spheres of interest.

On September 1, 1939, the German armies attacked Poland, and 17 days later, the Red Army crossed the Polish border to claim its share of the Pol-ish and Eastern European spoils. Contrary to Hitler's expectations, Britain and France did not shrink back but declared war instead. The Führer intentionally unleashed World War II by his desire for conquest. Stalin's complicity facilitated Hitler's invasion of Poland and the failure of the Western powers to resist German aggression earlier gave him the confi-dence to proceed with his plan for war.

The German armies used *Blitzkrieg* (lightning war) strategy to defeat the Polish armies in less than five weeks. After a six-month interlude of qui-etude broken only by occasional skirmishes on the French-German border, Nazi forces occupied Denmark and Norway in April 1940 in anticipation of British and French plans to send troops to their defense. In the follow-ing month, German armies launched a massive strike against the Low Countries and France and achieved a triumphal victory that seemed to confirm the remarkable success of Hitler's strategy. This victorious cam-paign placed the German dictator at the peak of his popularity in Ger-many and silenced opposition within the echelons of the officer corps. He now expected Britain to make peace but was surprised when British heroic resistance in the air Battle of Britain in the summer of 1940 resulted in a strategic deadlock.

Rather than subduing Britain, Hitler made the most crucial mistake of his career in launching an invasion of the Soviet Union in June 1941. True, the obliteration of Jewish Bolshevism and conquest of *Lebensraum* in Russia were his cardinal goals, but by moving east before defeating Britain, he plunged Germany into a two-front war that it could not win. The hitherto successful *Blitzkrieg* strategy failed miserably in the Soviet Union despite enormous Soviet losses at the outset of the German invasion. It ground to a halt in the wintry snow and ice before the gates of Moscow. A newly launched offensive in the spring of 1942 extended German lines far into the Soviet interior to the heights of the Caucasus mountains, but by early 1943, after the German defeat at the Battle of Stalingrad, the tide turned inexorably against Germany. When Japan attacked Pearl Harbor in early December 1941, the European war became a world war. Hitler quickly declared war on the United States, expecting Japan to keep the United States from helping Britain in the west and giving him a free hand against Russia. This miscalculation was only matched by Hitler's delusion of German global supremacy at this time.

Between 1941 and 1944, most of Europe was under the harsh rule of the *Wehrmacht* and the SS, and its human and material resources were relentlessly exploited for the German war effort. Germany annexed some conquered areas outright; other lands were treated as occupied areas or satellite or client states. In Western Europe, military occupation generally followed a traditional pattern, although the Gestapo committed brutal acts against civilians while pursuing partisans and rounding up Jews and Gypsies. In contrast, Poland and most of Eastern Europe experienced the full brunt of racist ideology. The Polish elites were either killed or confined to concentration camps. Many hundreds of thousands of Polish civilians and Jews were deported from their homes to make room for ethnic Germans from Eastern Europe. Millions of Soviet civilians and other eastern Europeans were conscripted and brought to Germany, where foreign labor (some voluntary but chiefly forced) from various European countries exceeded 7 million. Two-thirds of the 5.7 million Russian prisoners of war captured by the Germans perished in camps under ghastly conditions.

For Germans on the home front, these war years did not bring hunger as had happened in World War I. Until 1944, no serious food shortages developed since the resources of occupied countries were available to be plundered for German needs. Under the pressure of the war, the political influence of the Nazi party and the SS increased significantly. Public life became more militarized, increasing the organization of the formerly private sphere and bringing more social leveling. Rationing enabled the government to exploit envy and class differences by appealing to the solidarity within the "community of people." Party and state organizations came to include virtually every citizen with block wardens watching neighborhoods; neighbors were encouraged to spy on one another. The Gestapo relied heavily on anonymous denunciations. With the onset of Allied air raids, more and more people were forced to spend time together in bomb shelters. The Allied aim to break German morale by intensified bombing of civilians failed badly. Germans grimly faced the destruction of cities and loss of human lives in air raids by seeking ways to survive. These experiences tended to wear down class distinctions as millions of people tried to cope with the increasingly harsh conditions, while also listening to the same radio slogans, standing in line for rationed goods, and taking in the often uninspiring entertainment offered on the radio and in movie theaters for distraction. Nevertheless, morale remained high and support of the Hitler regime continued among civilians even though hopes for German victory were fading.

Apart from conquering *Lebensraum*, the Hitler regime concentrated during the war on the elimination of the Jews of Europe. As early as January 30, 1939, Hitler prophesied in the Reichstag that a world war would bring "the annihilation of the Jewish race in Europe." He believed that the Aryan race could not establish a lasting empire without the elimination of the divisive and corrupting influence of its age-old adversary, the Jews. The harsh persecution of Jews in prewar Germany gave way to the extermination of European Jews under Hitler's "Final Solution" during the war.

The Nazi New Order in Europe comprised an empire of concentration camps under Heinrich Himmler and, after 1941, death camps in Poland as well. As late as 1940, Nazi plans included the establishment of a super ghetto for Jews somewhere in Eastern Europe or as far away as the French island of Madagascar. As German armies advanced into the Soviet Union in 1941, summary executions of hundreds of thousands of Jews were carried out, largely by mass machine-gunning. Sometime in the summer or fall Hitler opted for the Final Solution, or physical destruction of European Jewry. By the end of 1941, Himmler and his associates extended the procedure of gassing the mentally impaired and physically disabled in the euthanasia program that began in 1939 to the mass killing of Jews. Large gas chambers were installed at six major death camps in late 1941 and in 1942; the largest and best known of these was Auschwitz-Birkenau. Mechanized racial genocide claimed the lives of close to 6 million Jews. In addition, millions of Gypsies, Slavs, and others perished as victims of Nazi political and racial persecution.

Even though the mass murder industry operated in secret, there were too many government agencies, organizations, and departments that participated in it for the existence of the extermination program not to become a matter of public knowledge within Germany. But habitual defense mechanisms, fallacious justifications, and the preoccupation of the people with war conditions that affected them immediately proved stronger than consciousness of guilt and revulsion.

Even though the regime felt threatened from within as well as from without, there was never any staunch unified resistance against National Socialist rule. The original resistance groups were centered in the remnants of the political parties, especially socialist and communist, during much of the 1930s. By 1938, a group of army officers formed a somewhat loosely organized resistance movement that lasted until the fateful assassination attempt of July 1944. It was this core of military officers that drew civilians and political leaders into its network and maintained a resistance organization that illegal political parties, labor unions, or existing but weak church organizations could not provide.

Although Hitler made every effort to beat the army leadership into submission, he was not able to gain total control over all segments of the officer corps, many of whom were conservative, aristocratic in origin and mindful of the Prussian military tradition in their attitude toward the state. They joined with several high-ranking civilian officials who were motivated by conservative ethical principles, Christian morals, and patriotic concerns for Germany. Several actions that they planned before the war to carry out a coup d'état against Hitler came to naught in the face of Hitler's diplomatic triumphs. Once the war broke out and Hitler was successful, any action against him would be viewed by the German people as treason. Few military leaders were willing to act. When the fortunes of war turned against Hitler, several attempts on his life were planned, but all of them either miscarried or had to be aborted. Meanwhile, the resisters lost all credibility in the eyes of the Allies. In the end, the leaders of the opposition, after several of them had been arrested, were ready to pay any price that might be exacted from taking action against Hitler and his regime and to proceed not out of expediency but on ethical grounds to demonstrate that "in the eyes of the world and of history the German resistance movement has dared to risk the decisive blow." The attempted assassination on July 20, 1944 failed, and the Hitler regime took frightful vengeance on the conspirators and on many of their families who had known nothing of the plot.

Prior to the assassination attempt, the Normandy invasion of June 1944 set the stage for the Allied liberation of France and the Low Countries and the conquest of Germany. While the Allies were forging ahead in France, the Soviets were advancing into Eastern Europe. They penetrated Germany and stood less than 50 miles from the outskirts of Berlin by the end of January 1945. Hitler was determined to fight to the bitter end, even if it brought the annihilation of Germany. According to his lunatic reasoning, if the German people were defeated, they had shown themselves weaker than their enemies and therefore did not deserve to exist. In March 1945, he gave an order to destroy all German resources and to leave Germany a wasteland for the Americans, British, and Russians. Fortunately, many courageous mayors and military commanders, several of whom were executed for disobedience, did not carry out Hitler's insane directive. Seven days after the Führer's suicide in his Berlin bunker, the war in Europe ended with the unconditional surrender of the *Wehrmacht* leadership to the Western Allies at Reims on May 7 and at a repeat ceremony in Berlin on May 9 that included the Russians.

The immediate legacy of the Hitler regime was millions of dead and even more maimed, displaced populations, widespread destruction of cities, and Germany divided into four military zones of occupation by the victorious powers. The eastern German territories were annexed by Poland and the Soviet Union and placed under communist regimes that lasted until the end of the 1980s. Until then the division of Germany into a Marxist-Leninist people's republic and a liberal, democratic, capitalist state accentuated the deep political and economic division of Europe. During the last few decades, but especially after the reunification of Germany and the collapse of communism, some historians have emphasized continuities in the development of Germany that carry over from Nazi Germany. They point out that the foundations for the robust car industry in West Germany date back to the Third Reich. Similarly, the massive Nazi rearmament program indirectly made possible the West German economic miracle of the 1950s. The war production peaked in 1943–44, and despite destruction and postwar dismantling, many elements survived and contributed to the later recovery. Socially, class differentiation lessened during the Third Reich as a result of Nazi policies and actions. Egalitarian ideas and attitudes without the antidemocratic and racial aims of the Nazis are reflected in the absence of distinction between workers and salaried employees in today's Germany. Also, the German Labor Front helped bring about the modernization of leisure by introducing mass tourism for the working class. Such a perspective on the Third Reich has only become possible due to lengthening historical distance and the realization that this harrowing 12-year period needs to be assessed in the evolutionary flow of twentieth-century German history, rather than be seen as a singular phenomenon confined to a limited era in the German experience.

SELECTED BIBLIOGRAPHY

Allen, William S. *The Nazi Seizure of Power: The Experience of a Single Town 1922–1945.* Rev. ed. New York: Franklin Watts, 1984. Classic study of the takeover of a town by the Nazis and their impact on the community.

Beck, Earl R. *Under the Bombs: The German Home Front, 1942–1945.* Lexington: University of Kentucky Press, 1986. Examines the Allied bombing campaign and its impact on the German populace.

Bessel, Richard, ed. *Life in the Third Reich.* New York: Oxford University Press, 1987. Very well informed short accounts of various social aspects of life in Nazi Germany by British, German, and American historians.

Bracher, Karl Dietrich. *The German Dictatorship: The Origins, Structure, and Effects of National Socialism.* Translated by Jean Steinberg. New York: Praeger, 1970. The best scholarly account of the Nazi regime by a distinguished German political scientist.

Broszat, Martin. *The Hitler State: The Foundation and Development of the Internal Structure of the Third Reich.* London and New York: Longman, 1981. Detailed study of the structure and organization of the Nazi state.

Bullock, Alan. *Hitler: A Study in Tyranny.* Rev. ed. New York: Harper & Row, 1964. The best early scholarly account of Hitler as a man and historical actor.

Burleigh, Michael. *The Third Reich: A New History.* New York: Hill & Wang, 2000. A comprehensive recent history of the Nazi regime that emphasizes its criminality.

Fest, Joachim C. *The Face of the Third Reich: Portraits of the Nazi Leadership.* Translated by Michael Bullock. New York: Pantheon, 1977. Good, short biographies of the leading personalities of the Hitler regime.

Fleming, Gerald. *Hitler and the Final Solution.* Berkeley: University of California Press, 1984. Elucidates Hitler's role in instigating the destruction of the European Jews.

Frei, Norbert. *National Socialist Rule in Germany: The Führer State, 1933–1945.* Translated by Simon B. Steyne. Oxford: Blackwell, 1993. Short, stimulating study of the Nazi regime and excellent complement to the Broszat volume.

Gellately, Robert. *The Gestapo and German Society: Enforcing Racial Policy, 1933–1945.* New York: Oxford University Press, 1990. Provides insight into how consensus and coercion served the secret police in its effort to control German society.

Grunberger, Richard. *The 12-Year Reich: A Social History of Nazi Germany, 1933–1945.* New York: Ballantine Books, 1971. A well-informed account of what it was like to live in Germany under Hitler.

Haffner, Sebastian. *The Meaning of Hitler.* Translated by Ewald Osers. Cambridge, MA: Harvard University Press, 1983. Thought-provoking account that attempts to assess the historical significance of Hitler.

Kershaw, Ian. *Hitler.* New York: Longman, 1991. Excellent short account of how Hitler acquired, maintained, and expanded his power.

————. *Hitler, 1889–1945*. 2 vols. New York: Norton, 1999–2000. The most detailed and best new biography of Hitler.

Leitz, Christian, ed. *The Third Reich: Essential Readings*. Oxford: Blackwell, 1999. Interpretive essays by leading historians on important aspects of the Nazi regime.

Noakes, Jeremy, and Geoffrey Pridham, eds. *Nazism, 1919–1945: A History in Documents and Eyewitness Accounts*. 2 vols. New York: Schocken Books, 1990. An excellent compendium of contemporary sources on a broad array of aspects of the Third Reich with informed and connecting comments.

Peukert, Detlev J. K. *Inside Nazi Germany: Conformity, Opposition, and Racism in Everyday Life*. Translated by Richard Deveson. New Haven, CT: Yale University Press, 1982. Excellent account of what life was like in the Third Reich.

Schoenbaum, David. *Hitler's Social Revolution: Class and Status in Nazi Germany, 1933–1939*. Garden City, NY: Doubleday, 1966. Argues that Hitler's regime transformed German ideas of class and society.

Speer, Albert. *Inside the Third Reich*. Translated by Richard and Clara Winston. New York: Avon Books, 1971. Memoirs of Hitler's architect and later armaments and munitions minister who was the only defendant at the Nuremberg Trial that showed some contrition for his part in the Nazi regime.

8 ———————————————————————

World War II, 1939–1945

INTRODUCTION

Early on the morning of September 1, 1939, units of the *Wehrmacht*, Nazi Germany's army, launched an attack on Poland, Germany's eastern neighbor. The onset of war surprised no one; armed conflict had long been anticipated. Moreover, unlike World War I, Europe did not accidentally slide into war; rather, most observers—with a few notable exceptions—view World War II as the logical consequence of German dictator Adolf Hitler's belligerency.

Well before he came to power on January 30, 1933, Hitler had formulated a foreign policy that boiled down to two major points. The first of these called for the destruction of the Treaty of Versailles, a goal that enjoyed universal support among the Germans who despised the World War I settlement. The second, which eventually became enshrined as the goal of *Lebensraum*, or "living space" for a growing German nation, envisioned a substantial expansion of Germany's borders. Since *Lebensraum* could be accomplished only through war (normally, countries do not voluntarily surrender territory to another country) and the German people were not anxious to shed blood so soon after the close of the murderous World War I, Hitler soft-pedaled this goal until he had created an omnipotent dictatorship that could not only ignore public opinion, but also crush any signs of opposition.

Hitler's first significant move on the international scene occurred in late 1933 when he withdrew Germany from the League of Nations, the international body established in the wake of World War I to maintain peace. Two years later he repudiated the clauses of the Treaty of Versailles that

A forlorn angel overlooks firebombed Dresden in February 1945. World War II demolished Hitler's Third Reich and destroyed numerous German towns and cities. At the conclusion of the war, Germany was occupied and subsequently divided. (Reproduced from the Collections of the Library of Congress.)

limited the size of the German military and openly began to rearm Germany at a furious pace. Buoyed by these successes, Hitler next took a bold step in March 1936, when he remilitarized the Rhineland. According to the Treaty of Versailles, Germany was forbidden to station any troops west of the Rhine River or in a 30-mile wide demilitarized zone along that river's eastern bank. The German dictator now denounced these clauses and moved his army to Germany's borders with France, Belgium, and Luxembourg. In the same year Germany also intervened in the Spanish Civil War on the side of Francisco Franco's fascist forces. Finally, in March 1938, Hitler carried out the *Anschluss*, or the absorption of Austria into Germany, in direct violation of the Treaty of Versailles.

In response to Hitler's disruptive actions, the Western powers—Great Britain and France—followed a policy of appeasement. Basically, appeasement called for the British and the French to give the bully (Hitler) what he wanted in the hopes that he would go away and leave them alone. The Czechoslovak crisis of 1938 graphically demonstrated how appeasement worked. Seizing on the fact that a German minority lived within the boundaries of the Czechoslovak state that had been created at the end of World War I, Hitler demanded a change in borders in order to bring many of these Germans (and not a few Czechs) into his Third Reich. Such a change would have made the Czechoslovak rump little more than a German satellite. Czechoslovakian resistance to Germany's outrageous demands rested on its defensive alliance with France and the belief that Great Britain would also lend its support. When Hitler threatened war over the issue, the Western powers panicked. At the subsequent Munich Conference in September 1938, Great Britain and France forced Czechoslovakia to accept Hitler's demands in the name of "peace in our time." Six months later Hitler demonstrated his trustworthiness when he devoured what was left of Czechoslovakia.

The demise of Czechoslovakia severely undermined faith in appeasement, and when Hitler began to menace Poland, Great Britain joined France in guaranteeing that country's independence. As the Polish crisis deepened in the summer of 1939, a startling shift in the balance of power occurred. From the beginning, Hitler had targeted Soviet Russia as Nazi Germany's number one enemy. The USSR reciprocated this animosity. Thus, one can imagine the world's astonishment in August 1939 when it learned that these two mortal enemies had signed a nonaggression pact stating that each party would remain neutral in the case of the other party going to war. The pact also contained secret clauses that called for the Nazis and Soviets to divide a conquered Poland and to split the remainder of east Central Europe into two spheres of influence. By virtue of the Nazi-

Soviet Nonaggression Pact, Hitler's Germany could now move to destroy Poland with the knowledge that unlike World War I, it would not have to fight on two fronts.

In launching their strike against Poland, Hitler and his generals employed a new grand tactic designed to forestall any repeat of the stalemated trench warfare that so debilitated Germany in World War I. During the interwar years, the German army's general staff had developed the concept known as *Blitzkrieg*, or lightning war. *Blitzkrieg* called for an army to mass overwhelming firepower and mobility against a single point in the enemy's defensive line. Using mechanized armor units, the army would punch a huge hole in the enemy's defenses and race to the rear where it would spread out and destroy the enemy's lines of communication. In the meantime, mechanized infantry would flood through the hole and pounce on the enemy from the rear and the flanks. To aid these movements, the air force would pound the enemy's cities and command centers. The desired result would be massive chaos that would lead to rapid collapse. Tanks and heavy bombers were key to *Blitzkrieg*'s success.

In the campaign against Poland, *Blitzkrieg* worked so successfully that within a few weeks Poland ceased to exist. Of course, its demise was hastened when on September 17 Soviet Russia joined its Nazi allies in attacking the hapless Poles. Great Britain and France declared war on Germany on September 3, but neither went on the offensive; rather, they assumed a defensive posture as they anticipated a repeat of World War I's trench warfare.

After vanquishing Poland, Germany's forces retired until the following spring. Germany ended this *Sitzkrieg*, or phony war, when it seized first Denmark and then Norway. These conquests were the prelude to the main event, the Nazi invasion of the Low Countries (Belgium, Luxembourg, and Holland) and France. That campaign opened on May 10 and proved to be as successful as the previous autumn's campaign against Poland. Once again *Blitzkrieg* carried the day, although one should note that the woeful condition of the French army (especially its commanders) and the puniness of Great Britain's expeditionary forces played no small role in Hitler's success. On June 22, 1940, France surrendered; earlier in the month Great Britain had managed to retrieve most of its soldiers (but not their equipment) and 120,000 French stragglers from the beaches at Dunkirk in a chaotic cross-Channel rescue operation. Hitler now ruled supreme in Europe. With the exception of Great Britain, every European country was either occupied by Germany, allied to Germany, or benevolently neutral.

Hitler now turned his attention to Great Britain. Unwilling to risk an amphibious invasion for which Germany was not prepared, Hitler tried to bomb Great Britain into submission. Beginning in July and continuing for several months, the Battle of Britain raged. Bolstered by its new prime minister, Winston Churchill, and taking advantage of superior aircraft production, intelligence, and technology (radar), Britain weathered the storm. Although this was the first instance of Germany failing to attain its objective, Hitler seemed unconcerned. Instead, he concentrated Germany's energies on a goal near and dear to his heart—the conquest of Russia.

Dubbed Operation Barbarossa, Hitler's plan to attack his unsuspecting ally took shape during early 1941. On June 22, Hitler unleashed an awesome *Blitzkrieg* against the Soviet Union. By early December, German armies were at the gates of Moscow and Leningrad, Germany ruled the Ukraine, and millions of Soviet troops had been killed and millions more had been captured. However, the war had reached a turning point. Soviet resistance stiffened, and Germany failed to take Moscow. Furthermore, the German army had outrun its lines of supply. German soldiers, dressed in their summer uniforms, froze to death in their tracks in the face of the coldest December on record. Finally, and perhaps most importantly, in the wake of Japan's attack at Pearl Harbor, Germany declared war on the United States, thereby bringing into the conflict the same country whose unlimited supply of men, money, and materiel had spelled defeat for Germany in World War I. Very quickly, Great Britain, the Soviet Union, and the United States formed the Grand Alliance directed against Germany and its allies.

The nature of the conflict changed radically after December 1941. Henceforth, World War II became a war of attrition, and that being the case, Germany was doomed. The history of World War II from early 1942 until its conclusion in May 1945 shows the Grand Alliance first fighting Germany to a standstill and then slowly but surely grinding Germany's armies (and its cities) into dust. The bulk of the fighting took place on the eastern front. Here massive German armies faced even more massive Soviet armies. The most significant battle occurred at Stalingrad, the industrial city on the Volga River renamed to honor the Soviet dictator. From August 1942 until February 1943, desperate fighting took place amidst the ruined city's frigid rubble. By the close of the battle, the German Sixth Army had been annihilated. The following summer, at the Battle of Kursk, the Soviets crushed the German armored corps, the famous Panzers. At the same time, in North Africa and Italy the British and Americans were defeating both the Germans and their Italian allies.

Within Germany itself, Hitler's initial victories were greeted with satisfaction if not wild enthusiasm. In order to maintain a high level of morale, the Nazis consciously decided to keep the German economy on a civilian (consumer) foundation for as long as possible. Moreover, Joseph Paul Goebbels, Hitler's minister of popular enlightenment and propaganda, organized a steady stream of favorable propaganda. However, when the military tide turned, the German people found themselves in a hopeless and helpless position. Albert Speer, the minister for armaments and munitions, instituted a war economy, and German war production actually peaked as late as September 1944 before plunging precipitously. Meanwhile, the casualty lists grew, Allied bombs rained down, and the Nazi organs of coercion quickly ferreted out and brutally destroyed what little resistance there was to Hitler and the war.

As the defeat of Nazi Germany became inevitable, Hitler and his most devoted followers determined to fight to the last German. In a sort of demonic *Götterdämmerung,* the Nazi leader expressed his belief that Germany's death was preferable to its continued existence as a defeated (and hence, in his mind, inherently inferior) nation. On this score, the Grand Alliance was more than willing to accommodate the German dictator.

With the Red Army methodically moving toward the German heartland, the Western Allies launched a cross-Channel invasion on June 6, 1944, and liberated France in short order. However, this western thrust toward Germany was checked during the December 1944 Battle of the Bulge, and western troops did not cross the Rhine River until March 1945. By that time, the Soviets had drawn close to Berlin's suburbs. The end of Hitler, the Nazis, and the Third Reich itself came during April and May 1945. As American and British forces swept eastward through Germany, the Soviets attacked the enemy capital. On April 30, 1945, Adolf Hitler committed suicide in the ruins of Berlin. On May 7, German forces in the west surrendered to U.S. general Dwight D. Eisenhower; one day later, representatives of the German high command surrendered to Soviet general Georgii Zhukov.

The last stages of the war confirmed horrific rumors that had surfaced concerning the fate of Europe's Jews who had fallen into Nazi hands. Place names like Auschwitz, Treblinka, Majdanek, Sobibor, and several more entered every western nation's vocabulary as sites of Nazi death camps. Even before the outbreak of war, Hitler's anti-Semitism had been venomous; with a large percentage of European Jewry under his control, Hitler took even more drastic steps. Setting up a series of concentration camps on the soil of conquered states, especially Poland, Hitler and his Nazi henchmen combined energetic efficiency and modern technology with their maniacal anti-Semitism to murder as many Jews as they could. This nadir of human history, the Holocaust, took the lives of approximately 6 million Jews. Perhaps an equal number of innocents such as the mentally retarded, the aged, homosexuals, prisoners of war, intellectuals, and common, ordinary men, women, and children died at the hands of the Nazis during World War II.

INTERPRETIVE ESSAY
Martin Berger

Germany initiated World War II by invading Poland on September 1, 1939. Britain and France had promised support for Poland, in the hope of deterring German aggression, and the two Western democracies declared war on Germany on September 3. It was clear that Britain and France went to war most reluctantly; they did nothing to aid Poland and carried out little activity of any kind until the Germans attacked them with devastating effectiveness in May 1940. It was less clear that Hitler's Germany, a militarized state whose economy and society were supposedly "coordinated" (*gleichgeschaltet*) into a single-minded, irresistible national purpose, was not entirely ready either. Total war, which Nazis had hailed as the ultimate test for nations and races, would demolish the Third Reich, leaving ruin and rubble from which new and quite different German societies would emerge.

Victories came quick and cheap; in the first stage of the war, the often-repeated line of the official weekly newsreel film was true: "Germany is victorious on all fronts!" Poland's hard-fought defense was hopeless against the larger and more modern German forces; German transport planes were able to circle above Warsaw's flames as crewmen shoveled incendiary bombs out the aircraft doors. Britain and France did nothing to aid the Poles, and the Soviet Union helped to finish Polish resistance as its troops moved in to occupy the Polish territories promised in the Nazi-Soviet Nonaggression Pact of 1939. In the north, Norway and Denmark fell quickly, and in May 1940, the Germans ended the *Sitzkrieg* ("sitting war") in the west, overrunning France, the Netherlands, and Belgium in a stunning seven-week campaign, expelling British forces from the Continent.

The conquest of western Europe was merely the introduction to the grander conquest that Hitler had been proclaiming for years: free from distractions in the west, he could move east to destroy "Jewish Bolshevism," gain "living space" for an expanded Germanic population, and acquire the vast material resources of the Soviet Union. Germany would become the greatest power on the globe. What were the chances for this vastly ambitious plan to succeed?

Propaganda created an image of a German military machine irresistibly superior in military technology. In fact, German military hardware was not always superior. In the French campaign the numbers of aircraft were fairly close, and the Western Allies had more tanks than the Germans. Most German troops traveled by train, horse, and foot. Planning and leadership favored the Germans, and their innovative "lightning war" (*Blitzkrieg*) concentrated armor and air strength against enemy weak points. Hitler's own intervention favored boldness over caution, and everything worked. Germany's successful domination of Europe proved the Führer's genius to him and to others. Later in the war he would be derisively called the *Gröfaz* (abbreviation for "greatest military commander of all time"), but in 1940 even the military professionals were awed. The conquest of western Europe had cost 30,000 German dead—tragic for many families, but a bargain in grand-strategy terms for a goal that had eluded generations of ambitious European rulers. Germany could afford to relax a bit, enjoying Dutch butter and French wine; Germany's obvious superiority over all rivals meant that weapons programs that did not promise a very prompt result could be canceled. The army was to be "de-motorized," increasing reliance on horse transport in order to save on fuel.

The German advantage lay in superior planning, training, and leadership. German armored units slashed ahead, supported by aircraft, moving too quickly for the sluggish Allied forces to respond. The easy, dazzling triumphs in 1939 and 1940 bred overconfidence. When Germany moved to a larger-scale conflict in Russia, where prompt and huge initial victories were insufficient to finish off the enormous Red Army, things turned out differently. When the United States joined the Allies, the balance of resources tilted absurdly against Germany, and the gap in tactical competence eventually closed, leaving German forces no better skilled or better equipped than their adversaries.

Few Germans had been enthusiastic at the war's outbreak (Hitler was bitterly disappointed by the general glumness), but the Führer seemed to be vindicated by the results. High party officials competed in looting art and other treasures from occupied countries; industrialists divided up factories and mines. Even some who disliked Nazi brutality and fretted over Hitler's risky diplomacy took pride in the country's success. Patriotism led many to support their country despite their differences with the Nazis. Martin Niemöller, imprisoned for objecting to Nazi religious policy, wrote from his concentration camp asking to return to submarine duty, as in

World War I. There was full employment, in part because so many workers were now soldiers. Grumbling was largely limited to such issues as the
price that dairy farmers received for their cheese. Any inclination toward
significant opposition was stifled; no one could argue with success.

What the war meant within Germany was an intensification of Nazi
rule. The Third Reich became *more so*. But in some respects, in the short
run, war interfered with Nazi inclinations toward major changes. Thus
Hitler and his propaganda chief Joseph Paul Goebbels reined in local
party officials who had offended churchgoers by taking down crucifixes in
Bavarian schools. After the war, Hitler declared in private conversations
that Christianity would be eradicated; for the time being, it was useful to
have the support of most Protestant and Catholic authorities for war to
defend the country. Even before the invasion of the Soviet Union, the
Nazis had defined their mission to include stamping out atheistic communism. Regular army and navy forces (not the Armed SS) retained their
Christian chaplains.

Plans to reform the army, too, would be deferred until after the war.
Hitler and the army leadership cooperated, but they were divided by their
different concepts of the army's role in society. Hitler's frequent and con-
spicuous public praise of the army served to cover the differences and to
reassure the military leadership. Nazis and the officer corps agreed on the
desirability of enlarging the military and casting off the Treaty of Versailles' ban on tanks, aircraft, and so on, and some officers saw the Nazi
Party as useful in building morale. The army's deep roots in pre-Nazi German history and its pride in that tradition, however, meant that much of
the leadership looked down on the party as an insubstantial and probably
temporary thing. In general, the officer corps had long been conservative
and nationalist but apolitical in that soldiers stayed clear of party politics.
Even common soldiers on active duty did not vote. Hitler's purge of the
SA (Storm Troops, the rowdy brown-shirted street-fighting organization)
and the murder of its leader Ernst Röhm in 1934 had quieted fears that
Hitler would replace the army with the SA. During the war, the Armed SS,
part of the more disciplined black-uniformed Protection Squad, expanded
rapidly (to more than 900,000 by the war's end), but the regime could not
afford to confront the army head-on. Not until after the attempt on
Hitler's life in June 1944, an event that involved many officers, did the
stiff-armed Nazi salute replace the traditional salute in the army.

Other sweeping changes remained dreams, such as the gigantic archi-
tectural and city-planning fantasies that Hitler entertained to the end. Like
the Führer's eventual intention to impose vegetarianism and stamp out
tobacco use and the speculative discussion among some party leaders of

allowing war heroes and party leaders to have multiple wives (the better to breed more superior Germans), these Nazi fantasies could be achieved only after victory, as could ambitious plans for planting forests that some scholars have seen as a green, environmentally conscious thread within Nazism. Some efforts were made toward the scheme of settling much of eastern Europe with racially superior families of hereditary small farmers, reversing the historic trend toward urbanization in favor of the Blood and Soil mystique that had preoccupied much of the German right since the late nineteenth century. The removal of the Slavic occupants from the "living space" or their transformation into laborers serving Germanic colonists would take some time. Only a few agrarian colonists were sent east, and as things turned out, they did not stay long. Indeed, one reason that Hitler was impatient for war in 1939 was his fear that too long a wait might leave him unable to accomplish all his projects in his lifetime.

All these projects were slowed down, deferred, or abandoned. Some of the regime's cherished schemes were sustained at some cost to the war effort, like the campaign to provide the ordinary worker with an affordable automobile. Production of the Porsche-designed People's Car (*Volkswagen*) was abandoned in favor of scout cars and airplane parts after only 210 civilian-style Beetles had been built. Only the massive effort dearest to Hitler's heart and most central to the Third Reich, the murder of Europe's Jews, was carried out to the fullest possible extent, despite its diversion of resources from the war.

Everything had to go right for the Nazis to achieve total victory, and everything did go right for the first year of war. Hitler offered total victory or total disaster. In retrospect, the odds seem so unpromising that scholars have suggested that deep-seated psychological desires for failure and punishment must have motivated Hitler to launch the war, invade the Soviet Union, and risk other bold gambles. At the time, many intelligent people, including highly trained military professionals in Germany and outside, thought that he would succeed.

The German war effort had its first significant setback in the Battle of Britain, which occurred during August and September 1940. It was obvious to almost everyone that Britain was defeated and would have to accept Hitler's generous peace terms: recognize German domination of Europe and keep the British Empire. When Hitler referred to Winston Churchill, the British prime minister, as a warmonger, it was because Churchill refused to be reasonable and persuaded his colleagues to continue the war. To encourage the British to give up, Germany began a bombing campaign intended to destroy British morale or, perhaps, to annihilate the British Royal Air Force so that German air power could protect a German cross-Channel invasion from the large and undefeated British navy. The invasion scheme, Operation Sea Lion, was improvised and iffy. Germany had none of the specialized craft that the Allies later developed for landing on hostile beaches. The plan was to put motors on river barges and to use the powered barges to pull trains of other barges, loaded with troops, horses, and equipment, in a short but exciting trip across the turbulent English Channel, hoping that waves were mild and nothing interfered with the process. The barge-trains could travel at a bit over four miles per hour if all went well. To be sure, if large numbers of Germans survived the crossing, Britain was ill-prepared to resist; more than 300,000 Allied troops had escaped from Dunkirk as France collapsed in June, but they had left most of their equipment and weapons behind. Many Germans worked hard preparing Operation Sea Lion, but everyone clearly hoped that Britain would yield without the invasion.

In 1940, no air force was yet able to do what Hermann Göring had promised. German bombers were twin-engine craft, "medium" bombers in Allied terminology, carrying less payload than the four-engine heavies that would later inflict terrible damage on Germany. Like the Allied bombers, they were vulnerable to fighter attack. Though the Germans quickly learned to send fighters to escort and protect the bombers, their fighters were short-range (like their British opponent's) because bigger fuel tanks would have made the aircraft heavier and less agile. German and British single-seat fighters were nearly equal in numbers at the start of the campaign and very similar in performance. The Germans had an edge in pilot experience, but they fought over enemy territory. A British pilot whose plane was damaged might survive and fight again, but for his downed German opponent the war was over (except for one German fighter pilot who was inadequately guarded and flew a British Hurricane to German-occupied France). As the British built new aircraft with desperate urgency, costly German losses continued, until Hitler called off the invasion preparations. A German decision to target London and other cities is often described as the decisive blunder, but even when the Germans were still concentrating on the Royal Air Force, they were not finishing their task. Britain continued to be bombed but remained in the war.

The British even hung on in North Africa, routing Italian forces. A small German force, led by the dashing Erwin Rommel, drove the British back and threatened to seize British-controlled Egypt. The Germans also transformed the bogged-down Italian invasion of Greece into a decisive victory and overran Yugoslavia. Then, in June 1941, Hitler broke the nonaggression pact with Stalin and launched the titanic struggle for which everything else had been a prelude. Operation Barbarossa, the

German invasion of the Soviet Union, was not only much larger in scale than previous campaigns but a different, more desperate, more total kind of war. In some campaigns, particularly against the British, German forces had generally adhered to the accepted rules of warfare. Russia would be a different story. The "commissar order" proclaimed that Communist morale officers who fell into German hands would be executed. It was made clear that Soviet citizens were regarded as subhuman; brutality against Soviet civilians was not a court-martial offense. German officers' enthusiasm for this departure from regular military practice varied. Many disapproved, and Colonel-General Johannes Blaskowitz objected in writing to SS atrocities, but the army was drawn into brutal activities against civilians and, especially, against the Jews. In North Africa, Rommel could maintain a reputation for sportsmanlike conduct; in Russia, no German officer could stay clean. It has often been pointed out that had the Germans behaved in a civil way toward the Soviet population, they might have been welcomed as liberators by long-suffering people oppressed by the Stalinist regime. This is true, of course. But had they been able to behave decently they would not have been Nazis and would not have been in Russia.

The Soviet army and air force were caught by surprise, and their ruinous losses far exceeded what happened a few months later at Pearl Harbor. Red Army troops died and surrendered in astonishing numbers (2 million would die in German captivity that first winter), and it seemed that once again Germany had gained a quick and decisive victory. At first, some Germans complained of the mud, which slowed their advance, and welcomed the frost that hardened the ground, but when the winter stopped the advance, the campaign was not over. Hitler forbade falling back, and German troops froze. Even before the freeze, the successful German forces noted that however many Soviet troops were killed or captured that there were always more. Germany had destroyed more Red Army tanks than were supposed to exist, and still more kept appearing. The newer ones were impressive machines. Fresh, well-equipped Soviet troops arrived near Moscow in early December 1941—freed from watching the Manchurian border because Japan had directed its energies elsewhere, attacking U.S. and British possessions. By December 10, 1941, Germany's Eastern Front had cost some 750,000 troops, including almost 200,000 dead. The winter of 1941–42 cost Germany 75,000 motor vehicles and 180,000 horses.

The war in Russia heated up in the spring of 1942, and Germany advanced again, reaching Stalingrad in late 1942. The German Sixth Army was cut off in that city by Soviet counterattacks, and in February 1943,

91,000 survivors surrendered, including Field Marshal Friedrich von Paulus. Only about 5,000 of the Stalingrad POWs returned to Germany after the war. One more German push in the east, crushed in a titanic tank battle at Kursk in the summer of 1943, was followed by relentless Soviet advances that led all the way to Berlin.

There were disasters on other fronts, too; more Germans surrendered in Tunis in 1943, as the British and Americans disposed of the Axis forces in North Africa, than at Stalingrad. (POWs from North Africa sent home postcards describing how well-fed they were in Canada and the United States.) Allied victories in Italy and the 1944 landing in France were major setbacks for Germany, and the bombing made an increasing impression. The postwar German memory of the war, however, featured above all else the misery in the Soviet Union—the genocidal brutality of the fighting, the cold that cracked engine blocks, solidified lubricants, and destroyed mere flesh, and the sheer immensity of Russia. The self-congratulation of the early war years was replaced by dread. Perhaps the propagandist Goebbels's cleverest stroke was the highly credible line that Germans must fight on regardless of the odds because the revenge of the Soviets, who had been characterized for years as vicious subhumans and who had been goaded into fury by German crimes in Russia, would be terrible beyond all imagining.

Until Stalingrad, a good deal of slack remained in the German economy. Only after that was it considered possible to call for "total war" and to draft some of the hairdressers who had previously been considered vital to maintaining civilian morale. Only after costly Allied bombing raids on Schweinfurt, a center of ball-bearing production, did the still-undamaged bearing factories go to round-the-clock work. Although German workers put in long hours, many continued to be grateful for their employment, seeing themselves as better off than in the Depression years of the early 1930s—at least until loss of family members at the fighting fronts and Allied bombs and invasion changed their points of view. Germany was able to supplement its labor force with foreigners. All Europe's human resources were available, as voluntary or semivoluntary paid workers or as outright slave labor, depending on Germany's political relations with each country. Nazi racial ideology meant that workers from western Europe and Italy were treated differently than Slavic eastern workers. German authorities and editorialists complained about the attraction between male foreigners (especially Frenchmen) and German women whose potential German mates were away in the army, but the enormous foreign workforce (7.6 million in August 1944) kept the German war economy running.

Nazi ideology, more vigorously male chauvinist than most thinking of the era, regarded women as breeders, essential to the propagation of the master race and the maintenance of male morale. Recruiting women for wartime factory work fit uneasily with the prevailing world view and seemed less urgent than in many other belligerent countries because of the easy availability of foreign labor. When girls were pressed to help the national effort as household aides (babysitters, etc.), many middle-class women simply exchanged daughters. Some young women were sent to help with farm work, their purity endangered by proximity to foreign male laborers. As the war went on, more German housewives were beset by shortages of fabrics and food and by the deadly dangers of bombs and invasion.

The Nazi youth organizations concentrated on boys and their preparation as fully Nazified, physically fit recruits for the military. Young men were supposed to be ready to die for their Führer, as many did. Most enjoyed the physical training and comradeship of the Hitler Youth, but some were alienated by the heavy-handed indoctrination. One means of expressing alienation was indulging in forbidden Western culture. Jazz music and the jazz-flavored swing dance bands were officially condemned as decadent products of black and Jewish culture (though the German Air Force had its own swing band, called—in English—"Charlie and His Orchestra"), so the music served as a means of protest. A few "swing kids" attacked Hitler Youth and engaged in sabotage, even damaging a Gestapo headquarters. Elements of juvenile delinquency mingled with anti-Nazi resistance in this countercultural fringe. Most of the young, however, stayed on track, sometimes seeing their educations abbreviated or interrupted. Many thousands, some as young as 13, served in hazardous antiaircraft duty, and at the end of the war, boys were sent off with antitank rockets to die in futile resistance to the Allied onslaught. When the war was over, surviving true believers emerged blinking into a different world where the interlocking web of Nazi ideology was no longer true.

The war economy fell short of its well-planned image. Everything was subject to several authorities—party, local government, military, and so forth—and their often-conflicting demands. The multiplication of authorities prevented any concentration of power that might challenge the Führer's primacy. It was impossible to resolve conflicts unless Hitler chose to adjudicate, and he was busy with grand strategy, postwar building schemes, and all-night monologues to his groggy companions. Young scientists were shipped off to die as infantry in Russia instead of assisting with the nuclear weapons project; a local party leader refused to allow a temporary plant-closing to permit the changeover to make necessary airplane parts, so obsolete products were turned out and immediately scrapped. New models of aircraft and tanks and improvements to existing weapons were needlessly delayed by bureaucracy. Hitler's personal meddling in the jet-fighter program, where he insisted on inappropriate conversion of the astonishingly advanced Messerschmitt 262 to a bomber, is perhaps the best-known instance, though metallurgical challenges made it hard to produce many turbojet engines in any case. Albert Speer, appointed to coordinate war production in 1942, strove mightily to reduce bottlenecks and duplication of effort, but German weapons still tended to be too fancy and too few. Total German arms production was ultimately limited by resources; it ended up slightly ahead of Britain's and far behind the Soviet Union's, which was far behind U.S. arms production.

Germany coped surprisingly well with Allied bombing, but the cumulative effect ground down production as well as morale. In 1942, the British conceded that, like the Germans in the Battle of Britain, they could not afford the aircraft losses of daylight bombing. Accuracy at night was so poor that German defense authorities were sometimes unable to determine what the Royal Air Force had intended to bomb. The British chose to target urban working-class housing (ironically occupied by the least Nazified portion of the German population) because it would burn. Though German defenses learned to inflict heavy losses on the nocturnal attackers, the Royal Air Force was increasingly able to ruin German cities. A symbolic thousand-plane attack on Cologne in May 1942 was meant to signal a large-scale assault. On two occasions—Hamburg in July 1943 and Dresden in February 1945—the fire-bombing campaign ignited a firestorm. Superheated air in the center of the storm rose miles into the air, hurricane-force winds rushed to bring more oxygen into the inferno, and people in their underground shelters died of heat or oxygen deprivation. Days after the attack, superheated corpses and possessions burst into flame when rescue workers opened up shelters and air rushed in; months after the war ended, cities reeked of the rotting bodies under the rubble. Workers with buckets spent years after the war clearing rubble so that cities could be reconstructed.

The United States insisted on daylight bombing. The heavily armed bombers could carry less bomb tonnage than the British, but when all went right they could hit particular targets. American formations, neatly arranged, making their way across German skies, were a discouraging sight for Germans on the ground. The bombs, night and day, often missed vital factories, but eventually the effort of dispersing production to avoid bomb damage, deploying a million men in antiaircraft gun and searchlight duty, and repairing or working around battered railways and canals exhausted German production. Attacks on oil fields in Romania and synthetic oil plants elsewhere, in combination with Soviet advances that disrupted supplies from the east, cut off fuel for pilot training and meant that jets had to be hauled around airfields by oxen. A late 1944 offensive in France was supposed to capture Allied fuel dumps; however, the Germans only had enough fuel to start their push but not to finish it. The air offensive meant that Germany virtually ceased to build bombers, concentrating on defensive fighters. However, since most of the fighters were engaged against the Anglo-American bombing offensive, Red Army troops encountered little interference from the German air force. As the Americans perfected long-range escort fighters, German fighter forces eroded almost to the vanishing point.

While the war against the Allies was being lost, the destruction of Europe's Jews surged forward. The Holocaust was not a war crime. Germans committed those in abundance—brutalities toward prisoners and civilians and other violations of the rules of war—but the murder of the Jews was not the use of excessively hideous means in pursuit of victory or indifference to those in the path of violence. It was conducted separately, even at the expense of the war against the Allies. Persons who could have done useful work were murdered; troops who could have helped hold off the Allies were busy murdering Jews. Yet the war made the Holocaust possible. Without Germany's initial victories, only Germany's Jews would have been vulnerable to the Nazi murderers, and emigration had reduced their numbers to about 215,000 at war's outbreak and 164,000 in October 1941.

Before the war, Germany's Jews had been set apart, labeled, driven out of occupations, and insofar as was possible, driven out of the country (sometimes to what turned out to be temporary refuge in Czechoslovakia or France). During the war, they were "deported to the east." Most Jews, like their Aryan neighbors, imagined the eastern destination as labor camps or detention camps. The truth about the murder program was kept as secret as possible; though many Germans (and other Europeans) favored extermination, most had been embarrassed and horrified by the riotous "Night of the Shattered Glass" in November 1938. When Heinrich Himmler, whose SS played the key role in what the Nazis termed the "final solution of the Jewish problem," spoke to SS leaders in October 1943, he emphasized the need to keep the extermination from the general public. The Nazi authorities did their best to conduct their colossal crime out of sight.

Nothing so massive could be hidden completely, of course. Trains crammed with suffering people from Germany and western Europe were not invisible; soldiers on leave from the east told of mass murders in Poland and Russia. For most Aryan Germans, inquiring into the horror was somewhat dangerous. Those who disapproved of the murders could not impede them, and it was more comfortable not to know the details. At first, killing teams did their work in the east, where most of their victims lived. Then centralized death factories were constructed—in the east, out of sight of most Germans—and Europe's Jews were collected into ghettoes to be shipped off to the killing centers. When U.S. and British troops liberated the hellish concentration camps at Dachau and Belsen, they could not imagine that those nightmares were modest compared to the industrial-scale facilities in the east. About 6 million Jews were murdered, as were about the same number of others, but the Jews were the center and reason for the process. The Jews and the Gypsies were to be exterminated totally, regardless of their actions or opinions. Other victims did something to inconvenience or annoy the Nazis. Even the despised Slavic peoples were to be preserved, for the most part, as brute labor. The mission of ridding the human race of Jews persisted and increased even as Germany lost the war. The bureaucrat Adolf Eichmann refused to allow diversion of his railway cars to carry medicine and ammunition to hard-pressed German troops; his job of murdering Jews was more important than defending Germany.

The Holocaust defined the essence of Nazism. Some who had detested the movement from its first appearance had the courage to look at what was being done in the name of the German people and were astonished at the incredible scale of the horror. Students at the University of Munich wrote and distributed statements of protest and were executed. Others attempted to kill Hitler, and the bomb attempt of July 20, 1944, nearly succeeded. That attempt involved army officers and members of the pre-Nazi elite. These traditional, conservative resisters were not the only anti-Nazis, but Socialists and Communists were in exile, in prison, or dead—in no position to threaten the Führer. The July 20, 1944 plotters have been criticized as German nationalists who objected to Hitler only because he was losing the war. But their moral outrage was genuine, and they paid a terrible price. Had they tried while Hitler was delivering victories, the public would have hated them. As it was, the assassination would create confusion and weaken a nation endangered by Russian vengeance.

That vengeance did come, and it was terrible. While troops of the Western Allies were not always polite to Germans who fell under their control and some troops were badly treated in U.S. and British confinement, those German civilians and military personnel who could drive or fly hastened to surrender in the west. In history's worst maritime disaster, about 9,500 refugees died on the *Wilhelm Gustloff,* torpedoed in the Baltic by a Soviet submarine. Those who fled had good reason. Soviet soldiers had much to avenge, and mass rape accompanied their bloody progress into Berlin. The contrast between Soviet brutality and the relatively civilized actions in the west had considerable influence on postwar attitudes in Germany and in Europe.

Exhausted, defeated, living in ruins, and confronted with the regime's crimes, Germans were compelled to recognize that the Nazi dream of European domination had been ugly as well as unsuccessful. Many were all too ready to blame everything on the dead Führer, forgetting how they had been swept along. Redefinition of what Germany was and what it was about would take very different paths in the Western and Soviet zones, occupying the minds of people busy digging out from ruin.

SELECTED BIBLIOGRAPHY

Bartov, Omer. *The Eastern Front, 1941–1945.* New York: St. Martin's Press, 1986. An overview of Germany's war in Soviet Russia emphasizing the unspeakably brutal nature of the warfare.

Beck, Earl R. *Under the Bombs: The German Home Front, 1942–1945.* Lexington: University Press of Kentucky, 1986. Detail-crammed, concentrating on miseries of ordinary Germans.

Browning, Christopher R. *Ordinary Men: Reserve Battalion 101 and the Final Solution in Poland.* New York: HarperCollins, 1992. The author closely traces the men and the activities of Reserve Battalion 101 as it carried out genocide in occupied Poland.

Dallin, Alexander. *German Rule in Russia, 1941–1945.* 2nd rev. ed. Boulder, CO: Westview Press, 1981. Originally published in 1957, this volume is the standard account of Nazi Germany's occupation policy in Soviet Russia.

Fleming, Gerald. *Hitler and the Final Solution.* Berkeley: University of California Press, 1984. Focuses on decision making and implementation of Holocaust measures.

Freidlander, Henry. *The Origins of Nazi Genocide.* Chapel Hill: University of North Carolina Press, 1995. A detailed study of the Nazis' homicidal orientation from the birth of the party.

Goldhagen, Daniel. *Hitler's Willing Executioners.* New York: Alfred A. Knopf, 1996. A lengthy and very controversial study that argues that years of anti-Semitism had predisposed ordinary Germans to embrace Hitler's "Final Solution."

Grunberger, Richard. *The 12-Year Reich: A Social History of Nazi Germany, 1933–1945.* New York: Holt, 1971. Readable, colorful; war years in context of Third Reich as a whole.

Herbert, Ulrich B. *Hitler's Foreign Workers: Enforced Foreign Labor in Germany under the Third Reich.* Cambridge: Cambridge University Press, 1997. Definitive, massive account of this aspect of wartime German society and economy.

Hilberg, Raul. *Perpetrators, Victims, Bystanders: The Jewish Catastrophe, 1933–1945.* New York: HarperCollins, 1992. Contexts of the Holocaust.

Hoffmann, Peter. *The History of the German Resistance, 1933–1945.* Cambridge, MA: Harvard University Press, 1977. Mammoth, thorough, even-handed assessment.

Kitchen, Martin. *Nazi Germany at War.* London and New York: Longman, 1995. Topically organized, coherent, and authoritative.

Jukes, Geoffrey. *Hitler's Stalingrad Decisions.* Berkeley: University of California Press, 1985. An expert on Soviet military matters contemplates Hitler's decisions at the Battle of Stalingrad.

Mayer, Arno J. *Why Did the Heavens Not Darken? The Final Solution in History.* New York: Pantheon, 1989. Eccentric but thought-provoking attempt to connect progress of the war with development of the Holocaust.

Milward, Alan S. *The German Economy at War.* London: Athlone Press, 1965. Milward, a British economic historian, has written the best one-volume history of Germany's World War II economy.

Read, Anthony, and David Fisher. *The Deadly Embrace: Hitler, Stalin, and the Nazi-Soviet Pact, 1939–1941.* New York: Norton, 1988. A massive but illuminating examination of the nonaggression pact that made temporary allies of Nazi Germany and Soviet Russia.

Rupp, Leila J. *Mobilizing Women for War: German and American Propaganda, 1933–1945* Princeton, NJ: Princeton University Press, 1978. Valuable comparison of German and U.S. efforts, illuminating tensions between ideology and economic necessity.

Steinert, Marlis G. *Hitler's War and the Germans: Public Mood and Attitude during the Second World War.* Athens: Ohio University Press, 1977. German public opinion; a well-organized, jargon-free analysis.

Weinberg, Gerhard L. *A World at Arms: A Global History of World War II.* New York: Cambridge University Press, 1994. Although global in its scope, this work gives an excellent overview of the rise and fall of Germany's army.

9

West Germany's Economic and Political "Miracle," 1949–1973

INTRODUCTION

In May 1949, the United States, Great Britain, and France—three of the four powers that occupied Germany at the close of World War II—cobbled together from their respective zones of occupation a new and artificial German state. The victors chose this course for a number of reasons, including the onset of the Cold War with their former ally the Soviet Union and a desire to free themselves of the burden of maintaining the Germans who lived under their control.

This new German state had several names. Officially, it was the Bundesrepublik Deutschland, or BRD; in the English-speaking world it was the Federal Republic of Germany or, as it was more commonly known, West Germany. West Germany began life with a population of about 47 million, growing to about 61 million by 1973, and a territory of 96,000 square miles. (In 1871, Bismarck's Reich had a population of about 40 million, growing to 65 million by 1914; in 1939, Hitler's Third Reich had a population of about 68 million.)

Several months after West Germany's establishment, a rival German state appeared. This was the Deutsche Demokratik Republik, or DDR, known best in the English-speaking world as the German Democratic Republic, or East Germany. The Soviet Union created East Germany from

Crusty old Konrad Adenauer led West Germany to political stability and economic prosperity during the years after World War II. In a surprisingly short time, West Germany emerged as Europe's economic engine and clearly aligned itself with the democratic states of Europe. (Reproduced from the Collections of the Library of Congress.)

its zone of occupation, and East Germany remained firmly under Soviet control until its demise in 1990.

In 1949, West Germany was untried, weak, and poor. However, by the onset of the 1973 oil crisis that seriously harmed all western countries, West Germany was stable, strong, and prosperous. Western-style democracy had put down deep roots, West Germany's voice was heard and listened to in European if not global councils, and West Germany provided the economic engine that drove post–World War II Western Europe's spectacular economic recovery. How did this all come about?

At the end of World War II, the German economy lay in ruin. It is estimated that in 1946 industrial production in the three western zones of occupation—those belonging to the United States, Great Britain, and France—was less than one-third of what it had been in 1936. In 1950, a superficial glance might have suggested that little progress toward economic recovery had occurred. There were more than 2 million unemployed; 17 million depended on some form of assistance; and 6 million families lacked permanent housing. The national debt totaled 13.5 billion deutsche marks (DM). However, this grim picture was inaccurate; rather, in the preceding years the foundation had been set for West Germany's astounding economic rebound.

The person chiefly responsible for this turnaround was Ludwig Erhard, West Germany's first minister of economics. Erhard was an academic who had been greatly influenced by the Freiburg school of economics that advocated a laissez-faire approach to economic issues. However, he combined his belief in the market economy with a commitment to a generous social welfare program. The result was the *soziale Marktwirtschaft*, or "Social Market Economy," which allowed capitalism to flourish while ensuring that all West Germans received a piece of the pie.

In the late 1940s, Erhard's evaluation of West Germany's industrial infrastructure was unusually perceptive. While acknowledging that Allied bombing had severely damaged Germany's transportation system and seriously depleted its housing stock, Erhard concluded that it had not truly devastated Germany's industrial infrastructure. In fact, the war had ruined only about 19 percent of Germany's capital stock and 6.5 percent of its machinery. In other words, Germany's industrial foundation remained largely intact. Moreover, the influx of German refugees from the east added to an already existing abundance of skilled labor. Furthermore, reparation payments in the form of machinery (sent chiefly to the Soviet Union) meant that West Germany's factories would retool with modern equipment.

West Germany's economic recovery received a much-needed boost in June 1947 when George C. Marshall, the U.S. secretary of state, announced the European Recovery Program. Under this program—almost always known as the Marshall Plan—the United States committed significant sums of money to jump-start Europe's moribund economy. West Germany received about $1.5 billion from the Marshall Plan; this represented about 7 percent of West Germany's capital and material requirements.

The restoration of fiscal order in June 1948 provided a major step toward West Germany's postwar economic miracle. Cooperating closely with occupation authorities, Erhard announced the creation of a new currency, the deutsche mark, to replace the discredited reichsmark. He also established a central bank, the Deutsche Bundesbank, and announced an end to price controls and rationing.

By the early 1950s, the West German economy was beginning to take off. Its acceleration continued in 1951 when West Germany joined the European Coal and Steel Community (ECSC), a six-nation consortium that rationalized the production of coal and steel throughout West Germany, France, Italy, Belgium, the Netherlands, and Luxembourg. In turn, the ECSC led in 1957 to the Treaty of Rome and the creation of the European Common Market, a development with significant positive consequences for both West Germany and its western European neighbors.

Other important factors help to account for West Germany's economic miracle. In May 1952, West Germany enacted the *Lastenausgleich*, or the Law for the Equalization of Burdens. Under this legislation, West German citizens whose property had not been destroyed during the war were taxed, with the proceeds going to refugees, the homeless, and those who had suffered significant property losses. By 1987, 57 million West Germans had shared in more than $68 billion of equalization money. Several months later, the *Vertriebenengesetz*, or Refugee Law, came into force. This provided meaningful sums for the even redistribution of the huge West German refugee population, then concentrated in a few regions, for job training programs and for much-needed housing.

Unquestionably, harmonious relations between business and labor contributed to the economic recovery. The 1951 *Mitbestimmung*, or Law of Codetermination, required that a representative of the workers be included on the board of directors of every large West German firm. Management-labor cooperation reduced the incidents of strikes to almost zero and increased both the profit margins for the owners and the standard of living for the workers.

Erhard's belief in the market economy and his conviction that a rising tide lifts all boats proved true. During the 1950s, the West German economy grew at an annual rate of 8.6 percent. Between 1950 and 1985, the

Gross National Product increased by a factor of 100 to 1,845 billion DM. At the same time, exports grew from 8.4 to 537 billion DM, and the balance of trade went from a deficit to a 112.6 billion DM surplus. By 1960, 7 million new jobs had been created, and the unemployment rate neared 1 percent.

Prosperity gushed rather than trickled down to the common man. Between 1950 and 1970, the average West German household saw its disposable income jump by 400 percent and its real wages jump by almost 300 percent. With more money in their pockets, the West Germans enjoyed an increased standard of living and greater consumption. By 1962, one-half of West German homes had a refrigerator, two-thirds had a vacuum cleaner, one-third had a washing machine, and there were well over 6 million television sets. Good times were also reflected in West Germany's intense love affair with the automobile. In 1950, there were 12 cars per 1,000 people; by 1984, that number had grown to 412 per 1,000. West Germans now had more meat in their diets and vacationed in other countries, sometimes to the annoyance of their hosts. Meanwhile, under *Marktwirtschaft* the workweek shrank to less than 40 hours, the federal government provided a large array of social services, and millions of government-sponsored housing units were constructed.

The establishment and growth of a stable and democratic West German government matched the spectacular economic recovery. The rapidly deteriorating relationship between the three western allies (the United States, Great Britain, France) on one hand and the Soviet Union on the other, which eventually resulted in the Cold War, prompted the former to allow German political activity to resume in their zones of occupation. In June 1948, German political leaders met at Coblenz, where they formed a parliamentary council to work on a new constitution for an envisioned West German state comprising the three western zones of occupation. Meeting in the Rhine River town of Bonn from September 1948 until May 1949, the parliamentary council produced the *Grundgesetz*, or Basic Law, that became West Germany's constitution after the various state legislatures ratified it.

The Basic Law was modeled after the Weimar Republic's failed constitution, but it contained some important changes that eliminated several of the flaws that had undermined the Weimar document. For one thing, the Basic Law changed the role of the state's president and greatly diminished his power. Henceforth, the president would play a chiefly ceremonial role as head of the nation rather than head of the state; that is, he would be a symbol of the new West Germany. Perhaps most importantly, the Basic Law denied the president any right to exercise emergency powers in times of crisis.

The authors of the Basic Law also worked to end the parliamentary chaos that had crippled the Weimar Republic by adopting what was known as the "constructive vote of no-confidence." Under this provision, no vote of no-confidence could pass the legislature unless those bringing the vote could demonstrate that they were capable of forming a government.

Finally, the Basic Law enshrined the "five percent principle." In order to eliminate the fringe groups and splinter parties that had fragmented the Weimar Republic's legislature and made coalition-building nearly impossible, the Basic Law set a threshold of five percent of the vote for representation in the parliament. In other words, unless a political party or group garnered at least five percent of the vote, it could not seat any representatives in the legislature.

The Basic Law extended civil liberties and human rights to every West German. It called for a bicameral legislature with real power given to the popularly elected lower house, or *Bundestag*. Suffrage was granted to all West Germans over the age of 18. The Basic Law provided for the equivalent of a supreme court to rule on constitutional questions. Acutely aware of Germany's recent past, the Basic Law also specified that any future German military force could only be used for defensive purposes and expressly forbade any offensive actions. The western occupying powers endorsed the Basic Law and transformed their military governors into civilian high commissioners.

While the Basic Law provided an excellent foundation for West Germany, the new state's success owed much to the sagacity of its initial political leaders, especially Konrad Adenauer, its first chancellor. Well over 70 years old when he became chancellor, Adenauer had been in German politics for decades. A leading member of the old Center Party, Adenauer had been mayor of Cologne for many years until ousted by the Nazis. During the Third Reich, he remained in Germany, but he withdrew from politics. His disapproval of the Nazis was well known. Although irascible and inclined toward authoritarianism, Adenauer worked diligently and skillfully to make the West German political experiment a success.

Adenauer led the Christian Democratic Union (CDU) which together with its Bavarian ally, the Christian Social Union (CSU), dominated West Germany's politics for the first 15 years. Conservative in orientation, Adenauer's CDU/CSU tried to rehabilitate Germany in the eyes of Europe. Under Adenauer, West Germany stood at the forefront of efforts to either create or strengthen multinational European institutions ranging from the European Coal and Steel Community (ECSC) and the Common Market, or European Economic Community (EEC), to the North Atlantic Treaty Organization (NATO) and the European Defense Community (EDC). Adenauer and the CDU/CSU also cultivated a special relationship with the United States, becoming that country's most reliable continental partner.

The chief opponent of the CDU/CSU was the revived Social Democratic Party (SPD). Although failing to gain power, in 1959 the SPD made a grand gesture toward ensuring political stability in West Germany when it jettisoned its Marxist rhetoric during its annual meeting at Bad Godesberg. The Bad Godesberg Program officially placed the SPD on the path of reformist, revisionist socialism rather than revolutionary Marxism.

While the "five percent principle" eliminated the fringe elements, it did not make West Germany a two-party state. Rather, a third party survived and came to play an important role in West German politics. This was the Free Democratic Party (FDP), which occupied the middle ground between the CDU/CSU and the SPD. For much of West Germany's political life, the FDP, with usually somewhere between 6 and 10 percent of the vote, held the balance of power.

Throughout the 1950s, a CDU/CSU-FDP coalition held sway. During the 1960s, the CDU/CSU gradually lost popularity. In 1963, Adenauer, now old and more crotchety than ever, was eased from power. His successors, Ludwig Erhard and Kurt Kiesinger, failed to capture the electorate's imagination, and in 1966, the CDU/CSU was forced into a "grand coalition" with the SPD, whose popularity was on the rise. In 1969, a milestone was reached when the FPD threw its weight behind the SPD, and the first socialist government since the waning days of the Weimar Republic came into office under the leadership of the young, charismatic Willy Brandt. This democratic changing of the guard passed without disturbance.

INTERPRETIVE ESSAY
Richard A. Leiby

As ground troops fought their way into Hitler's Reich, Allied planners turned their attention to the impending occupation of Germany. For the European Advisory Commission (EAC), the group charged with creating a plan for the administration of occupied Germany, the Allied insistence on unconditional surrender posed some intriguing problems. How should the German people be treated once the war was over? Who should be responsible for the reconstruction of the country? In the absence of the Nazi government, how should Germany be administered? Had some politicians gotten their way, there would have been no "Germany" in the postwar European order at all. One plan, devised by Henry Morgenthau, the U.S. secretary of the treasury, called for Germany to be dismembered, stripped of its industry, and turned into seven agricultural states. Although Morgenthau's extreme suggestion was soon discarded as impractical, the idea of partitioning Germany was still a viable option as the Yalta Conference convened in February 1945. There, the "Big Three" agreed to accept the EAC's recommendation that Germany be divided into zones of occupation pending a final determination on how Germany as a whole should be governed. This decision was reconfirmed at the Potsdam Conference in July, and what had been intended as a temporary measure became official policy. Each victorious nation (Great Britain, the United States, the Soviet Union, and now also France) assumed administrative control over a region of Germany for the immediate postwar period.

Although the creation of occupation zones divided the responsibility for the occupation, the Allies still intended Germany to be treated as a single economic entity. An Allied Control Council (ACC), composed of the four military governors and their staffs, met regularly to devise policies for governing Germany as a whole. Despite managing to agree on a general framework for occupation policy, the members of the ACC found it difficult to set aside their political and ideological differences on more specific matters. Consequently, the ACC never became the instrument of quadripartite governance as was originally intended. Instead, each zone became a semiautonomous entity, ruled by a military governor whose primary responsibility was to decisionmakers in his home country.

At least initially, Germany would be rebuilt by the occupying powers individually. All too often, zonal commanders had a paucity of clear directives to inform and guide their work. For example, the U.S. Joint Chiefs of Staff had hammered out an official occupation policy early in 1945, but it was not officially issued to the field until the last week of the war. JCS 1067, as the directive is commonly known, contained policies that may, in retrospect, be described as punitive or even draconian. Germany was to be treated as a defeated enemy nation and not as a liberated country. Military government was to conduct itself in a "just, but firm and aloof" manner with whatever German civil authority it encountered. Most importantly, JCS 1067 ordered military government to "take no steps looking toward the economic rehabilitation of Germany or designed to maintain or strengthen the economy." All indigenous resources were to be made available for use by the occupation forces, displaced persons, prisoners of war, and United Nations nationals before they might be applied to the needs of the Germans themselves.

Thus, the reconstruction of Germany began in an atmosphere of confusion and disunity. The most difficult work had already begun during the combat phase. As the Allied armies advanced into Germany, they found a civil infrastructure on the verge of complete collapse. Destroyed or damaged roads, bridges, and municipal installations were in dire need of repair. In addition, essential social services such as police, fire, sanitation, power, water, and sewerage systems had stopped functioning as the authorities who had overseen them fled for fear of capture and punishment. Getting the civil infrastructure back into operation might have been manageable on a small scale, but the Civil Affairs Units in charge of administering conquered German territory quickly proved ill-equipped, understaffed, and overextended as more and more territory fell to the Allied advance.

Fortunately, the end of hostilities in May 1945 allowed the zonal commanders to devote more of their attention to the reconstruction effort. Despite the colossal task at hand, the Allies managed to make substantial headway on many of the initial goals of the occupation within the first twelve months after the surrender. By summer 1946, most municipal services were functioning again (albeit in reduced capacities), and government, complete with functioning political parties, had been reestablished on the local level in all zones. In many ways, Germany seemed on the road to a speedy recovery. Unfortunately, the most critical sector—the economy—still showed few signs of improvement. One might blame the lackluster performance on the destruction of Germany's industrial capacity by strategic bombing, but that conclusion is contradicted by the postwar surveys of aerial bomb damage, which revealed that much of German industry had survived more or less intact and was still in operation at the war's end. Similarly, the stagnation was not a by-product of the crippling of Germany's labor force. While it is true that civilian and military casualties did cut a large swath through the population of Germany, there was still a sizeable sector of skilled labor available to industry, one that was growing all the time with the influx of refugees.

Why, then, did the German economy continue to sputter for so long? The disruption of the supportive infrastructure, particularly the scarcity of adequate transportation, fuel, and food, was certainly a reason. Zonal organization was also partially at fault, for it had chopped a single marketplace into four autonomous economic units, each one incapable of dealing effectively with the others. The most pernicious problems, however, were structural. First of all, there was too much money in circulation. The Nazis had printed great quantities of the *Reichsmark* (RM) in order to pay for the war. The resulting devaluation of the currency led to wage and price controls designed to halt inflation. The occupation authorities could do little about either of these difficulties without a complete overhaul of Germany's economic system; therefore the German economy languished. Manufacturers refused to produce goods of any value, since their products would be both underpriced and purchased with a nearly worthless currency. Some companies compensated for the dysfunctional marketplace by shifting production to newer products that were not regulated under the price-control mechanism. This led to what the Swiss economist Wilhelm Röpke called a "hair oil-ash tray-herb tea" economy, where unregulated consumer goods of little lasting value abounded but durable goods remained scarce. Other manufacturers simply withheld their best commodities from the marketplace entirely, by either hoarding them for future use or selling them on the black market at highly inflated prices. In many instances, such items were used for "compensation trading," that is, bartered for other valuable goods. Some commodities became a currency in their own right. It was not unusual for businessmen to purchase goods or services with cigarettes, eggs, or other scarcities instead of paper currency.

Despite these serious faults, the German economy was hardly dead; it contained all the preconditions for expansion except an incentive for workers and employers to produce. Restoring public confidence in the currency would be the first and most important step in rehabilitating the economy. That was the conclusion of the Colm, Dodge, and Goldsmith report of May 1946, which urged the occupation authorities to enact a currency reform as soon as possible. The United States, eager to relieve the financial burden of occupation, received the report favorably and was inclined to put the recommendations into motion. The Soviets and the French, however, given their ideological and social reservations about the Germans, demurred. Consequently, currency reform remained on the ACC's agenda for months while the details could be worked out to the satisfaction of all.

The dispute over currency reform was not the first, nor would it be the last, battleground between the Soviet Union and the Western Allies now that the Cold War had begun. Each side determined to remake Germany in its own ideological image and neither proved very willing to make compromises unless its own geopolitical interests were served. Faced with what it perceived to be Soviet intransigence, the Truman administration decided to forge ahead with its own vision of Germany's future. At a meeting of foreign ministers in July 1946, Secretary of State James F. Byrnes announced that the United States would be willing to merge its zone with that of any other power for the purpose of creating an economic unity. The next day, Byrnes's British counterpart, Ernest Bevin, announced his government's agreement in principle to the proposal. During a speech delivered in Stuttgart in August 1946, Byrnes explained that this new administrative unit was the first step in a completely new approach to the occupation. In at least the British and U.S. zones, the Germans would be allowed to achieve the highest standard of living they could. The punitive overtones of JCS 1067 were suddenly gone, replaced by policies framed in the language of reconciliation. Germany was no longer the enemy; it was now rapidly becoming a partner in the struggle to contain communism.

Although the Stuttgart speech astounded everyone who heard it, average German citizens did not notice any immediate change in their lot when "Bizonia," a merger of the U.S. and British zones of occupation, came into being on January 1, 1947. Most were too busy foraging for food to augment their meager rations and trying to stay warm during one of the coldest winters on record. Nevertheless, the administrative fusion of the British and U.S. zones did mark an important initial step toward a possible reunion of all four zones and indicated a willingness to give the Germans more say in their own affairs. By now, political parties and state governments were well established across Germany. In June, the Bizonal authority invited the state minister-presidents to meet in Bavaria to discuss a common economic plan. Out of this gathering emerged the Economic Council, which convened for its first meeting in Frankfurt on June 25, 1947. Its functions were mostly advisory, since the occupation authority had veto power over its decisions. Still, the council represented the first institution of centralized decision making since the collapse of Nazism, and in spite of the fact that the delegates were not allowed to discuss politics, most citizens of Bizonia considered it to be a nascent central government.

The emergence of Bizonia can in retrospect be interpreted as the beginning of Germany's bifurcation. At the time, however, there was still some hope for a union of all four zones into a single nation. In an August meeting of the ACC, Marshall Vasili Sokolovsky, the Soviet military governor, announced that his government would agree to the creation of a single new German currency if the Soviet occupation authority were given a duplicate set of printing plates. When the United States refused, the mudslinging resumed and quickly devolved into a propaganda battle over who was to blame for Germany's continuing economic misery. This was a pointless debate, since the British and U.S. authorities had already decided to introduce a new currency with or without Soviet participation. The new banknote, called the deutsche mark (DM), had already been printed in the

United States and shipped to Germany for distribution. All that remained was to introduce it into the Bizonal economy.

The changeover procedure was fairly straightforward. Each citizen would be permitted to exchange 60RM for 60DM; 40DM could be taken at once and the remaining 20DM within a few weeks. Thereafter, all bank balances would be converted to the new currency at the rate of 10RM to 1DM, with larger accounts at the rate of 10RM to .65DM. Wages, rents, and pensions were converted at a rate of one to one. This process managed to eliminate 93.5 percent of the paper money in circulation and give everyone (at least temporarily) the same spending power. The reform went into effect on June 20, and the effects were nothing short of amazing. Hoarded goods reappeared on store shelves practically overnight, signaling the impending demise of the black market. Compensation trading was no longer necessary now that a trusted currency was available. Manufacturers quickly resumed production of durable goods. Laborers, lured by the promise of more spending money, came to work asking for overtime hours. The "hair-oil, ash-tray, herb-tea" economy had become a thing of the past.

The introduction of the deutsche mark solved the currency crisis, but the economy was still unable to operate freely because the artificial wage and price restrictions remained in force. The job of eliminating them fell to Ludwig Erhard, a Bavarian economist, who near the end of the war risked his life at the hands of the Nazis by publishing an article on monetary policy in a defeated Germany. Erhard had made a name for himself as a proponent of laissez-faire economics at a time when wage and price controls seemed the only solution to Germany's problems with shortages. At some risk to his own professional reputation, Erhard used his authority as Economic Council chairman to remove the price controls on most commodities. Despite the misgivings of many, the results were dramatic. Once the Bizonal economy was finally open to market forces, production rates rose by 30 percent (compared to 5 percent the previous year) and continued to increase steadily over the next two years.

The success was not without some sacrifice, however. As the economy retooled itself, unemployment rates rose concomitantly. This was a harsh reminder that economic progress can entail social costs. Consequently, the Economic Council had a difficult time deciding what form the German economy as a whole should take. The political parties were understandably divided on the issue. The Christian Democratic Union (CDU), formed out of prewar centrist and confessional political parties, believed in the virtues of the open market and laissez-faire economics. The economic resurgence following Erhard's elimination of controls seemed to make a strong case for capitalism. Still, there was an equally strong sentiment in the Council in favor of socialism. Most delegates could still remember both the inflation following World War I and the Great Depression and could argue that structural faults within capitalism were responsible for the rise of Hitler and the horrors that befell Germany after 1933. The Social Democratic Party (SPD) therefore found fertile intellectual ground for its platform of economic planning and state intervention in the marketplace. It needed only to point to the unemployment figures, which were rising rapidly as industries laid off workers in an effort to rationalize production, as justification.

Despite their differences, both the SPD and the CDU ultimately agreed that some restraint on the free market system was desirable. As Erhard himself put it, what was needed was "a sound middle way between out-and-out freedom and totalitarianism." The resulting compromise has often been called the "new liberalism," that is, a belief that the free market system must be tempered with a sense of social responsibility and government oversight. Thus was created the Social Market Economy, a bold experiment to see whether a national economy could be based on not just economic or political considerations but on moral principles as well. The Social Market Economy is, like much of West Germany's postwar reality, a compromise between contradictory ideas. In some ways it is classical liberalism. It decries government intervention in the marketplace of any kind, and it distrusts Soviet-style directed economies. Yet at the same time it accepts that government would and should intervene to mitigate social wrongs that might result from free market action. For example, the central government is expected to protect small businesses from the unfair competition of larger ones and to subsidize struggling sectors of the economy. The Social Market Economy also continued Germany's extensive (and expensive) social welfare system, providing all workers with sickness and unemployment insurance, old-age pensions, and paid five-week vacations. It is, as some have quipped, "capitalism with a conscience."

The western zones now had both the macro- and microeconomic preconditions necessary for recovery. As they worked their way back toward economic vitality, it became increasingly clear that those advances had been gained at the expense of any possible reunification with the Soviet zone. Following its refusal to go along with the currency reform, the Soviet occupation authority retaliated by issuing its own currency (subsequently referred to as the *Ostmark*) and by blockading West Berlin. As the Cold War intensified, the Western Allies saw little reason to include the Soviets in any subsequent deliberations on Germany's future. So, in the summer of 1948, the military government presented the minister-presidents of the

western German states with a blueprint for the reconstruction of a permanent central political authority. A parliamentary council, composed of delegates chosen by the states, gathered to draw up a new constitution for a
united German state.

The council delegates faced a terrible dilemma. They understood that
the Soviets would not participate, so any new constitution would effectively divide the country, perhaps permanently. No one wanted to participate in an endeavor that would partition the nation, but then again, the
opportunity to work toward reestablishing Germany's political future
was too good to pass up. With yet another inspired compromise, the
Council figured out a way to move forward without completely abandon-
ing all hopes of reuniting Germany. Building on a recommendation made
by the minister-presidents, the Council decided that this new constitution
should be transitional, not permanent, and contain two articles addressing
a possible future union with areas not yet under its jurisdiction. The
resulting document, called the Basic Law in deference to its temporary
nature, became the foundation of central government across the three
western zones. As expected, the Soviets retaliated by permitting their zone
to craft a separate constitution. Thus, two German states were born in
1949. In the west, the first elections of the fledgling Federal Republic of
Germany brought the CDU to power. Governing from a capital in Bonn,
its chancellor was Konrad Adenauer, and Ludwig Erhard was its first economics minister. In the east, the German Democratic Republic came into
being. Its leader, Walter Ulbricht, ran a Soviet-style government based on
single-party rule from the eastern sector of Berlin.

The early years of the Federal Republic of Germany put the Social Market Economy to the test. The currency reform inaugurated a period of
industrial growth that lasted (with minor seasonal adjustments) well into
1950. While this success was the result of the freeing of internal production and demand, it was also due in part to the external stimulus provided
by the U.S. European Recovery Program, more commonly called the Marshall Plan. By 1949, the initial shipments of raw materials and industrial
goods purchased with Marshall Plan credits began to work their way into
the German economy. Food imports may have been the most important
deliveries, as they helped insulate the populace from the threat of starvation and allowed them to devote their time to working instead of foraging.
West Germany was well on its way to economic self-sufficiency.

Just as the West German economy began to heat up, the outbreak of the
Korean War in 1950 threatened to reverse all the gains made so far. Ini-
tially, the worldwide demand for finished goods was a godsend for West
Germany's economy, and it experienced what has been called the "Korea

boom,"—a continual period of increasing production and economic expansion. Unfortunately, the supply of raw materials could not keep up with the demand, and rapidly rising prices thrust West Germany into a serious balance of payments crisis. Suddenly, Germans had to face the specter of scarcity again. Some West German legislators called for a return to rationing and price controls, but Erhard refused to retreat from his belief in free market forces. Luckily, the payments crisis passed, leaving the neoliberal order (and Erhard's reputation) intact. West Germany had survived its first major economic crisis and the biggest test of the Social Market Economy so far.

The Korea boom ended in the first quarter of 1952, but the steady increase in industrial production continued apace. Within the next two years, the rate of West German industrial production was double that of prewar Nazi Germany. This affluence allowed the government to address the inequities that had accompanied the transition from the wartime to the peacetime economy. True to the spirit of the Social Market Economy, in 1952 West Germany passed the *Lastenausgleich*, or Law for the Equalization of Burdens, designed to help those who had suffered from the war and the postwar economic stagnation (refugees, people on fixed incomes, small savers, etc.). The law levied a payment on citizens and institutions, based on the value of the assets owned in 1948. Over 80 billion DM would be redistributed over the next 19 years. While an excellent humanitarian gesture, the Law for the Equalization of Burdens had only a marginal effect on the overall economy. Most who received benefits never saw anything close to full restitution for the losses they had sustained. A much more important consequence was that the law demonstrated that the West German government was serious about providing some measure of economic justice. For those ethnic German refugees seeking integration into the mainstream of West German society, this was a welcome sign.

By 1955, the West German economy was growing at the staggering rate of 10 percent per annum. Most of the unemployment problems that had characterized the formative years of the economy were gone, and employers had to turn to refugees and non-German guest laborers to fill the demand for workers. Expansion continued throughout the remainder of the 1950s and into the 1960s, transforming the German living standard into the highest in Europe and making the deutsche mark one of the most stable and coveted currencies in the world. The ultimate recognition of the success of the free market approach came in 1958 when the Social Democratic Party of Germany (SPD), after almost 10 years of failure at the polls, finally discarded what was left of its revolutionary Marxist underpinnings and reinvented itself as a mainstream party of reform. The Bad Godesberg

Program, as it is known, was more than just a repudiation of Marxism. It was a tacit recognition that the ideas of Adenauer and Erhard were right all along—that the pursuit of profit in an open and free marketplace was a precondition for economic success.

It would be erroneous to assume that internal factors alone accounted for the dramatic economic boom of the 1950s and 1960s. To complete the picture, one must also consider the impact of West Germany's participation in Europe's first supranational economic institutions. In 1951, West Germany was a principle partner in the creation of the European Coal and Steel Community (ECSC), the first agency designed to share the benefits of coal and steel production across national boundaries. Ultimately, West Germany joined with Italy, France, and the Benelux nations to create the Common Market. These economic initiatives had political consequences as well. By committing itself to work within the framework of a larger Europe, Adenauer's government had demonstrated that German expansionism was a thing of the past. Former enemies were now economic partners, and the thought of a future German-instigated European war became more and more distant.

A new threat had replaced such fears, namely the threat of communist expansion. What would Germany's role be in a nuclear conflict between superpowers? Many thought that both West and East Germany should stay out of the Cold War dispute. Although the Soviets tempted Germany with the carrot of unification should both nations agree to neutrality, Chancellor Adenauer insisted that his fledgling nation remain aligned with the West. As a reward, the United States accepted West Germany as a partner in the western alliance. On May 5, 1955, almost 10 years to the day after the Nazi surrender, the Western Allies granted West Germany its sovereignty. The Federal Republic of Germany took its place in NATO and the United Nations as an equal partner with the countries that had once defeated and occupied it. However, the price of legitimacy was high. As West Germany became more and more integrated into the West, East Germany became further entrenched as a satellite of the Soviet Union. It seemed that nothing short of nuclear war or perhaps the internal collapse of communism would ever reunite them.

Many students of German history consider the currency reform to be the beginning of the German recovery. As the French political scientist Alfred Grosser put it, currency reform "marked the spectacular debut of an economic renaissance." Recently, however, some experts have questioned whether the currency reform played as large a role in recovery as was previously thought. They point out that the preconditions for recovery were already in place well before 1948, and they note that some economic gains had been made before the reform went into effect. While it would be an error to assume that the recovery began with the creation of the deutsche mark, it would be an even greater error to underestimate the currency reform's role in the West German revival. There is no denying that the reform marks the turning point of the occupation. One look at the statistical indicators shows how central the new currency was to a revitalization of the economy. Its impact was more than just economic, however. To a population struggling with scarcity, the deutsche mark was a psychological boost; it was a symbol that Germany was back on its feet and that life would soon be normal again. Perhaps the best metaphor to describe the impact of the currency reform is that it served as a catalyst, speeding up the pace of an economic renewal that to some extent had already begun.

A similar debate concerns the role of the Marshall Plan in the German economic recovery. The traditional interpretation, one that was very popular among western historians during the Cold War, holds that the Marshall Plan moneys were the engine driving the economic revival of both West Germany and Europe as a whole. Economic historian Alan Milward's work has questioned this conclusion. While it is true that the amount of aid the United States sent to West Germany totaled in the billions of dollars, that sum seems more impressive than it actually is. Indeed, the Marshall Plan aid represented less than three percent of West Germany's yearly national income. While the evidence seems conclusive that the Marshall Plan was not the decisive factor in West Germany's revival, it nonetheless did help contribute to it. U.S. funds lent valuable support to West Germany's balance of payments situation, helped keep its export sector busy, and gave a psychological boost by signaling the United States' willingness to commit to the economic well-being of West Germany and Europe. The Marshall Plan aid primed the pump of recovery and accelerated the drive to economic stability.

How was West Germany able to sustain its "miraculous" rise to economic power? The answer lies in a combination of internal and external factors. Contrary to the conventional wisdom that holds that new industries were responsible for West Germany's economic explosion, the recovery was fueled by the same sectors where Germany had always been powerful, namely the electrical, chemical, and machinery industries. What is amazing is that these sectors had relatively little difficulty reclaiming their prewar position in the world marketplace, despite being cut off from it by six years of war and three years of stagnation. This dramatic reemergence is a testament to the quality of German products and the skill and workmanship of the German labor force. Another reason the West

German economic "miracle" continued for so long was the availability of skilled labor. As the boom period of the 1950s progressed, the demand for industrial labor was satiated by millions of refugees and expellees from East Germany. Many of them, including those who had lost their homes east of the Oder and Neisse rivers due to postwar border rectifications, were highly skilled and educated and therefore easily reincorporated into the social and economic fabric of West German society. West German industry also benefited from the flight of East German citizens until 1961, when the erection of the Berlin Wall ended the westward migration. In fact, the labor shortage caused German employers to offer Yugoslavian and Turkish guest workers jobs in the burgeoning economy, thereby forever changing the ethnic makeup of Germany. This ever-growing and eager labor force had a doubly stimulating effect on the West German economy. It not only helped keep the price of labor at reasonably low levels, but it also handcuffed the ability of unions to strike effectively. These are two critical ingredients in any employer's recipe for success.

As impressive as these internal stimuli were, West Germany's economic "miracle" was also the by-product of the international initiatives to promote economic cooperation. The economic successes of the ECSC and the Common Market definitely played a role in sustaining West Germany's economic revival by eliminating tolls and tariff impediments that had hampered trade between the member nations for decades. We may never be able to quantify how much impact these institutions had on the German recovery, simply because it is impossible to replay history and compare what the West German economy would have been like without them. It will have to suffice to say that the relationship between the West German economy and the supranational economic organizations was synergistic; success in one area helped propel the success in the other.

Perhaps the most fundamental question of all concerns the term "economic miracle" itself. Just how "miraculous" was it? Given the widespread destruction of the war and the complete political collapse in 1945, it seems a fitting description of what appears to be a swift and dramatic reconstruction. Those who use the word "miraculous" most often base their conclusions on a conflation of three distinct but interrelated assumptions: (1) that Germany had suffered the most horrendous devastation as a result of war; (2) that the speed at which the recovery took place was remarkable; and (3) that these accomplishments were unusual, unexpected, and unmatched elsewhere. Each of these premises can be attacked in turn. First, we have seen that Germany's economic infrastructure survived the war reasonably well, and a great deal of underutilized plant, human, and material resources was available immediately after the war's end. Therefore, the devastation was not nearly as total or widespread as has always been assumed. Second, was the recovery all that speedy? This question defies a definitive answer. Speed is a relative phenomenon, requiring fixed starting and ending points for measurement. History rarely gives us such distinct signposts, nor does it provide many analogous situations with which West Germany's experience can be compared. While it may seem that Professor Grosser's "economic renaissance" of 1948 began quickly, it is arguable that recovery might have begun sooner had it not been delayed by the bickering of the four occupation powers over issues such as currency reform. Likewise, statistical information yields no definitive conclusions regarding the speed of recovery. If we compare West Germany's index of industrial production (using 1936 as a base) to those of other nations over the 10-year period following from 1945–55, West Germany's levels did not surpass the western world's until 1954. Lastly, the West German economic revival was far from unique. Other countries experienced comparable "miracles," and the data show that Japan's economic resurgence may well have been more impressive than Germany's. It is also important to remember the social cost of the German "miracle." While the living standard the West Germans achieved is admirable, it should not be forgotten that this might not have happened at all had German politicians not tacitly accepted the partitioning of their country. The reverie with which we celebrate West Germany's postwar economic success must be balanced by the sobering reality that millions of Germans had to endure 40 years of repression and economic hardship under a dictatorial regime.

Still, there is plenty of evidence, both direct and circumstantial, to support the notion that something "miraculous" happened in the 20 years following the Nazi surrender. Consider, for example, the 10 percent growth rates per annum in the 1950s, the elimination of unemployment, and industry's recapture of its share of the world market as indications of West Germany's transition from political pariah to economic powerhouse. Certainly, contemporaries were sufficiently amazed by their dramatic recovery to call what they had experienced a miracle. How else does one explain the 20 years of success the CDU enjoyed at the polls and the eventual transformation of the SPD into a mainstream party of liberal economics, except as evidence of the potency of the German economic revival?

In the final analysis, perhaps the source of contention is the word "miracle" itself. Its use is unfortunate, in that it implies some foreign or even supernatural intervention. However one interprets the events of West Germany's dramatic reemergence as a world economic power, it was no fortuitous accident. It was the result of hard work, done by an industrious people who wanted nothing more than to build a secure and prosperous future while avoiding the mistakes that had plagued them in the past.

SELECTED BIBLIOGRAPHY

Backer, John H. *Priming the German Economy: American Occupation Policies, 1945–1948*. Durham, NC: Duke University Press, 1971. A particularly good book on the reemergence of German infrastructure in the U.S. zone of occupation. Includes a chapter on U.S. and U.K. efforts to kick-start German foreign trade.

Balabkins, Nicholas. *Germany under Direct Controls: Economic Aspects of Industrial Disarmament*. New Brunswick, NJ: Rutgers University Press, 1964. A dated but still very useful overview of the economics of the occupation period. A good first stop for anyone studying the effects of postwar economic controls.

Borchert, Knut. *Perspectives on Modern German Economic History and Policy*. Cambridge: Cambridge University Press, 1991. A collection of essays previously published in a variety of journals by one of Germany's preeminent scholars of economic history. Only one of the chapters (chapter 7) is devoted entirely to the Federal Republic, but it is well worth reading for its insights into the so-called economic miracle.

Clay, Lucius D. *Decision in Germany*. Garden City, NY: Doubleday and Company, 1950. The reminiscences of the commander of the Office of Military Government, United States. Meant to be a record of the events of four years of occupation and rebuilding, this volume is an invaluable look into the decisions and personalities of the occupation from the military governor's perspective.

Erhard, Ludwig. *The Economics of Success*. London: Thames & Hudson, 1963. Printed as a follow-up to *Prosperity through Competition*, this volume is a collection of contemporary newspaper and periodical articles, speeches, and papers written by Erhard. It provides an interesting look at the contemporary arguments in favor of the social market approach to economics.

———. *Prosperity through Competition*. New York: Frederick A. Prager, 1958. First-hand account of the economic revival from the architect himself. The book begins with the events of 1948.

Giersch, Herbert, Karl-Heinz Paqué, and Holger Schmieding, eds. *The Fading Miracle: Four Decades of Market Economy in Germany*. Cambridge: Cambridge University Press, 1992. Part of the Cambridge Surveys in Economic Policy and Institutions series, this work is written by economists and is aimed more at economists and less at historians. It accepts the concept of an "economic miracle" but holds that it has continually "faded" since the early 1950s. Highly technical but still very useful.

Gimbel, John. *The American Occupation of Germany: Politics and the Military, 1945–1949*. Stanford, CA: Stanford University Press, 1968. As the title suggests, this book is mostly about U.S. decision making in occupied Germany. Nevertheless, it contains valuable chapters on the formation of Bizonia and the development of the West German political and economic infrastructure.

Hardach, Karl. "The Economy of the Federal Republic of Germany: Structure, Performance, and World Position." In *Contemporary Germany, Politics and Cul-*

ture, edited by Charles Burdick, Hans-Adolf Jacobsen, and Winfried Kud-szus, pp. 107–27. Boulder, CO: Westview Press, 1984. Concise and direct assessment of Germany's economic performance from the occupation period into the 1980s.

————. *The Political Economy of Germany in the Twentieth Century.* Berkeley, CA: University of California Press, 1980. A valuable survey of German economic history from World War I. The last three chapters provide an overview of the development of West and East Germany from the occupation zones through the creation of rival economies.

Hartrich, Edwin. *The Fourth and Richest Reich: How the Germans Conquered the Postwar World.* New York: Macmillian, 1980. An insightful look into the West German economic resurgence after World War II, written by a *Wall Street Journal* correspondent.

Kettenacker, Lothar. *Germany since 1945.* Oxford: Oxford University Press, 1997. A survey akin to that of H. A. Turner but containing more in-depth analysis. Of particular value is the statistical appendix, which quantifies much of the labor and immigration trends in the Federal Republic.

Kramer, Alan. *The West German Economy, 1945–1955.* Oxford: Berg Publishers, 1991. Excellent overview of economic forces and trends of the immediate postwar period. The author synthesizes the best research of German scholars, particularly that of Werner Abelshauser and presents the conclusions in a readable form to an English-reading public.

Milward, Alan. *The Reconstruction of Western Europe, 1945–1951.* Berkeley: University of California Press, 1984. A revisionist scholar of great influence, Milward downplays the role of the Marshall Plan in stimulating western Europe's post–World War II economic recovery.

Nicholls, A. J. *The Bonn Republic: West German Democracy 1945–1990.* New York: Addison Wesley Longman, 1997. Excellent single-volume history of the Federal Republic of Germany.

————. *Freedom with Responsibility: The Social Market Economy in Germany, 1918–1963.* Oxford: Clarendon Press, 1994. Probably the best English-language explanation of the historical origins and philosophical underpinnings of the Social Market Economy. Especially useful for understanding Erhard's role in its creation.

Turner, Henry Ashby. *Germany from Partition to Reunification.* New Haven, CT: Yale University Press, 1992. A survey of the history of the two Germanies since the end of World War II. Its usefulness as a research volume is limited; however, as an introduction or textbook it is quite valuable. A must for students new to postwar German history.

Wallich, Henry C. *Mainsprings of the German Revival.* New Haven, CT: Yale University Press, 1960. A description of the German "miracle" through the eyes of a contemporary economist. This volume is full of statistical information and analysis, some of which may be daunting to those unfamiliar with the discipline of economics. Nevertheless, amid all the technical narratives are excellent accounts of the currency reform, the birth of the free market economy, and the political fallout of the Cold War. It is still a good starting point for serious research on the postwar period.

10

The Reunification of Germany, 1990

INTRODUCTION

Although the reunification of Germany clearly was of vital importance to the German people, it was an event that happened *to* them rather than an event initiated *by* them. Fundamentally, German reunification was a function of the Cold War and its unexpected end. While Germans did play a part in their reunification, the major roles in the drama fell to the United States and, especially, the Soviet Union.

At the close of World War II, the victorious allied powers—Great Britain, the United States, the Soviet Union, and, belatedly, France—occupied an utterly defeated and ruined Germany. An independent German state ceased to exist, and the victors carved out zones of occupation. However, the victors soon fell out and prostrate Germany became a bone of contention for them. Disagreements among the erstwhile allies gradually intensified leading to the Cold War, a struggle featuring the Soviet Union on one side opposed by a coalition of states led by the United States and including Great Britain and France on the other side. While the Cold War eventually became a global struggle lasting about 40 years, its first and for a long time most passionate "battlefield" was Germany.

Bitterly disagreeing over what to "do" with Germany, the Cold War adversaries went their separate ways. The controversy over Germany continued to deepen until 1949, when the opposing parties independently of each other recreated not one but two Germanys. In May, the western powers organized the Federal Republic of Germany or, as it was commonly known, West Ger-

In 1961, the Berlin Wall was erected, physically dividing democratic and capitalistic West Berlin from totalitarian and communist East Berlin. Its destruction in November 1989 signaled the end of East Germany and the subsequent reunification of Germany. (Reproduced from the Collections of the Library of Congress.)

many. The following October, the Soviets established from their zone of occupation the German Democratic Republic, or East Germany.

Over the course of the next 40 years, East Germany, with its capital at Berlin, developed into the Soviet Union's most loyal and reliable satellite country. Not only did it faithfully follow the Soviet Union's lead in international politics, but its leaders—if not its people—also enthusiastically adopted the Soviet domestic model. This included the collective ownership of the means of production, a one-party political system, an ubiquitous and at times vicious security apparatus maintaining close scrutiny over the population's daily activities, isolation from Western Europe, but especially West Germany, and integration into Soviet-sponsored Eastern European organizations including economic and military ones.

West Germany, with its capital at the small Rhine River town of Bonn, moved in a very different direction. Turning westward, it allied itself with the United States and its European friends. West Germany embraced a vigorous capitalism, a multiparty democratic system, and a commitment to civil liberties and human rights common to the Western world. It shunned East Germany and only slowly developed relations with the Soviet-dominated Eastern European states. It became a leading force in such western organizations as the European Coal and Steel Community and its successor, the Common Market, and it joined the North Atlantic Treaty Organization (NATO), the West's military arm.

The unexpected reunification of Germany actually got under way in 1985 in Moscow when Mikhail Gorbachev became Soviet leader as General Secretary of the Communist Party of the Soviet Union. The Soviet Union that Gorbachev inherited had been in decline for a number of years. While its military might remained unquestioned, its economy was stagnating, its standard of living was falling, and its industrial infrastructure was growing obsolete. The Soviet Union had missed the technological revolution featuring the arrival of the computer, its people were demoralized, and its leadership was ancient, unimaginative, and corrupt. Gorbachev recognized the serious nature of the problems confronting the Soviet Union and committed himself to a program of extensive reform.

The Soviet Union's poor relations with the United States and its support of global communism complicated matters for Gorbachev. The former was leading to a new round in the decades-old arms race, a development the Soviet Union could ill afford given its financial and economic difficulties; the latter had already led to a serious draining of dwindling Soviet resources and worsening relations with the United States.

Gorbachev's reform program rested on three concepts. The first was *glasnost*, or openness. Gorbachev reasoned that the Soviet people had been lied to for so long that they believed nothing their government said. In order to reverse this attitude and to enlist the wholehearted support of the Soviet people for reform, the Soviet government would henceforth be honest and aboveboard with its citizenry. The second was *perestroika,* or renewal. Gorbachev proposed to revitalize and modernize the Soviet economic infrastructure through an infusion of controlled market capitalism, a truly radical idea for a Marxist-Leninist state. Finally, Gorbachev committed to *demokratizatsia,* or the infusion of a small degree of public participation in the country's civil and political life. For example, while the Soviet Union would remain a one-party state, henceforth there would be two communist candidates for a post instead of the usual formula of "one post-one candidate."

Gorbachev also kept his eye on the East Central European states. In the wake of World War II, the Soviet Union had not only adjusted that region's borders in its favor, but it had also established a string of satellite states insulating the Soviet homeland from possible invasion from the West. The Soviet Union's European satellite empire included Bulgaria, Romania, Hungary, Czechoslovakia, Poland, and East Germany. The Soviet grip on this empire had always been somewhat tenuous. The vast majority of people living in these countries aspired to independence and wanted the Soviet Union out. Many disliked the Russians; virtually all despised the communist system. In each country the Soviets had installed a compliant leadership and stationed Soviet troops in order to keep that leadership in power and to prevent popular uprisings. Nevertheless, hostility toward the Soviet Union and its puppets periodically boiled over. In those instances, the Soviet Union usually relied on force to bring the opposition to heel. For example, the Red Army had crushed revolution in Hungary in 1956 and destroyed a Communist reform movement in Czechoslovakia in 1968.

East Germany also had an early encounter with the Red Army. In June 1953, growing disenchantment with Communist hard-liner Walter Ulbricht's puppet regime and a declining standard of living brought hundreds of thousands of workers into the streets of East Berlin, Halle, Leipzig, Dresden, Magdeburg, and other East German cities. Soviet troops quickly and violently put down the unrest. In 1961, another serious challenge arose as an increasing number of disgruntled East Germans made their way to East Berlin where they crossed freely into West Berlin and moved on to West Germany. Most alarmingly, these emigrants tended to be young and well educated. East Germany's future was disappearing before its very eyes! The regime responded in August 1961 by constructing a wall that cut Berlin in two and put a quick end to the brain drain. The Berlin Wall came to symbolize both the Cold War and the post–World War II division of Germany.

Yet another serious challenge to Soviet control of East Central Europe emerged in 1980 in Poland when an independent trade union called Solidarity spread throughout the country. Within a few months, fully one-third of Poland's population joined Solidarity, and Poland's Communist leadership collapsed. Luckily for the Soviet Union, a handful of Polish collaborators appeared, enabling it to salvage its position in Poland without having to resort to a bloodbath. Nevertheless, the Solidarity movement clearly demonstrated the Soviet Union's continuing unpopularity in East Central Europe and its need to expend significant resources to keep that region quiet.

This reality was not lost on Gorbachev. He realized that maintaining Moscow's tight grip on its European satellites retarded his reform program in several important ways. For one thing, it hindered his drive for improved relations with the Western world, especially the United States. Moreover, it cost Moscow significant amounts of scarce cash and resources to station huge troop contingents in each of these unhappy countries. Finally, in order to keep its empire afloat Moscow generously subsidized the failing economies of its satellite states. Gorbachev badly needed those funds to promote his own reform plans.

The first concrete sign of the Soviet Union's new attitude toward East Central Europe came in 1988 when Gorbachev announced in a speech at the United Nations that the Soviet Union would significantly reduce the number of men and armaments that it maintained in the satellite countries. He also quietly signaled the communist leadership of the satellite countries that Moscow would not be as willing to put down incidents of popular discontent as it had in the past. East Germany's leadership, headed by Erich Honecker, who had replaced Ulbricht in 1971 as head of the communist Socialist Unity Party (SED), and Erich Mielke, who directed the ubiquitous and dreaded Ministry for State Security or Stasi, ignored Gorbachev's warnings and resisted his calls for reform. These hard-liners preferred to maintain the Stalinist status quo.

Sensing that the Soviet grip was weakening, the peoples of East Central Europe became emboldened. In 1988, Solidarity reemerged in Poland and through strikes and work slowdowns forced the government of communist military dictator Wojciech Jaruzelski to the bargaining table. There the Communists capitulated, relegalizing Solidarity and promising free elections. When those elections took place in June 1989, Solidarity candidates triumphed, and in August a noncommunist coalition government was formed. Meanwhile, in June 1989 Gorbachev made a highly successful trip to West Germany where he was wildly cheered, and a month later in a speech before the Council of Europe at Strasbourg, he renounced the Brezhnev Doctrine, which had been Soviet policy since 1968. Under the Brezhnev Doctrine, the Soviet Union reserved for itself the right to intervene in any other "socialist" country if it concluded that said country was veering from the "socialist" path prescribed by Moscow. The East German leadership steadfastly ignored what was happening, and Honecker even went so far as to say that the Berlin Wall would last for another 100 years.

However, despite the bold rhetoric dark storm clouds loomed on the horizon for East Germany's communist leadership. Hungary soon followed Poland along the path to liberalization. One of the most important steps it took was to open its heretofore closed border with Austria. At that, thousands of East Germans took vacation in Hungary and then "voted with their feet"; that is, they took advantage of the open border to go to Austria and then on to West Germany. In September alone it was estimated that 57,000 East Germans "voted."

Meanwhile, Honecker and his allies dug in. On September 5, he announced that East Germany categorically rejected the wave of reform sweeping over both the Soviet Union and its satellites, and he rejected the attempt of Neues Forum, a grassroots reform organization, to register as a legal body. Nevertheless, the pressure for change was growing. Monday night prayer services at Leipzig's St. Nicholas Church—a form of nonviolent protest against the regime—drew crowds in the tens of thousands. In Warsaw and Prague, the grounds of the West German embassies were packed with thousands of East Germans who waited for transit visas that would enable them to go to West Germany.

The reform movement received an important boost when Gorbachev visited East Berlin in early October to celebrate the fortieth anniversary of the founding of the German Democratic Republic. During his public presentation, the Soviet leader undercut Honecker to the wild applause of the assembled East Germans. Meanwhile, attendance at the demonstrations in Leipzig grew to approximately 200,000 by the middle of October. When Honecker ordered the use of force to break up the demonstrations, his colleagues on the ruling Politburo overruled him, and he was forced from office on October 18. Egon Krenz, a young and more pragmatic communist leader, replaced Honecker, but the handwriting was on the wall. In early November, more than 1 million East Germans took to the streets of East Berlin, and it appeared as though the collapse of the state was imminent.

The symbolic end of the German Democratic Republic came on November 9, 1989, when the hated Berlin Wall was opened, and East Berliners mingled freely with their western cousins. The Stasi, as despised as the

Wall, was shut down on December 7. Meanwhile, several days earlier West German chancellor Helmut Kohl had announced a "10-point plan" for German reunification. The Socialist Unity Party surrendered its position of absolute authority and a multiparty "Round Table" arrangement provided an interim government for the fading East Germany. When Kohl visited Berlin on December 22, 300,000 ecstatic Germans watched him reopen the Brandenburg Gate.

Germans now provided the driving force for the reunification of Germany, although the four victorious wartime allies were now reunited in their desire to have some input into the reunification process. The result was the two-plus-four talks on German reunification that opened in Ottawa, Canada, in February 1990. Featuring the two Germanys and the four allies, Kohl and the West Germans dominated these talks, bringing them to a successful conclusion in September. On September 12, 1990, the two-plus-four countries signed a treaty in Moscow granting full sovereignty to a reunified Germany. The treaty obligated the new Germany to accept the Oder-Neisse Line as the permanent boundary between Germany and Poland, to reduce the all-German army to 370,000, to keep the army firmly within the NATO command structure, to renounce all weapons of mass destruction, and to indemnify the Soviet Union for 8 billion dollars for its costs in continuing to station and then withdrawing its troops from East Germany.

In the meantime, free elections were held in East Germany on March 18, 1990. The big winner was Kohl's conservative Christian Democratic Union with Lothar de Maizière at its head. In May, Kohl and de Maizière signed an agreement calling for the political and social union of East and West Germany beginning on July 1. That date also marked the commencement of a currency union between the east and the west. Finally, on October 3, 1990, Germany was reunified, 45 years after it was defeated, occupied, and subsequently divided.

INTERPRETIVE ESSAY
Jean E. Abshire

It is a tremendous task to integrate two peoples who, after 40 years of separation, have developed significant differences in their expectations of themselves, their fellow citizens, and their government. The effects of this effort on Germany, its people, and its international status have been undeniably profound. The average German, whether eastern or western, has likely felt the economic impacts as much as or more than any of the other changes. That said, the political shifts and the implications of reunification on German society are also ones that leave lingering marks, both positive and negative, on Germany's people.

Many of the developments in the economic sphere relate to the approach used by the government in integrating the two very different economies. Early in the process, Chancellor Helmut Kohl assured his people that within three to five years the standard of living in the eastern part of the country would be similar to that of the western part. Eastern Germany would become a "flourishing landscape" and, with even greater optimism, Kohl said that this transformation could be paid for with "petty cash." Like in Russia, Poland, and other economies in transition, the Germans opted for "shock therapy." Rather than a gradual opening of the markets to competition, a gradual introduction of the West German mark to replace the old East German currency, and a gradual restructuring of wages and prices, the West German economic system was transplanted in the former East Germany overnight. For example, the true market value of the East German mark was four to five times less than the West German mark, but they were instantly converted at a 1:1 exchange rate for everything but savings over a certain amount. This dramatically increased the cost of eastern German labor, but labor productivity in the eastern part of Germany lagged well behind the productivity of workers in the western part of the country. What resulted was a rapid and complete collapse of the eastern German economy.

There were a variety of reasons for this economic collapse. The overvalued exchange rate, which increased wages and helped preserve people's savings but devastated the industrial sector, was only one reason. The problems with the exchange rate were heightened by overestimating the productivity of eastern German workers. Their productivity was thought to be approximately 50 percent of that of western workers, but it turned out to be about 30 percent. A number of the major East German industries, including steel and chemicals, proved to have obsolete technology and produced goods that could not compete with western goods on the open market. Many of these production facilities had to be closed. Some industries, including textiles, leather, optics, and electronics, fared somewhat better but still faced significant restructuring before they could hope to be competitive. Indeed, in the first year after the collapse of communism, eastern industrial output dropped by 28 percent, and the following year it fell a further 30 percent.

The evaporation of most of their previous markets further diminished the market competitiveness of eastern German goods. Special trade arrangements had existed among the members of Comecon, the economic organization of the Soviet Union and eastern European countries. East Germany exported approximately 75 percent of its products to other member countries. However, the rapid collapse of communism throughout the region meant that all the member states were undergoing economic transitions, and they no longer needed or wanted to buy the others' inferior goods.

Further contributing to the problems of overpriced and underproductive labor were the tactics adopted by the western labor unions, which quickly assumed bargaining authority for eastern workers. Germany has traditionally practiced a neocorporatist policy-making process in which trade unions, employer associations, and the government negotiate and seek consensus on policies relating to wage levels, systems for health, retirement, unemployment provisions, working hours, vacation time, and more. The agreements are then applied to all workers and employers in the sector. This institutionalized role in policy making gives labor unions a great deal of power and influence. However, in seeking to protect their traditional support base and see that western wage levels were not undermined by cheap labor in the east, the labor unions pushed for wage equalization between west and east. Employers in the west also had an interest in seeing that they were not undersold by eastern producers employing lower cost labor. The immediate imposition of the 1:1 exchange rate facilitated this, but at the time of economic unification, wage rates in the east were only 37 percent of the wage levels in the west. Naturally, increasing wages was appealing to eastern workers and, as indicated, also protected the western labor market.

The eastern workers' benefits from the equalization of wage levels was extremely brief for many. Combined with the lack of a market for eastern-produced goods, the inefficiencies of production, and the factory closings, the wage equalization policies helped bring a sharp increase in unemployment. Eighty percent of the manufacturing workforce lost their jobs. Overall unemployment in eastern Germany quickly rose to and remained at 15 percent, though some calculate it as high as 25 to 30 percent when factoring in early retirements and other such mechanisms for coping with labor surpluses. In some towns with factory closings, unemployment reached 35 percent or higher.

The lower levels of productivity and higher wages relative to western Germany had the further effect of discouraging investment. While the opening of new businesses and the retrofitting of old ones would have helped the unemployment problem, investors saw little incentive when more could be gained by keeping or investing their money in the western part of the country. Investment was further hindered by the difficulties and uncertainties surrounding the privatization process. Known as the *Treuhandanstalt,* this government-created privatization agency was charged with "privatization, restructuring, and lastly closure of wholly unprofitable enterprises." The privatization aspect led to many problems. In seeking to put property and enterprises previously owned by the East German government in private hands, many doors were opened to competing property claims. Indeed, the first priority claimants would be those who were considered "original owners," meaning those whose land had been confiscated by the East German government upon its creation or sometime thereafter. In some cases, these original owners were people who had been displaced during World War II and who had been residing in West Germany during the entire existence of East Germany. East Germans who had been living in homes and working land for decades were not given priority. The process of privatizing these state-owned properties was slow and made slower by court cases, the most significant of which was not concluded until a Constitutional Court decision in 1995. Not surprisingly, investors hesitated until property rights questions could be addressed. When enterprises were sold, they were sold primarily (about 75 percent) to western German owners, with only about 20 percent being sold to eastern Germans. The implication was that many of the profits would flow westward rather than remaining in the east.

The government response to these economic problems was to inject money in the form of massive transfer payments. After promising that reunification could be financed from "petty cash" and after resisting tax increases, the need for these transfer payments placed a great financial burden on the western Germans. German federalism has had as a central element that resource flows from the national government to states and from wealthier to poorer states to equalize revenues. Because of the economic weaknesses of the five new eastern states, western states would all have been net contributors, and they resisted this. The national government was, thus, left to bear the responsibility almost alone. The German Unity Fund, with a new "solidarity tax," was the primary vehicle for the transfers to the eastern states. Even when, in 1993, the Fund was dissolved and the eastern states were integrated into the state equalization system, the national government was forced to yield some of its other tax revenues to the states to compensate for the transfer payments from western states to eastern states. Of course, either way, it was the taxpayer who assumed the burden.

The transfers from the national government amounted to 75 billion marks in 1991 and quickly grew to and stayed in the range of 135 to 139 billion marks per annum. This, over time, constituted a decreasing percentage of the nation's gross domestic product (GDP) but remained, nevertheless, a great financial drain on the government. Throughout the 1990s, the transfer funds were targeted heavily toward social security benefits, including pensions and unemployment assistance, at a rate of 40–45 percent of transfer funds being used in this area. Subsidies to firms constituted a 6–10 percent share of transfer funds, while investment incentives received a 15–18 percent share. Other, not categorized, cash transfers generally ranged from 29–33 percent of total transfer funds.

Along with the increased tax burden, the western Germans were also subject to decreases in social services. The costly unemployment compensation that had to be paid to the many displaced eastern workers led to policy restructuring, with a decrease in benefits. This affected many western Germans as the cost of reunification, the approaches used in reunification, and a worsening global environment for German business led the whole country into a recession. While unemployment in eastern Germany was undeniably worse, unemployment in western Germany increased from 5.5 percent in 1991 to 9.9 percent in 1997. All in all, the increased tax burden, reduced services, and a mammoth public debt are the negative financial outcomes of reunification for the western Germans and have led to much public dissatisfaction.

Despite all of these difficulties, the economic picture is not completely bleak. During the 1990s, more than 1.3 trillion marks were invested in capital equipment and structures in eastern Germany. There is a completely new infrastructure, including highways, train service, electricity and water delivery systems, and one of the world's most advanced telecommunications systems. Cities and their many cultural and historical treasures have been rebuilt and restored. Perhaps more importantly, when lower living costs are factored in, the real household income in eastern Germany now stands at 90 percent of that in western Germany. Labor productivity has increased dramatically. The investment that was slow in coming, when it did finally arrive, exceeded investment in western Germany by 52 percent. These must be seen as indications of success despite all the problems.

However, there are lingering concerns over the sustainability of the success. Critics are quick to note that while there has been progress, it has been paid for to a very large degree by the fund transfers from west to east. The possibility of the "Mezzogiorno effect"—which refers to the relatively impoverished region in southern Italy that suffers from chronic joblessness and is sustained, seemingly permanently, through transfer payments from much more prosperous northern Italy—frequently arises.

Time alone will determine if, in the next decade or so, eastern Germany develops to the point where it can stand on its own economically.

Given the aforementioned dissatisfaction of western Germans, it is perhaps ironic that many of the government's policy choices were shaped by political and particularly electoral concerns for the western voter. The initial reluctance to raise taxes, which delayed development in the east, was due to doubts over the willingness of western Germans to sacrifice for reunification. Eastern Germans were initially euphoric over reunification, and Chancellor Helmut Kohl, the "father of reunification," was a regional hero. The westerners had to be reassured through political promises: no tax increases, a return of property lost in the communist takeover, and a short-term transition period. The approaches to wage and production competition by trade unions and employers associations were also determined with an eye toward keeping westerners content at the expense of easterners.

Despite these efforts to confine negative outcomes of reunification, change has occurred and has reshaped the political landscape. Germany has a multiparty, parliamentary form of government. The political executive is selected from and by the legislative branch, which is composed of a coalition of parties that form temporary partnerships to govern together. West Germany's party and coalition systems were characterized by a high level of stability and predictability. There were two dominant parties, the Christian Democrats (CDU) and the Social Democrats (SPD), and a smaller party, the Free Democrats. There were other smaller parties as well, but not ones that had a chance of governing. A coalition would be composed of either the Christian Democrats with the Free Democrats or the Social Democrats with the Free Democrats. For a time a grand coalition of the Christian Democrats with the Social Democrats governed, but generally a change in government happened when the Free Democrats switched sides.

In post-reunification Germany, this predictability and the composition of the party landscape have altered. The Party of Democratic Socialism, the successor party to East Germany's communist party, is a significant regional party in the east but draws virtually no support from the west. Its electoral successes have eroded in the last decade at the national level, and it is likely that this will continue. For the past 10 years, though, it has served as an advocacy party for the troubled eastern Germans and is an important actor in eastern state governments. The Free Democrats have been weakened and draw support almost exclusively from the west. Another development of note is the rise of the Green Party. It existed in West Germany for years but was radical and thus not considered a viable coalition partner. In post-reunification Germany, however, that has changed, and since 1997, Germany has been governed by a "red-green coalition," that is, the Social Democrats with the Greens. This is a dramatic change, as it opens up an entirely different option for the Social Democrats, who could now govern with either the Greens or the Free Democrats, while the Christian Democrats retain only the Free Democrats as an option. This lessens the predictability of Germany's governing coalitions and widens the range of significant political parties to an even higher degree at the state level.

The opening of the system, however, also meant internal but difficult changes for the Green Party. For a time the Greens were deeply divided between those who thought the compromises needed to participate in a coalition would mean selling out the party's principles (fundamentalists) and those who thought the only way to effect change was to participate in government (realists). The realists have clearly won and at an important time, since cleaning up the environmental devastation left by the East German government required a serious commitment of money and effort.

Also decreasing the predictability of governing coalitions and electoral outcomes is weaker party loyalty. This is a trend that has appeared in many western democracies in the last few decades, and because of this the CDU and SPD were plagued with weakening support bases prior to reunification. There has been no lessening of this trend since reunification. Moreover, with the western party system being simply transplanted to the east, as happened with reunification, the easterners do not have a sense of ingrained party loyalty that would serve as a reliable support base for the parties. In the first all-German election, the CDU with Chancellor Kohl at its head won overwhelming support for its rapid unification proposal, while the SPD suffered greatly in the east for raising concerns about the economic effects of a quick state merger. When the economic problems of reunification manifested themselves, the CDU was held accountable, and as stated previously, the SPD took control of the government in 1997. This government, however, has also faced stiff challenges due in large part to ongoing economic stresses and has paid at the ballot box, especially at the state level. Despite these adjustments, however, the traditional core of German party politics remains quite similar: The CDU and SPD are still the two main parties, and the country is governed by a coalition composed of one of the larger parties with a smaller party as partner.

One area of the political realm that has undergone real change is the traditional neocorporatist policy-making system mentioned previously. One aspect of the government response to many of the economic problems of reunification has been to introduce more classic liberal economic policies, which allow a greater role for the market with less government intervention. Various public service monopolies, such as the post and telephone service, have been privatized. Moreover, the self-regulation that existed and was maintained through the negotiated agreements of labor unions, employers associations, and the government has been weakened through a combination of freer market forces in some areas and greater government regulation and oversight in others. Neocorporatism was a hallmark of West Germany's policy making, and to have it diminished is a meaningful post-reunification development.

Another significant political shift that may still be on the horizon relates to the German federal system of power sharing between the state and national governments, known as "cooperative federalism." Traditionally, the system has functioned with very few powers assigned strictly to either the national or state governments. Rather, the national government has had primary authority for creating legislation, while the states have retained primary authority for implementing that legislation in the way that is most suitable. This relationship is institutionalized in the upper house of the parliament, the Bundesrat, which is composed of representatives from the state governments. It has only very limited veto power, but considerable consultative power over the laws passed by the lower house of parliament, the Bundestag.

This cooperative system of national legislation and state implementation has relied heavily on the states presenting a united front in the face of national power. The system began coming under stress in the 1980s because of increasingly divergent interests between the traditional coal and steel industry states and the high-tech industry states. Scholars considered the possibility that less unity among the states would allow the national government to use the divisions to assume greater power vis-à-vis the states. Since reunification there have been discussions about restructuring the federal system, which like the economic and party systems was simply transplanted to eastern Germany. However, this has not yet occurred, and some worry that the even greater disparities between the western and eastern parts of Germany will give rise to impossibly deep rifts between the states and preclude a unified state front. There is indeed evidence for this, with the eastern states taking common stances on certain issues without consultation and coordination with western states and, of course, the western states being very concerned about the drain on resources for rebuilding the east. Eastern states, which were reconstituted after the collapse of the very centralized East Germany, have also found somewhat daunting the responsibilities of state authority in German federalism and seem less interested in protecting state authority from federal incursions.

If the previously mentioned "Mezzogiorno effect" transpires and the east becomes permanently reliant on fund transfers from the western states and the national government to survive, then greater problems in federal relations can be anticipated. In Italy this has even led to a regional separatist movement in the northern areas where many people are tired of seeing their tax money permanently prop up the south. In response to these potential problems with German federalism, a number of reforms have been proposed. Thus far, however, nothing has occurred, and some scholars believe the western states may have lost the chance that came with reunification to adjust the system to the challenge of a less cohesive group of states that cannot stand unified against the national government.

The divisions in government interests are naturally reflections of diverse interests in society, which also have grown and developed anew as an outcome of reunification. Within a short time, people began speaking of the "wall of the mind" that replaced the Berlin Wall, separating "Wessis" (westerners) from "Ossis" (easterners). With western managers being sent to operate many of the eastern companies that had been purchased by westerners, the Ossis soon became frustrated with the know-it-all westerners directing their lives and living a much more prosperous life than the easterners around them. They also missed various amenities of East German life, which gave rise to the term "Ostalgia," or *Ostalgie*—nostalgia for East Germany. Surveys show that eastern Germans now respond favorably to the idea of socialism with support ranging from 58 to 72 percent (in contrast to 30 to 35 percent among westerners) and that easterners associate socialism with desirable provisions that they have lost such as guaranteed employment, equality, affordable housing, and guaranteed childcare.

For their part, westerners grew impatient with the easterners who kept expecting handouts, would not adapt to new ways, and would rather whine than work for what they needed. Westerners tended to think that easterners should complain less, as most were better off than before, and show more gratitude. This mindset further alienated easterners, who were displeased that reunification was more of a takeover by the west than a merger, whose existence—that easterners had worked toward for 40 years—was thereby devalued and deemed inferior. Indeed, opinion polls through the years have indicated a steady feeling among eastern Germans of being second-class citizens.

Perhaps the most disturbing attitudinal gap between Germans is directed toward government institutions. Western Germans generally have a high degree of faith and satisfaction in their institutions. Eastern Germans express a high degree of faith in democracy, but much lower levels of confidence in existing government structures. For example, in 1995 polls indicated 63 percent of westerners versus 38 percent of easterners thought democracy could solve Germany's problems. Two years later, another poll showed 81 percent of easterners supporting the idea of democracy, but only 40 percent found its performance in Germany satisfactory, as compared to 60 percent of people in the west.

While the "wall of the mind" continues to be problematic, there are signs of hope. In a 1999 survey, 70 percent of Germans associated the word "reunification" with positive feelings. In a different poll that same year, in which people were asked to rank a list of 17 hopes, "That German unity might succeed" ranked third on the list in both parts of Germany.

On a negative note, as so often occurs with economic want, scapegoating, right-wing extremism, racism, and hate crimes have increased. Incidents of racial violence rose alarmingly in the first two years after reunification. There was actually a decrease in 1990 from the previous year with 270 racial attacks reported. However, in 1991 there were 1,483 such attacks, and in 1992 there were 2,584 attacks. The severity of the problem has decreased some since then, but elevated levels of racial violence remain a characteristic of the new Germany. The greatest numbers of attacks have fallen into the category of homicides, arsons, assaults, bombings, and property damage. These have occurred at higher levels in both parts of Germany. The second category of racial violence, large-scale riots, has been confined to eastern Germany.

The most frequent targets are immigrants, including many asylum seekers. In 1992, Germany received 79 percent of the asylum applications that were tendered to European Community countries. Adding these numbers to the many ethnic Germans entering the country from former communist areas of Eastern Europe and the former Soviet Union, the number of immigrants in Germany was relatively high. Prior to reunification, a meaningful percentage of West Germany's population—up to one-third—had resulted from immigration. Many post-reunification immigrants, including asylum seekers, were settled in eastern Germany. In towns where factories had closed and unemployment was high, it proved an explosive mixture to establish housing for hundreds of asylum seekers who may also have been looking for employment.

While the extreme right grew in strength all over Germany after reunification, surprisingly, the number of right-wing organizations and their memberships did not increase significantly. There was, however, an increase in right-wing voting behavior, particularly in state and local elections. Several rightist political parties, including the Republicans and the German People's Union, experienced high enough levels of support to gain seats in state and local governments. However, they failed to gain the five percent threshold required for representation at the national level. Significantly, this occurred primarily in western states. As is characteristic of most such parties, they tended to draw their support from young, working-class males, and from the unemployed. The economic stresses across the country, combined with high levels of media attention to the numbers of immigrants and asylum seekers, in particular, provided fertile ground for these parties. The government response was to pass a law in the early 1990s that restricted the rights of asylum applicants and facilitated the deportation of those applicants who had been denied. In turn, the number of asylum applications dropped significantly by the end of 1993.

More recently Germany has grappled with the difficult question of citizenship rights for its immigrant population, many of whom have been in the country for decades and may even be second or third generation. A liberalized citizenship law was passed in 1999, the first change since a blood-based law was created more than 80 years ago, but it has undergone various court challenges and has become a political hot potato. The term "foreign co-citizens" has even been coined, as many Germans seem incapable of considering immigrants to be bona fide Germans.

The domestic changes have also had international implications. Beginning in the 1950s, West Germany became a primary actor in the early efforts at European integration in order to prove itself tied to the democratic west; so too did the newly reunified Germany seek to reassure its nervous neighbors through greater European integration. The memories of an aggressive united Germany from the earlier World Wars had not been forgotten, and French president François Mitterand was quoted during international discussions prior to reunification as saying, "We like Germany. We like it so much, we'd like to have two." In order to allay such concerns, the new Germany pushed for greater cooperation among the members of the European Union, including the ultimate step of monetary union. The result of this is that the German mark, of which western Germans were very proud as it reflected their post–World War II recovery and success, has ceased to exist, having been replaced by the European single currency, the Euro.

More negatively, Germany's post-reunification economic bumps also created disturbances for those concerned neighbors. The deficit spending the government used to finance eastern reconstruction led the German Federal Bank to raise interest rates. This caused a ripple effect in many economies of the European Community, which had currency values tied together through the European Exchange Rate Mechanism (ERM) as a step toward monetary union. The currencies of France, Italy, and the United Kingdom were exposed as weaker than had been thought, and across Western Europe countries were forced to quickly buy French, Italian, and British currencies or sell German marks in order to keep their own currency values from falling. These currency shocks led to the demise of the ERM and likely hastened the creation of the Euro. Moreover, Germany and the Federal Bank were blamed by some western neighbors for causing unemployment and other economic problems in those countries.

Unified Germany, considered more confident by many scholars, has also demonstrated greater interest in taking on a larger international role. Germany has made clear its desire for a permanent seat on the United Nations Security Council, though its willingness to accept the responsibility that accompanies influence does not always seem as strong. It has also been a leader in advocating the expansion of NATO eastward to include eastern European countries formerly in the Soviet alliance. It has undergone a dramatic shift and accepted more responsibility for a military role within NATO. In 1995, amid much debate, the German military participated in bombing Serbian positions as part of the NATO peacekeeping mission in Bosnia. For the first time since World War II, the German military was engaged outside the NATO theater. A similar debate arose in 1999 concerning the NATO action in Kosovo, and Germany once again chose involvement in military action. This has continued into the new century with German military aircraft patrolling American skies after the terrorist attacks on September 11, 2001, and also with German participation in the peacekeeping mission in Afghanistan after the U.S. war, its first deployment outside NATO territory or Europe. This pattern of engagement lapsed when Germany stood with France and many other countries in opposition to the U.S.-led war in Iraq in 2003. While Germany withstood much criticism from the United States and Great Britain, there was no "wall of the mind" among the German electorate, which strongly opposed U.S. President George Bush's policy of preemptive action. Germany's foreign policy is tightly bound with international organizations, particularly as Germany's push for deeper European integration has led the European Union, with some difficulty, to assume a greater foreign policy role on behalf of its member states.

The effects of German reunification have been tremendous. Significant changes have occurred in the economic sphere, and the political outcomes may still not be fully evident. Likewise, the social divisions between the two parts of Germany linger. The risk of the "Mezzogiorno effect" with long-term regional disparity, economic dependency, and unemployment is a serious threat indeed. If eastern Germany can develop enough self-sufficiency not to rely on the national and western state governments for financing, problems may be averted, and greater social and political harmony will likely grow. If not, the long-term implications of reunification for Germany could be quite negative.

SELECTED BIBLIOGRAPHY

Anderson, Jeffrey. *German Unification and the Union of Europe.* New York: Cambridge University Press, 1999. This book provides an in-depth analysis of the relationship between German reunification and European integration.

Bender, Peter. *10 Years of German Unity: A Political Essay.* Bonn: Inter-Nationes/IN-Press, 2000. A short but insightful essay reflecting on national unity from one of Germany's leading journalists.

Flockton, Chris, Eva Kolinsky, and Rosalink Pritchard, eds. *The New Germany in the East.* Portland, OR: Frank Cass, 2000. This book examines various aspects of social policy and their implications in the former East Germany.

Fulbrook, Mary. *Interpretations of the Two Germanies, 1945–1990.* 2nd ed. New York: St. Martin's Press, 2000. A short volume that gives a brief overview of post–World War II German history, but provides more depth on steps to reunification.

Heneghan, Tom. *Unchained Eagle: Germany after the Wall.* New York: Reuters, 2000. A detailed journalistic account covering 1989 to early 2000.

Jeffrey, Charlie, ed. *Recasting German Federalism: The Legacies of Unification.* New York: Pinter, 1999. This book examines structures, issues, and reform in the relationship between the German national and state governments since reunification.

Kahn, Charlotte. *Ten Years of German Unification: One State, Two Peoples.* Westport, CT: Praeger, 2000. This compelling book is structured around interviews with both eastern and western Germans.

Kurthen, Hermann, Werner Bergmann, and Rainer Erb, eds. *Antisemitism and Xenophobia in Germany after Unification.* New York: Oxford University Press, 1997. This volume provides analysis of many aspects of racism in post-reunification Germany with examinations of organizations, target groups, public responses, and more.

Larres, Klaus, ed. *Germany since Unification: The Development of the Berlin Republic.* 2nd ed. New York: Palgrave, 2001. An excellent volume giving overviews of developments across a wide range of economic, political, social, and international topics.

Libal, Gisela, ed. *10 Years of German Unity: A Discussion.* Bonn, Germany: Inter-Nationes/IN-Press, 2000. A series of short essays from well-known German politicians and journalists from both parts of Germany.

Leonhard, Jörn, and Lothar Funk, eds. *Ten Years of German Unification: Transfer, Transformation, Incorporation?* Birmingham, AL: University of Birmingham Press, 2002. An interdisciplinary look at different facets of reunification from historical and contemporary perspectives.

Mayr, Alois, and Wolfgang Taubmann, eds. *Germany Ten Years after Reunification.* Leipzig, Germany: Institut für Länderkunde, 2000. A volume of essays addressing changes in the areas of demographics, economics, transportation, and environment.

Merkl, Peter H., ed. *The Federal Republic of Germany at Fifty.* New York: New York University Press, 1999. This edited volume provides analysis of a range of issues including identity, politics, and international relations.

Quint, Peter E. *The Imperfect Union: Constitutional Structures of German Unification.* Princeton, NJ: Princeton University Press, 1997. This book provides a detailed examination of many constitutional questions relating to reunification and the blending of two social and legal systems.

Rittenberger, Volker, ed. *German Foreign Policy since Unification: Theories and Case Studies.* New York: Manchester University Press, 2001. An overview of leading foreign policy theories and in-depth investigations of foreign policy toward the United Nations, NATO, and the European Union.

Sinn, Gerlinde, and Hans-Werner Sinn. *Jumpstart: The Economic Unification of Germany.* Cambridge, MA: MIT Press, 1992. A seminal work providing in-depth analysis of the economic aspects of reunification.

Sinn, Hans-Werner. *Germany's Economic Unification: An Assessment after Ten Years.* Working Paper 7586. Cambridge, MA: National Bureau of Economic Research, 2000. A paper describing the economic status quo in Germany with suggested reforms.

Smith, Patricia J., ed. *After the Wall: Eastern Germany since 1989.* Boulder, CO: Westview Press, 1998. This edited book addresses the conditions of economic reconstruction, political changes, foreign policy, and the cultural and social implications of reunification in the east.

Thomaneck, J. K. A., and Bill Niven. *Dividing and Uniting Germany.* New York: Routledge, 2001. A brief volume providing a concise overview of the conditions surrounding division and reunification in Germany and afterward.

Von Hagen, Jürgen, and Rolf R. Strauch. "East Germany: Transition with Unification, Experiments, and Experiences." In *Transition: The First Decade,* edited by Mario I. Blejer and Marko Skreb, pp. 87–120. Cambridge, MA: MIT Press, 2001. A chapter focused on economic transition as part of a larger work looking at the transitions across Eastern Europe.

Appendix A

Glossary

Balkans. The Balkans refers to the southeastern corner of Europe, a swath of land dominated by the Balkan Mountains. Many different (and fractious) nationalities live in the Balkans, including the Serbs, Croats, Albanians, Bulgarians, Bosnians, and Romanians.

Benelux. Benelux is a shorthand way of referring to the three independent but similar states of Belgium, the Netherlands, and Luxembourg.

Bernstein, Eduard (1850–1932). Bernstein was the leading proponent of revisionist socialism, a form of socialism that gained ground in the 1890s. Revisionist socialism denied the infallibility of Karl Marx and advocated a peaceful, evolutionary way to socialism that took into account both a rising standard of living for the working class and the important and constructive role that unions and the right to vote could play in achieving workers' goals.

Big Three. This World War II term refers to the leaders of the Grand Alliance, Winston Churchill, Franklin D. Roosevelt, and Joseph Stalin, or to their respective countries, Great Britain, the United States, and the Soviet Union.

Boer War (1899–1902). This war pitted British troops against Afrikaner, or Dutch, settlers in southern Africa and represented an effort to bring the Boers and their lands into the British Empire. William II meddled in this matter to the detriment of Anglo-German relations.

Bolshevism. Derived from the Russian word *Bolshevik*, or man of the majority, the term *Bolshevism* became a synonym for Soviet-style Communism.

Brandenburg Gate. Constructed in 1791, the Brandenburg Gate sits in the heart of Berlin. It is perhaps that city's most famous landmark, and after being incorporated into the infamous Berlin Wall, it was opened anew with the reunification of Germany.

Carlsbad Decrees (1819). Alarmed by signs of rising German nationalism, Austrian chancellor Clemens von Metternich assembled the principal German states at Carlsbad where he persuaded them to issue a set of decrees suppressing the German press and universities. The Carlsbad Decrees retarded liberalism and nationalism in Germany for many years.

Colm, Dodge, and Goldsmith Report (1946). Named after its U.S. authors, this important study urged the reformation of Germany's monetary system. It served as a starting point for discussions that eventually resulted in a new currency for the western zones of occupation.

Common Market. By virtue of the 1957 Treaties of Rome, six European countries, including West Germany, pledged themselves to the elimination of customs barriers and the creation of a free trade zone. The Common Market helped to bring unprecedented prosperity to West Germany.

Congress of Vienna (1814–15). Meeting in the Austrian capital at the conclusion of the Napoleonic Wars and dominated by Clemens von Metternich, the Austrian chancellor, the Congress of Vienna redrew the map of Europe and defined European political orthodoxy.

Cottage Industry. The *American Heritage Dictionary* defines cottage industry as "a usually small-scale industry carried on at home by family members using their own equipment."

Great War. The Great War is a synonym for World War I.

Jameson Raid (1896). The Jameson Raid was a failed attempt by Cecil Rhodes, head of Great Britain's Cape Colony, to foment revolution in the neighboring Transvaal, which was controlled by the Boers, or Dutch settlers. The raid not only prompted a controversial telegram from Germany's William II congratulating the Boers, but it also helped to lead to the outbreak of the Boer War.

Junkers. This is the name given to the traditional German landed aristocracy, especially those who lived east of the Elbe River. The Junkers dominated Prussia and exercised great influence within imperial Germany.

League of Nations. Created at the close of World War I, the League of Nations was an international body composed of sovereign states committed to the settlement of international disputes in a peaceful manner.

Low Countries. This is another name for Belgium, the Netherlands, and Luxembourg.

Marshall Plan. This is the popular name given to the European Recovery Program. Under the Marshall Plan, the United States poured billions of dollars into Europe, including Germany, in order to revive the continent's economy after World War II.

Mein Kampf. Written in 1924, *Mein Kampf* is Adolf Hitler's autobiography. Concocted while Hitler served a prison term for attempting to overthrow the Weimar Republic, *Mein Kampf* is full of Hitler's ideas about race, politics, and Germany's future.

Midlands. This term refers to the highly industrialized central region of Great Britain, including cities such as Birmingham and Manchester.

Napoleon (1769–1821). Born Napoleon Bonaparte on the island of Corsica, Napoleon crowned himself emperor of the French in 1804. His attempted conquest of Europe brought his armies into the heart of the German-speaking world, where they spread the ideas of the French Revolution and provoked a patriotic backlash.

Napoleon III (1808–73). Nephew of Napoleon, Napoleon III ruled as emperor of France from 1852–70. He abdicated the throne after his humiliating defeat at the hands of Bismarck in the Franco-Prussian War.

NATO. This is the acronym for the North Atlantic Treaty Organization. NATO is a military alliance created in 1949 to contain the expansion of communism. West Germany joined the alliance in 1954, marking a significant step in Germany's post–World War II rehabilitation.

Niemöller, Martin (1892–1984). Niemöller was a former U-boat captain turned Lutheran pastor who in the 1930s courageously led that branch of the Lutheran Church opposed to Hitler's attempt to dominate the church and use it as a vehicle for Nazi political ends.

Oder-Neisse Line. This is the eastern boundary of post-1945 Germany. It runs along the Oder and western Neisse rivers. By virtue of this boundary, considerable territory that had belonged to Germany was incorporated into Poland.

Particularism. Prior to German unification (and for a number of years afterward, as well), many German-speakers felt a greater degree of loyalty to their particular German state (e.g., Bavaria, Hesse, Saxony) than to the unified country. This desire to put local interests first and for local political units to maintain as much independence as possible is called particularism.

Polish Corridor. At the end of World War I, a Polish state was reestablished. In order to provide the new Poland with access to the Baltic Sea, the valley of the Vistula River and the lands of Posen province were taken from Germany and given to Poland. Of mixed German and Polish population, these lands became known as the Polish Corridor and proved to be a serious bone of contention during the interwar years.

Potsdam Conference (1945). The Potsdam Conference took place in the Berlin suburb of Potsdam in July 1945. Formal agreements on several major issues were reached; however, the divergent views on Germany's future expressed by Great Britain, the Soviet Union, and the United States foreshadowed the breakup of the Grand Coalition and the subsequent division of Germany.

Prussian Tariff Union. This is another name for the *Zollverein*, the custom's union established in 1834 under Prussian auspices that economically drew much of Germany together prior to political unification.

Realpolitik. Literally, the politics of reality. Usually associated with Bismarck, who is frequently given credit for perfecting *realpolitik,* the adherents of this political methodology claim to base both their policies and actions on a dispassionate, objective reading of the facts at hand.

Red Army. Founded by V. I. Lenin in 1918 and built into an effective fighting force by Leon Trotsky, the Red Army defended the Soviet state from its external enemies. After World War II, its name was changed to the Soviet Army.

Romanticism. A chiefly nineteenth-century cultural and intellectual development that reacted to the Enlightenment's emphasis on reason by placing great value on emotion and feeling. Romanticism was a particularly strong force in the German-speaking world.

Social Darwinism. Derived from Charles Darwin's pioneering nineteenth-century work on evolution, Social Darwinism concluded that the struggle for existence and survival of the fittest applied to individuals and nations as well as plants and lesser animals. This concept both justified and encouraged belligerent, aggressive nationalism and racism.

Stresemann, Gustav (1878–1929). Stresemann was perhaps the most important political figure of the Weimar Republic. He dealt effectively with the crisis of 1923 and was particularly successful in integrating Germany back into the European community through a policy of compromise and compliance with the Treaty of Versailles.

Vormärz. This term refers to the period immediately before the outbreak of the Revolutions of 1848. It was characterized by a growing intellectual ferment that culminated in revolution.

Yalta Conference (1945). A few short months before the end of World War II, the Big Three met at Yalta, a Soviet resort on the Black Sea. Building on earlier discussions, Churchill, Roosevelt, and Stalin now agreed to a division of both Germany and Berlin into zones of occupation, the de facto recognition of Germany's eastern border with Poland, imposition on Germany of reparations with the lion's share going to the Soviet Union, and the demilitarization, denazification, and democratization of Germany.

Young Plan (1929). Following on the 1924 Dawes Plan, the Young Plan reworked Germany's reparations payments from World War I in a manner more favorable to the Weimar Republic.

Appendix B

Timeline

1814–1815	Congress of Vienna
1815–1866	German Confederation
1819	Carlsbad Decrees
1827	Beethoven dies
1831	Hegel dies
1832	Goethe dies
1834	Founding of the *Zollverein*
1835	First rail line in Germany
1840–1861	Frederick William IV, King of Prussia
1848–1849	Revolutions of 1848
1848–1916	Franz Joseph I, Emperor of Austria
1848	Revolution in southwestern Germany
	Revolution in Berlin
	Revolution in Vienna; Metternich flees
	Frankfurt Assembly
1849	Prussian constitution promulgated
1850	Punctation of Olmütz
1853–1856	Crimean War
1859	Austro-Italian War

1861–1888	William I, King of Prussia
1862	Otto von Bismarck named Prussian chancellor
1863	Ferdinand Lassalle founds the General German Workers' Association
1864	Austro-Prussian War against Denmark
1865	Bad Gastein Convention
	Napoleon III and Bismarck meet at Biarritz
1866	Austro-Prussian War
	Battle of Sadowa (Königgrätz)
	Treaty of Prague
	Siemens perfects electric dynamo
1867–1871	North German Confederation
1869	Social Democratic Workers Party founded
1870–1871	Franco-Prussian War
1870	Bad Ems Dispatch
	Battle of Sedan
1871	German Empire proclaimed
	Constitution of the German Empire promulgated
1873–1887	*Kulturkampf*
1873	May Laws
1875	*Reichsbank* founded
	Social Democratic Party of Germany founded
1878	Congress of Berlin
	Anti-Socialist Laws passed
1879	Dual (Germany and Austria-Hungary) Alliance
1882	Italy joins the Dual Alliance
	Kolonialverein founded
1883–1889	Bismarck pushes a package of advanced social legislation through the Reichstag
1883	Rathenau forms Allgemeine Elektrizitäts Gesellschaft (AEG)

	Wagner dies
1884	Germany begins to acquire African colonies
1887	Reinsurance Treaty with Russia
1888	William I dies
	Frederick III, emperor of Germany
	Frederick III dies
1888–1918	William II, emperor of Germany
1890	Bismarck resigns
	Anti-Socialist Laws expire
	Reinsurance Treaty not renewed
1891	Pan German League founded
1893	Agrarian League founded
1894	Franco-Russian alliance
1896	Kruger telegram
1897	Brahms dies
1898	Eduard Bernstein and the "revision" of Marxism
	Germany leases Kiaochow in China
	Germany adds South Pacific islands to its empire
	First Navy Law passed
	Flottenverein founded
	William II visits Palestine
1900	Germany sends troops to put down Boxer Rebellion in China
	Nietzsche dies
1904	Great Britain and France create Entente Cordiale
1905	First Moroccan crisis
	Schlieffen Plan developed
1906	Algeciras Conference
	Britain launches its first Dreadnought
1907	Great Britain and Russia settle their differences

1908	*Daily Telegraph* affair
	Austria annexes Bosnia-Herzegovina
1909–1917	Bethmann-Hollweg serves as German chancellor
1911	Second Moroccan crisis
1912	SPD largest party in Reichstag
1913	Military mission under General Liman von Sanders to Ottoman Empire
1914–1918	World War I
1914	Austrian Archduke Franz Ferdinand assassinated
	Battle of Tannenberg
	First Battle of the Marne
	Battle of the Masurian Lakes
	Turkey enters war on side of Central Powers
1915	Italy enters war on side of Allies
	Lusitania sunk
	Bulgaria enters war on side of Central Powers
1916	Battle of Verdun
	Battle of the Somme
	Battle of Jutland
	Romania enters war on side of Allies
	Generals Paul von Hindenburg and Erich Ludendorff rise to power
	Franz Joseph dies
1917	Unrestricted submarine warfare commences
	The United States enters the war on the side of the Allies
	Revolution in Russia
	German Independent Social Democratic Party (USPD) founded
1918	U.S. President Woodrow Wilson's Fourteen Points
	Treaty of Brest-Litovsk
	Massive offensive on the Western Front

	Germany collapses, William II abdicates
	Germany proclaimed a republic
	Armistice signed at Compiègne
	German Communist Party founded
1919–1933	Weimar Republic
1919	Spartacist Revolt
	Election of National Assembly
	Treaty of Versailles
	Promulgation of a constitution for the Weimar Republic
1920	Kapp Putsch
1922	Rapallo Treaty
	Franco-Belgian occupation of the Ruhr
1923	Runaway inflation
	Beer Hall Putsch
1924	Dawes Plan
	Hitler writes *Mein Kampf*
1925	Hindenburg elected president
	Locarno Pact
1926	Germany enters League of Nations
1929	Young Plan
	Gustav Stresemann dies
	Great Depression begins
1930	Heinrich Brüning named chancellor
	National Socialists make significant electoral gains
1931	Creation of Harzburg Front
1932	Hindenburg reelected president
	Unemployment at 6 million
	National Socialists become largest party in Reichstag
	Franz von Papen named chancellor
	Kurt von Schleicher named chancellor

1933–1945	Third Reich
1933	Adolf Hitler named chancellor
	Reichstag building burns; state of emergency declared
	Enabling Act
	Opening of first concentration camp at Dachau
	Organized boycott of Jewish businesses
	Public burning of books
	Trade unions outlawed
	All political parties declared illegal with the exception of the Nazis
	Germany resigns from the League of Nations
1934	German-Polish Nonaggression Treaty
	"Night of the Long Knives"
	Hindenburg dies
	Nazi-inspired unrest in Austria
	Hitler named *Führer und Reichskanzler*
	German Labor Front established
1935	Saar votes to join Third Reich
	Nürnberg Laws
	German rearmament
1936	Remilitarization of the Rhineland
	Olympics in Germany
	Rome-Berlin Axis
	German-Japanese agreement
1937	Hossback Conference
1938	Army nazified
	Anschluss
	Munich Conference
	Reichskristallnacht
1939–1945	World War II
1939	Germany seizes Czechoslovakia

	Nazi-Soviet Nonaggression Pact
	Germany invades Poland
1940	Germany conquers Denmark, Norway, Luxembourg, Holland, and Belgium
	Germany defeats France
	Battle of Britain
1941	Germany invades the Soviet Union
	Hitler declares war on the United States
	Battle of Moscow
1942–1943	Battle of Stalingrad
	Battle of the Atlantic
1942	Wannsee Conference to organize the Final Solution (the extermination of European Jewry)
	Battle of El Alamein
1943	Battle of Kursk
	Mussolini overthrown; Italy leaves war
	Teheran Conference
1944	Western allies land in Normandy
	Failed attempt to assassinate Hitler
1945	Yalta Conference
	Dresden firebombed
	Hitler commits suicide
	Germany surrenders unconditionally
	Potsdam Conference
	Nürnberg Trials begin
1945–1949	Germany occupied and divided
1946	Formation of Socialist Unity Party (SED) in Soviet zone of occupation from a forced merger of the SPD with the KPD
1947	United States and Great Britain merge their zones of occupation to form Bizonia
	Marshall Plan presented

1948	Currency reform in the western zones of occupation
	Berlin Blockade
1949	Berlin Blockade lifted
	Establishment of the Federal Republic of Germany (West Germany) with capital at Bonn
	Establishment of the German Democratic Republic (East Germany) with capital at Berlin
	Konrad Adenauer named chancellor of West Germany
	Walter Ulbricht leads East Germany
1951	European Coal and Steel Community
	Law of Codetermination
1952	Law for the Equalization of Burdens
	European Defense Community created
1953	Refugee Law
	Workers' rebellion in East Germany
1954	West Germany joins NATO
1955	Western occupation of Germany ends
	East Germany joins the Warsaw Pact
	West Germany establishes diplomatic relations with the Soviet Union
	Thomas Mann dies
1956	KPD outlawed in West Germany
1957	Saarland rejoins West Germany
	Hallstein doctrine
	Treaty of Rome establishes the Common Market
1959	Bad Godesberg program
1961	Berlin Wall erected
1962	Conscription in East Germany
	Der Spiegel scandal in West Germany

1963	Franco-German Friendship Treaty
	Ludwig Erhard succeeds Adenauer as chancellor of West Germany
1966	The "Grand Coalition" succeeds Erhard
1968	Student unrest in West Germany
	Warsaw Pact invades Czechoslovakia
1969	Willy Brandt named chancellor of West Germany
1970	Height of *Ostpolitik:* German-Soviet Non-Aggression Treaty signed; German-Polish Treaty signed
1971	Erich Honecker succeeds Walter Ulbricht as leader of East Germany
	Four power agreement on Berlin
1972	Olympics in Munich
	Basic Treaty between West Germany and East Germany signed
	Heinrich Böll awarded Nobel Prize for Literature
1973	Both West Germany and East Germany join the United Nations
	OPEC oil crisis
1974–1977	Height of "Red Army Faction" terror in West Germany
1974	Helmut Schmidt succeeds Brandt as chancellor of West Germany
1975	Helsinki Accords
1976	Wolf Biermann, East Germany dissident, exiled
1978	Establishment of the Green Party in West Germany
1979	Nuclear missiles deployed in West Germany
	Economy of West Germany continues to decline
1982	Helmut Kohl succeeds Schmidt as chancellor of West Germany
1985	Mikhail Gorbachev comes to power in the Soviet Union
1987	Honecker visits West Germany
1989	Berlin Wall falls

	East Germany collapses
1990	Germany reunified
1992	Maastricht Treaty
1993	Honecker goes into exile
1995	Germany participates in NATO's war against Serbia
1997	SPD-Green coalition wins election; Gerhard Schroeder succeeds Kohl as chancellor
1999	Germany participates in NATO's military action in Kosovo
	Günter Grass awarded Nobel Prize for Literature
2001	Germany participates in NATO's peacekeeping mission in Afghanistan
2002	The euro replaces the deutsche mark
2003	German elections reflect growing anti-U.S. sentiment

Appendix C

German Election Results

German Empire

Percent of Seats in Reichstag

Party	1871	1874	1877	1878	1881	1884	1887	1890	1893	1898	1903	1907	1912
Center	16%	23%	23%	24%	25%	25%	25%	27%	24%	26%	25%	26%	23%
Conservatives	14%	6%	10%	15%	13%	20%	20%	18%	18%	14%	14%	15%	11%
National Liberals	31%	39%	32%	25%	12%	13%	25%	11%	13%	12%	13%	14%	11%
Progressives	12%	13%	13%	10%	29%	19%	8%	19%	12%	12%	9%	12%	11%
Free Conservatives (Reichspartei)	17%	9%	10%	14%	7%	7%	10%	5%	7%	6%	5%	6%	4%
Social Democrats	–	2%	3%	2%	3%	6%	3%	9%	11%	14%	20%	11%	28%
Others	9%	9%	9%	10%	9%	11%	9%	11%	14%	16%	14%	15%	13%

Weimar Republic

Percent of Seats in Reichstag

Party	1919	1920	May 1924	Dec. 1924	1928	1930	July 1932	Nov. 1932	1933
Center	22%	14%	14%	14%	13%	12%	12%	12%	11%
Communist	–	–	13%	9%	11%	13%	15%	17%	13%
Democrats (Prewar Progressives)	18%	9%	6%	7%	5%	4%	–	–	1%
Independent Socialists (Prewar Social Democrats)	6%	18%	–	–	–	–	–	–	–
Majority Socialists (Prewar Social Democrats)	39%	22%	21%	27%	31%	25%	22%	21%	19%
National Socialists	–	–	7%	3%	2%	19%	38%	34%	45%
Nationalists (Prewar Conservatives and Free Conservatives)	11%	15%	20%	21%	15%	7%	6%	9%	8%
People's Party (Prewar National Liberals)	5%	14%	10%	10%	9%	5%	1%	2%	–
Other	–	7%	10%	10%	14%	16%	5%	5%	4%

Federal Republic of Germany (West Germany)

Party	Percent of Seats in Bundestag														
	1949	1953	1957	1961	1965	1969	1972	1976	1980	1983	1987	1990	1994	1998	2002
C.D.U./C.S.U.	35%	51%	52%	49%	48%	48%	45%	49%	46%	49%	45%	48%	44%	37%	41%
F.D.P.	13%	10%	8%	12%	9%	6%	8%	8%	10%	7%	9%	12%	7%	6%	8%
Greens	–	–	–	–	–	–	–	–	–	5%	9%	3%	7%	7%	9%
K.P.D.	4%	–	–	–	–	–	–	–	–	–	–	–	–	–	–
P.D.S.	–	–	–	–	–	–	–	–	–	–	–	1%	4%	5%	–
S.P.D.	33%	31%	35%	37%	39%	46%	47%	43%	44%	39%	37%	36%	38%	45%	42%
Others	15%	8%	5%	2%	4%	–	–	–	–	–	–	–	–	–	–

C.D.U./C.S.U. = Christian Democratic Union/Christian Social Union

F.D.P. = Free Democratic Party

K.P.D. = Communist Party of Germany

P.D.S. = Party of Democratic Socialism

S.P.D. = Social Democratic Party

Index

About the Editor and Contributors

JEAN E. ABSHIRE received her Ph.D. from Indiana University. Currently, she is assistant professor of political science at Indiana University Southeast and director of International Programs. She recently published "Politics in Paint" in *Peace Review*. Her main research areas are ethnic political movements and European policies for accommodating ethnic minorities.

MARTIN BERGER is professor of history at Youngstown State University. He earned his Ph.D. from the University of Pittsburgh. Professor Berger is the author of *Engels, Armies, and Revolution: The Revolutionary Tactics of Classical Marxism* (1977). His current research interests include jazz and World War II.

ROBERT D. BILLINGER, JR., is professor of history at Wingate University. He received his Ph.D. from the University of North Carolina at Chapel Hill. He is the author of *Metternich and the German Question: States' Rights and Federal Duties, 1820–1834* (1991) and *Hitler's Soldiers in the Sunshine State: German POWs in Florida* (2000). Professor Billinger is a former Fulbright Scholar in Austria.

GEORGE P. BLUM is professor emeritus of history at the University of the Pacific in Stockton, CA. He received his Ph.D. from the University of Minnesota. In recent years, he has contributed articles and chapters to a number of volumes including *Events That Changed the World in the Twentieth Century* (1995). He is also the author of *The Rise of Fascism in Europe* (1998). His current research interest centers on German refugees in the aftermath of World War II.

JOHN K. COX is associate professor of history and director of the Laut Honors Program at Wheeling Jesuit University. He received his Ph.D. from Indiana University. He is the author of *The History of Serbia* (2002) and *Slovenia: Evolving Loyalties* (forthcoming). Current research interests include the life and works of the Albanian intellectual Ismail Kadare and literary translations from German, Slovene, French, and other languages.

GESINE GERHARD is assistant professor of history at the University of the Pacific. She received her Ph.D. from the University of Iowa in 2000. Her most recent publication, "R.W. Darré: Naturschützer oder 'Rassenzüchter'?," appeared in *Naturschutz und Nationalsozialismus*. Her research interests include environmental and agrarian history, and she is working on a study of Nazi agrarian politics.

RICHARD A. LEIBY received his Ph.D. from the University of Delaware. He is associate professor of history at Rosemont College. His book, *The Unification of Germany, 1989–1990* (1999), chronicles the fall of the Berlin Wall and the collapse of the East German communist state. Among his other publications are book chapters dealing with Jean Monnet, Margaret Thatcher, the European Unity Movement, and Nazi resettlement policy in occupied France. At present he is working on an anthology dealing with effects of World War II on European cultural and political institutions.

CHARLES F. PENNACCHIO is associate professor of history and political science at the University of the Arts in Philadelphia. He is the author of "The East German Communists and the Origins of the Berlin Blockade" in *East European Quarterly*.

GREGORY F. SCHROEDER earned his Ph.D. from Indiana University. He is assistant professor of history at St. John's University in Collegeville, MN. His article, "Ties of Urban Heimat: West German Cities and Their Wartime Evacuees in the 1950s," was recently published in *German Studies Review*. He is currently working on a manuscript concerning the evacuee problem in postwar West Germany.

FRANK W. THACKERAY received his Ph.D. from Temple University. He is professor of history at Indiana University Southeast and director of the history program. He is the author of *Antecedents of Revolution: Alexander I and the Polish Congress Kingdom* (1980), as well as several articles on Russian-Polish relations in the nineteenth century. With John E. Findling, he edited *Statesmen Who Changed the World* (1993), *Events That Changed the World* (1995–2001), *Events That Changed America* (1996–2000), and *Events That Changed Great Britain* (2002–04). He is a former Fulbright Scholar in Poland and is currently researching constitutional issues in Poland and Russia.

ELEANOR L. TURK is professor emerita of history at Indiana University East. She received her Ph.D. from the University of Wisconsin–Madison.

Her recent publications include *The History of Germany* (1999), which was named a CHOICE Magazine Outstanding Academic title, and *Issues in Germany, Austria, and Switzerland* (2003). Her current research focuses on the history of German emigration.